The Economics of Ec

In an important contribution to educational policy, Daniele Checchi offers an economic perspective on the demand for and supply of education. He explores the reasons why, beyond a certain point, investment in education has not resulted in reductions in social inequalities. Starting with the seminal work of Gary Becker, Checchi provides an extensive survey of the literature on human capital and social capital formation. He draws on individual data on the intergenerational transmission of income and education for the United States, Germany and Italy, as well as aggregate data on income and educational inequality for a much wider range of countries. Checchi explores whether resources spent on education are effective in raising students' achievement, as well as analysing alternative ways of financing education. As a result, this book provides the analytical tools necessary to understand the complex relationships between current income inequality, access to education and future inequality.

DANIELE CHECCHI is Professor of Economics at the University of Milan. He has published books on income inequality and the economics of education, and articles in refereed journals on the intergenerational mobility of incomes and labour market institutions.

The Economics of Education

Human Capital, Family Background and Inequality

DANIELE CHECCHI

CAMBRIDGE
UNIVERSITY PRESS

CAMBRIDGE UNIVERSITY PRESS
Cambridge, New York, Melbourne, Madrid, Cape Town, Singapore, São Paulo

Cambridge University Press
The Edinburgh Building, Cambridge CB2 8RU, UK

Published in the United States of America by Cambridge University Press, New York

www.cambridge.org
Information on this title: www.cambridge.org/9780521793100

First published 2006
Reprinted 2007
This digitally printed version 2008

A catalogue record for this publication is available from the British Library

ISBN 978-0-521-79310-0 hardback
ISBN 978-0-521-06646-4 paperback

Contents

Figures

Tables

Preface

When I began to think of writing the present volume, the economics of education was a topic for specialists. I became interested in the process of acquiring education through the study of the intergenerational mobility of incomes. I wondered how it was possible that countries with free access to public education could be characterised by such different degrees of persistence of family backgrounds across generations. As soon as one starts wondering why people attend school, and for how long, a host of additional questions emerge. Does family income affect the educational choices of children? Does schooling affect labour productivity? Are educational resources (in particular, the quantity of teachers, and how well remunerated they are) effective in raising educational attainment in a population? This book aims to provide an overview of possible answers to these and similar questions, which have been posed in the recent economic literature.

I am indebted to several colleagues and fellow authors, and quite often to friends as well, for the development of most of the ideas reported in this volume. In particular, I would like to express my gratitude to Giorgio Brunello and Luca Flabbi for commenting on specific parts of the book, and to Tullio Jappelli and Giuseppe Bertola for lengthy discussions about the optimal configuration of educational systems. Hospitality from the Department of Economics and the Department of Social Sciences at the Universidad Pompeu Fabra (Barcelona), from the Department of Economics at the University of York and from the research centre Cepremap (Paris), where some of the themes presented in this volume have been finalised over the years, is gratefully acknowledged. Parts of this book have been used in graduate teaching in Milan, Pisa and York, and I would like to thank those students who commented on the initial versions of these chapters.

Finally, my thanks go to Dafne Hugh for revising my rather basic English. Last, but not least, I am indebted to Chris Harrison of Cambridge University Press. He supported the initial project, had confidence in the prospects for completing it (even when I had doubts), and was patient with my repeated postponements of the final delivery.

1 | The relevance of education

In many people's opinion it is the poor, not
the rich, who are social parasites, the more
benign version of which opinion adds that
the poor lack the ability to be productive.

Arrow, Bowles and Durlauf (2000),
Meritocracy and Economic Inequality
(p. x)

This is the crucial question. Since there are
no overt forces of coercion, educational
destinations have somehow to be reached
through individual preferences and
decisions, which leave one wondering how
it comes about that what at a macro level
takes the form of a partially reproductive
pattern can, at the same time, be the results
of decisions individually taken.

Gambetta (1987), *Were They Pushed or
Did They Jump? Individual Decision
Mechanisms in Education* (p. 2)

We will start our investigation into the role of education in modern
societies by reviewing some well-established facts. In the aftermath of
the Second World War we observe *a generalised rise in school attendance* across the globe (see table 1.1). Enrolment rates (as defined by
the ratio between the numbers enrolled at a given stage of education
over the whole population in the same age cohort) rose in particular
in the developing countries, reducing the education gap vis-à-vis the
OECD (Organisation for Economic Co-operation and Development)
countries, as witnessed by the coefficient of variation computed across
countries.[1]

1

Table 1.1 *School enrolment rates by world regions, 1960–1995*

	Primary education				
	1960	1970	1980	1990	1995
OECD countries	98.3%	97.4%	98.9%	99.1%	99.3%
North Africa and Middle East	62.6%	72.1%	87.9%	91.1%	94.3%
Sub-Saharan Africa	41.3%	53.8%	71.8%	72.6%	77.6%
South Asia	44.1%	57.1%	76.3%	80.6%	89.5%
Far East and the Pacific	85.4%	90.8%	96.0%	95.7%	95.4%
Latin America and the Caribbean	85.5%	91.5%	95.4%	95.2%	95.7%
Centrally planned economies	100.0%	96.5%	98.8%	91.3%	96.1%
Worldwide	**69.2%**	**76.0%**	**87.1%**	**87.5%**	**87.8%**
Cross-country dispersion (coefficient of variation)	0.46	0.37	0.24	0.22	0.21
Worldwide (women)	**69.2%**	**75.5%**	**84.2%**	**83.8%**	**84.6%**
Cross-country dispersion (coefficient of variation)	0.48	0.38	0.28	0.27	0.26

	Secondary education				
	1960	1970	1980	1990	1995
OECD countries	49.0%	69.5%	81.0%	90.9%	96.7%
North Africa and Middle East	20.7%	31.8%	48.6%	62.0%	62.8%
Sub-Saharan Africa	3.5%	7.8%	16.5%	21.2%	24.5%
South Asia	11.9%	20.3%	26.2%	32.4%	37.8%
Far East and the Pacific	25.8%	42.1%	58.4%	56.7%	59.7%
Latin America and the Caribbean	18.9%	31.3%	46.1%	50.8%	55.4%
Centrally planned economies	36.5%	53.0%	69.3%	68.0%	76.2%
Worldwide	**21.0%**	**31.9%**	**44.9%**	**51.4%**	**54.4%**
Cross-country dispersion (coefficient of variation)	0.99	0.82	0.65	0.60	0.59
Worldwide (women)	**19.2%**	**31.5%**	**45.2%**	**48.0%**	**52.8%**
Cross-country dispersion (coefficient of variation)	1.09	0.86	0.68	0.69	0.64

Table 1.1 (*cont.*)

	Tertiary education				
	1960	1970	1980	1990	1995
OECD countries	8.9%	16.2%	24.7%	38.1%	49.4%
North Africa and Middle East	1.7%	3.9%	9.1%	13.2%	16.7%
Sub-Saharan Africa	0.2%	0.6%	1.5%	2.5%	3.1%
South Asia	0.9%	2.6%	3.6%	4.2%	4.8%
Far East and the Pacific	4.3%	7.7%	12.4%	20.5%	24.1%
Latin America and the Caribbean	2.8%	6.2%	13.3%	18.6%	19.1%
Centrally planned economies	7.8%	13.3%	17.4%	14.2%	22.0%
Worldwide	3.1%	6.1%	10.9%	16.4%	18.9%
Cross-country dispersion (coefficient of variation)	1.48	1.24	1.02	0.99	1.00
Worldwide (women)	2.2%	4.9%	10.2%	—	19.0%
Cross-country dispersion (coefficient of variation)	1.59	1.33	1.08	—	1.10

Source: Barro and Lee (1997) and updates from World Bank (1998); unweighted mean averages.

Educational achievements rose quickly during the first two decades (the 1960s and the 1970s) but slowed down during the 1980s. By the beginning of the 1990s many countries had succeeded in having their entire school-age population enrolled in primary education (the OECD countries, Latin America, the Far East and the Pacific, and the centrally planned economies). However, while the OECD countries had by now reached almost complete saturation for secondary education as well, all the others were still lagging behind, the worst situation being recorded for Sub-Saharan and South Asian countries. A similar picture emerges with respect to higher education, though by this stage the differences between countries and/or regions have become more pronounced: while about 50 per cent of recent cohorts in developed countries gained access to university, the level went down to less than 5 per cent in the poorest countries of Africa and Asia.

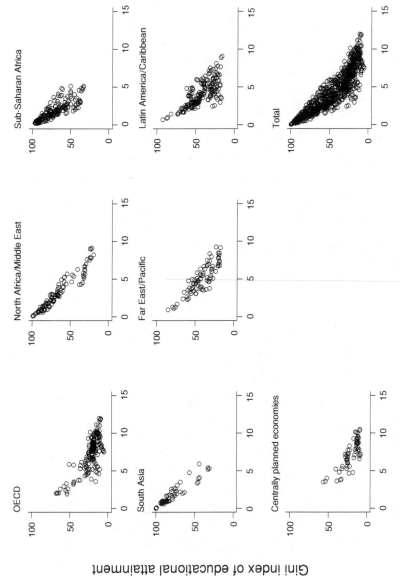

Figure 1.1 Average educational attainment and its dispersion by world regions, 1960–1995

The generalised increase in access to education has reduced the disparities not only between countries but also within countries. If we compute a measure of inequality in educational achievement (like the Gini concentration index)[2] within the population of each country, we can analyse its temporal evaluation in combination with the average educational attainment in the population (here measured by the average number of years of schooling). In figure 1.1 we scatter-plot these two measures by world regions. Each point is a specific combination of country and year. As can easily be seen from the graphs, *countries with higher educational achievements are also characterised by lower differences in educational achievement in the population.* This is due to the fact that, although in theory the total amount of achievable education is boundless, in practice it has its limits for the vast majority of the population. In addition, economic reasoning considers it irrational for schooling to continue beyond a certain age.[3]

Notwithstanding the generalised increase in educational attainment at world level and the contemporary reduction in education inequality, we do not observe a contemporary decline in income inequality. In figure 1.2 we scatter-plot country-average educational attainment and a measure of income inequality (the Gini concentration index) for a sub-sample of country/year combinations where both measures were available.[4] Without embarking here on a much wider discussion as to whether income inequality has risen or declined at the world level,[5] it suffices to note that *income inequality tends to be lower in countries where average educational achievement is higher.*[6] This could result either from the fact that more people have access to education and therefore better employment opportunities, or because greater equality in educational achievement enhances social mobility, thus lowering long-term inequality.

Thus, we face our first question: *why do people demand education, and what underlines this rapid growth in educational access?* Economic theory gives us some understanding of what underlies the demand for education from families, but is less forthcoming about the aggregate implications of this increasing preference for education.

Looking at the individual consequences of education is relatively easy, and nowadays there is a wide consensus on it. Table 1.2 reports some information about the labour market consequences of acquiring education for some developed countries and for the OECD country mean. Despite some apparent differences in education distribution

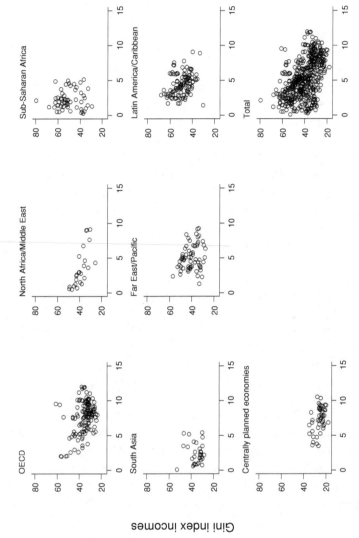

Figure 1.2 Income inequality and average educational attainment, 1960–1995

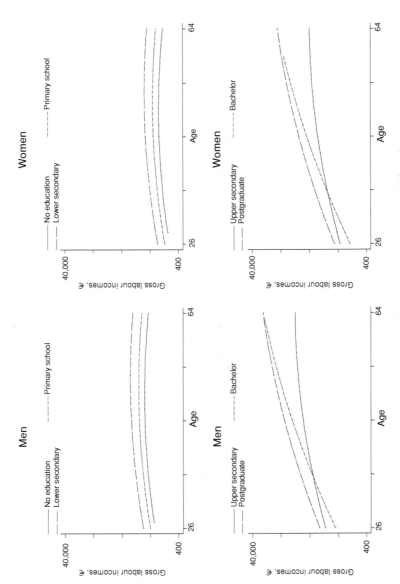

Figure 1.3 Age–earnings profiles on annual incomes: Italy, 2000

Table 1.3 *The return on education in selected areas of the world*

	Private return on education		
	Primary	Secondary	Tertiary
Sub-Saharan Africa	41.3	26.6	27.8
Asia	39.0	18.9	19.9
Europe, Middle East and North Africa	17.4	15.9	21.7
Latin America and the Caribbean	26.2	16.8	19.7
OECD countries	21.7	12.4	12.3
World	29.1	18.1	20.3

Source: Psacharopoulos (1994, table 1).

But this does not answer the question of why this occurs. We therefore ask our third question: *why are education and incomes positively related?*

There is a final point that we need to discuss. If it is worth going to school (and we have seen that it is, in terms of both employment probability and prospective earnings), why is it that not all families make such an investment in their children? In principle, we would expect all individuals to be grouped at the highest educational level, in order to benefit from the increased income opportunities. But, as often in economics, there is a fallacy of composition here. As more and more people go to school, so the relative advantage of better educated people declines. In table 1.3 we report some summary figures on the return on education – the expected increase in earnings associated with an additional year of schooling. As is clear from comparing table 1.1 with table 1.3, the returns are higher where access to education is limited, and they tend to decline with the widening of educational attainment.[10] But it is impossible to believe that this is the main reason for people not attending school. Families are often unaware of the economic benefit of education, or they are prevented from sending their children to further education by their financial needs. This leads us to our fourth and final question: *what does prevent full access to education?*

If we want to summarise the issues raised in this introduction, we could list the following points. For several reasons (to be discussed further on in the book), there has been an increase in access to education in most parts of the globe. Common sense tells us that going to school improves individual destinies. But, despite these radical changes, inequalities have not declined. Large numbers of families are still prevented from gaining access to schools. And, despite widespread scholarisation, wage differentials remain high even in most developed countries.

Is there a blanket explanation for all these phenomena? We doubt it. However, the economist's viewpoint has an important contribution to make. To begin with, it may help us understand the costs and benefits at the individual level of deciding whether to acquire more education. This is the main content of the second chapter, on THE DEMAND FOR EDUCATION. After a general discussion on what kind of a good education is (basic capabilities, a consumption good, a merit good, an investment good, etc.), this chapter introduces a formal model of investment in human capital. The return on education in the labour market is given exogenously, and aggregation problems are disregarded at this stage. Standard predictions are obtained in this framework: people will demand more schooling whenever family resources are high, borrowing rates are low, access to education is cheap and expected returns are high.

Once we consider the possibility of financial market imperfections, the educational choices become the mere reflection of family wealth distribution. Limited access to education is proved to contribute to income inequality persistence over generations. The empirical verification of previous propositions is analysed in the third chapter, on LIQUIDITY CONSTRAINTS AND ACCESS TO EDUCATION. Assuming the existence of a loglinear relationship between demand for education and family income, a simple linear relationship can be derived between the Gini index on income inequality and enrolment rates. This relationship is subsequently estimated for a group of countries for the period 1960 to 1995. The main findings of this analysis are that, once we control for the degree of development with the (log of) per capita output, financial constraints seem mainly relevant in limiting access to secondary education. However, when considering gender differences, there is evidence that female participation in education is more conditioned by family wealth, in some cases starting from primary education. There is also some slight evidence that public resources spent on education raise the enrolment rates.

Once we have completed the presentation of the demand side we go on to analyse the supply of education, which is, on the whole, publicly provided in most countries. The determinants of available supply are discussed in the fourth chapter, on THE SUPPLY OF EDUCATION. This chapter begins by reviewing the concept of the educational production function, and then proceeds to analyse its main ingredients.

The problems of class size and peer effect are discussed, both theoretically and empirically. The central issue in class formation is, however, whether to integrate or segregate students of different abilities: relevant conditions related to the substitutability/complementarity of talents in human capital formation are discussed. In so doing it was impossible to avoid reviewing the existing literature on resource effectiveness, an argument related to (but not coincident with) the problem of efficient use of resources in education. The optimal design of an educational system faces a trade-off between equity (equality of opportunity in access) and efficiency (selectivity), in order to concentrate higher resources on the ablest individuals.

Once we have set the stage for supply and demand in education, we ask how these two elements interact in the education market. This is the main content of the fifth chapter, on EDUCATION FINANCING. It considers the optimal educational investment when individuals and their families differ in terms of talent and wealth. The existing trade-off is then exploited to show why there is often an incentive for the private provision of education, despite a public supply freely available for all citizens. The size of the private sector in education may have an impact on the potential growth rate of an economy since it strengthens the incentive for human capital accumulation. Chapter 5 then presents the reasons why we observe the coexistence of mixed public–private systems of education provision in many countries. Public provision has the advantage of lowering access barriers, but at the same time it reduces the incentives for richer families to invest more in the education of their children. As in other cases of public good financing, decentralised provision and financing may help solve this problem. One section of the chapter is devoted to a discussion of the importance of school vouchers as a possible solution to the low educational investment of poor families.

Everything so far has taken it for granted that human capital is productive, and therefore that, on balance, the marginal cost (for the family) and the marginal benefit (for the firm) of education are equated. However, the empirical evidence of direct productivity gains when better-educated workers are used is scant. The sixth chapter, on THE RETURN ON EDUCATION, considers alternative explanations for the empirical evidence where the return on education is concerned. Attending school may either induce good traits (such as obedience) that are appreciated by managers; or be a way to signal individual ability; or provide a screening device to distinguish between individuals. However, all these explanations assume a zero barrier in accessing education, whereas such an assumption is hard to justify in the real world. Additional returns on education can be offered by an increased opportunity for on-the-job training, which typically is offered to better educated workers. A final section discusses the problem of measuring and estimating the private return on education.

The seventh chapter, on INTERGENERATIONAL PERSISTENCE, studies the intergenerational implications of alternative equilibria in the education market within each generation. It opens with a basic model of intergenerational mobility, followed by some empirical evidence. In this literature the intergenerational transmission of cultural traits (talent, for short) becomes crucial in guiding the assessment of the efficiency of different degrees of mobility. The properties of equilibrium distribution depend crucially on whether or not the agents know in advance the talent endowment of their children.

Notes

1. The *coefficient of variation* is a measure of dispersion normalised in order to preserve scale invariance. It is computed as the ratio between the *standard deviation* and the *mean* of a variable. In symbols, given a population made up of n individuals and denoting with x_i the value corresponding to the i-th individual and with $\mu = \frac{1}{n} \sum_{i=1}^{n} x_i$ the sample mean, the coefficient of variation is defined by $\frac{1}{n\mu} \sqrt{\sum_{i=1}^{n} (x_i - \mu)^2}$.

2. See Checchi (2004) for the derivation of this measure.

3. See the next chapter for a formal proof of this claim.

4. The income inequality measure is derived from Deininger and Squire (1996). See Checchi (2004) for details.

5. There is a growing literature on the current trends in income inequality at world level: see Atkinson (1999) and Cornia (2004), and the references therein. Recent contributions attempting to investigate the determinants of income inequality include Barro (2000 – where he finds some evidence on the existence of an inverted U-shaped relationship between output per capita and income inequality; he also controls for educational achievement by introducing average educational attainments at three levels – primary, secondary and tertiary), Deininger and Squire (1998 – showing that initial inequality in assets – land – is relevant in predicting both

income growth and changes in income inequality) and Li, Squire and Zou 1998 (finding a positive effect of (initial-period) average secondary school years on income inequality, which they interpret as a proxy for a political effect: the more political freedom there is the more informed is society, and the more difficult it will be for the rich to appropriate extra resources).

6. The uncontrolled regression coefficient of the Gini index of income inequality onto average years of education is -1.99 for the period 1960
   $\qquad\qquad\qquad\qquad\qquad\qquad\qquad\quad (12.94)$
   to 1995. However, when we control for country/year fixed effects, we get an estimate of -0.82, with a lower statistical significance.
   $\qquad\qquad\qquad\qquad\quad (1.58)$

7. The employment rate can be obtained from the participation rate and the unemployment rate through the following formula:

$$\frac{\text{employed}}{\text{population}} = \frac{\text{labour force} - \text{unemployed}}{\text{population}}$$

$$= \left(\frac{\text{labour force}}{\text{population}}\right)\left(1 - \frac{\text{unemployed}}{\text{labour force}}\right).$$

8. These can include the presence of unions, as well as minimum wage levels and centralised bargaining activity. See Kahn (2000).

9. Figure 1.3 plots the predicted value of a regression of the (yearly) gross labour income onto gender, age, age squared, educational standard and its interaction with age. The data come from the Bank of Italy's Survey on Household Incomes, conducted in 2001, and cover 6,204 individuals with positive labour income (the age ranging between fifteen and eighty-eight).

10. For a detailed discussion of this issue, see Bils and Klenow (2000) and Teulings and vanRens (2002).

2 | *The demand for education*

In this chapter we analyse the reasons why people go to school. Our initial answer will call into play the notion of *functioning*, formulated by Nobel laureate Amartya Sen. We then move on to the theories of another Nobel laureate, Gary Becker, who portrays education as an investment in *human capital*. Other alternative approaches, based on the idea of *signalling*, *screening* or *convenient human traits*, will be reviewed in chapter 6. The human capital approach derives from the assumption that perfect financial markets exist. When we remove this assumption, first family, then family income distribution, become limiting factors, and income inequality persistence arises as an equilibrium outcome.

2.1 Education as creation of minimal capabilities

When discussing equality and justice, we typically consider the distribution of economic resources such as income and wealth. Amartya Sen, however, has repeatedly drawn our attention to the fact that mere ownership does not necessarily imply an increase in utility, since a person might be unable to benefit from the additional economic resources. Yet this may not depend so much on individual heterogeneity[1] as on individual capability to transform resources into behaviours so as to function adequately.[2] Being able to read, calculate and process information can be thought of as a *functioning* necessary for conducting a normal social life (namely, appearing in public without shame). To convince the reader, here is a list of ordinary life acts that require some education in order to be performed successfully: using public transport, finding a street address, checking a bill in a restaurant, signing a cheque, enrolling your child at school, reading the instructions on an electrical appliance, and so on.

We should be convinced that the capabilities of reading and computing in the entire population constitute a non-excludable public good, since they allow a more complex organisation of social life.[3] In such a case, the public provision of compulsory education is equivalent to the provision of any other public good. Whenever the externalities from individual choices are strong enough, there are good (at least from the economic viewpoint) reasons to ensure a positive production of it. Public goods are characterised by underproduction in a market solution, because private demand would fall short of optimal provision.[4] This may offer a rationale for the widespread diffusion of some compulsory and freely provided education in all modern states since the French Revolution.[5] However, the nature of public goods requires there to be free access (as in the case of civil defence or road building) but not necessarily compulsory attendance. One possible explanation for this may come from the difference existing between those who decide (the parents) and those who obtain the benefits of the decision (the children). In addition, in many countries where poverty is endemic and child labour is not prohibited, children are a significant source of income for poor families. In such cases, society will aim to protect children from 'wrong' choices by their parents, as happens in the case of vaccination against infectious diseases.[6]

When we try to match an empirical content with the idea of literary and numerical capabilities, we encounter several problems. In principle, we would like to test a representative sample of the population of interest. But this would lead to an overestimate of the deprivation in the older segment of the population, due to the natural decline in general abilities with age. In addition, the set of minimal capabilities evolves with time, and it is inappropriate to require the same set of competences from different age cohorts.[7] Both considerations would suggest that capabilities should be assessed within each generation, more than in an intergenerational framework. Indeed, most international comparisons of educational attainments sponsored by the OECD are conducted with populations of the same age cohorts.[8]

But, if we are interested in assessing the extent of capability deprivation in the entire population, we should resort to differentiated tests across the population, which would lead to insurmountable difficulties. For this reason, the easiest strategy is to use proxy measures, based on enrolment rates, on the assumption that attending school provides a basic level of literacy and numeracy. In table 2.1 we report some indicators that are used to produce the Human Development Indicator proposed by the United Nations Development Programme (see UNDP,

Table 2.1 *Indicators of the diffusion of capabilities, life expectancy and per capita income, 1999*

	Combined primary, secondary and tertiary gross enrolment rates (%)	Adult literacy rate (% of population above 15)	People lacking functional literacy skills (% aged 15–65)	Life expectancy at birth (years)	GDP per capita ($, PPP[a])
High human development countries	91.0	98.5	n.a.	73.8	14,922
Medium human development countries	67.0	78.5	n.a.	67.0	3,044
Low human development countries	38.0	48.9	n.a.	56.0	1,241
Entire world	65.0	79.2	n.a.	66.7	6,980
France	94.0	99.0[b]	n.a.	78.4	22,897
Germany	94.0	99.0[b]	14.4	77.6	23,742
Italy	84.0	98.4	n.a.	78.4	22,172
Japan	82.0	99.0[b]	n.a.	80.8	24,898
United Kingdom	106.0	99.0[b]	21.8	77.5	22,093
United States	95.0	99.0[b]	20.7	76.8	31,872

[a] Purchasing power parity.
[b] Estimate.

Source: UNDP (2001) tables 1 and 4.

2001 and previous issues). The first column shows an aggregate indicator of school attendance. By comparing it with the last column, it is easy to see that school enrolment is positively correlated with per capita income. While school attendance is a *flow* measure (i.e. it records the population fraction attending school per unit of time), the second column proposes a *stock* measure (i.e. the distribution of a given characteristic in the population in a specific date). In this case we observe that, in almost the entire developed world, primary school attendance is universal, leading to the presumption that basic capabilities are generally achieved. However, when we look at the third column (with measures available for only the subset of OECD countries[9]) we realise that having attended school is by itself insufficient to attain competence in literacy ability. The fourth column reminds us that cultural deprivation can be only one aspect of multifaceted deprivation. Even without being able to assess the direction of causality (higher mortality can be the consequence of ignorance of basic sanitation rules, or the other way round; given the high rate of child mortality, there are other social priorities, so that schools are neglected), we realise that the possibility of delivering the public service of compulsory education varies significantly across countries (and even within countries).

2.2 Education as investment in human capital

In the previous section we have outlined the idea that the state may oblige its citizens to attend a school of some sort in order to acquire basic capabilities so as to improve the organisation of social life. However, we know that many individuals choose to attend school beyond the minimum requirement, and we will now go on to analyse this behaviour.[10]

A first approach conceives of education as a commodity: people go to school because they enjoy acquiring new knowledge.[11] In such a case the standard theory of utility maximisation predicts that the optimal demand for education will equate the marginal utility of additional knowledge to the marginal disutility of renouncing alternative uses of the time involved. Thus, as for any luxury item, income effect raises optimal consumption more than proportionally, which helps us to understand why rich countries have higher enrolment rates than poor countries. However, this explanation is at odds with most of the educational choices regarding tertiary education. At this stage of schooling, cost increases significantly when compared to secondary education, without any evidence of increased pleasure in attending university lectures. Thus education cannot be conceived of merely as a commodity.[12]

We can look at educational choice as investment decisions, where current income opportunities are renounced in exchange for better income prospects in the future. This is equivalent to purchasing a production unit today in order to obtain the rents associated with its ownership, net of depreciation associated with its usage. The close similarity with the investment theory of the firm, where physical capital is demanded up to the point where its marginal productivity equates its user cost, has led many economists to think of education as *investment in human capital*.[13] However, on deeper scrutiny the analogy between investment in physical capital and investment in human capital proves somewhat imprecise. The main difference is that human capital is incorporated in human beings, and cannot be resold. While physical capital can be acquired at (almost) any desired amount in boom periods and be resold during recession on secondary markets, human capital can be acquired mostly at the beginning of individual life, its pace of accumulation is determined by physiological factors, and it cannot be resold.[14]

The features of being embodied in human beings and being irreversible open the door to many potential market failures, which are absent in the case of physical capital. To begin with, human capital cannot be collateralised, apart from the case of slavery. While offering a machine as collateral eases the cost of borrowing from a bank in order to buy it, it is impossible to finance the education of your children by offering their incorporated knowledge as collateral! Thus, whenever financial markets are plagued with informational asymmetries (as they typically are), the difference between investment in physical and human capital will amplify. A second, and even more important, difference is given by the possibility of moral hazard behaviour, which is relevant for human capital, but not for physical capital. The future benefits of acquiring education now are conditional on exerting adequate effort in the labour market, but the impossibility of checking for future effort renders it non-contractible. Seen in this perspective, any current investment in education is riskier than any financial investment (at least from the point of view of investing agents – i.e. the parents).[15] Last, but not least, the apparent similarity between the two concepts of capital conceals substantial differences in the degree of control of the resource. The owner of physical capital can be properly termed a *capitalist*, since he or she is in control of either employing it in a production process or converting it into a liquid asset, living on it as a *rentier*. In contrast, an educated person who owns his/her own human capital cannot employ it in a production process unless hired as a dependent worker, thus becoming a *wage earner*. Thus, human capital does not command the same market power as does physical capital.[16]

Despite all these differences, the use of the term 'investment in human capital' as synonymous with 'acquisition of education' has become so pervasive that we will not refrain from using the same terminology. There is an additional reason for doing so. If we consider human capital, embodied in people, as a production input, we then obtain an (endogenous) explanation of the returns to education from profit-maximising behaviour by firms. Each worker is paid up to the point corresponding to his/her marginal productivity, which will differ in accordance with the embodied human capital input. Though convenient, this remains nothing but an analogy, because we do not have compelling evidence that education increases workers' productivity per se. In general, education induces the self-sorting of individuals, who therefore differ not only in terms of acquired education but also in terms of many other unobservable characteristics that may be valuable to a firm.[17]

Let us now present a simple model that allows the identification of the main determinants of educational choices as investment in human capital.[18] Suppose that, for simplicity, the life of an individual i, $i = 1, \ldots, n$, can be divided into two periods: youth (in period t) and adulthood (in period $t + 1$). The i-th individual can devote a fraction S_{it} of his/her time in each period of life to schooling, in order to increase his/her stock of human capital H_{it}. Human capital is rewarded in the labour market at its marginal productivity rate β_t.[19] Thus, the incentive to accumulate human capital is provided by the prospect of future gains.

$$W_{ij}(H_{ij}) = \beta_j H_{ij}, \quad j = t, t + 1 \qquad (2.1)$$

where W_{ij} indicates the labour earnings of individual i in period j. The accumulation of human capital is not instantaneous, but requires time;

in addition, human capital depreciates with time at rate δ, as assumed by the following relationship:

$$H_{it+1} = H_{it}(1 - \delta) + \Delta H_{it} \qquad (2.2)$$

where $\Delta x_t = x_t - x_{t-1}$ denotes first-time differences. Devoting a fraction S_t of time to schooling produces new human capital. If we indicate with A_i individual unobservable ability, we assume that abler individuals are advantaged in acquiring education (either because they need less effort to study or because they are characterised by a better family environment).[20] We also assume that more human capital is produced when more resources E_{it} are used in schooling (say, more and/or better teachers, libraries and so on). Finally, it is also assumed that there are decreasing returns on time spent in education. All these factors are imperfect substitutes (i.e. it is possible to compensate low talent with greater effort or better educational resources). All these assumptions are summarised in the following equation:

$$\Delta H_{it} = (A_i S_{it} E_{it} H_{it})^{\alpha}, \quad \alpha < 1 \qquad (2.3)$$

Finally, we have to specify individual preferences that consist of the discounted value of lifelong earnings:

$$\begin{aligned}
V_i &= W_{it}(H_{it}) - S_{it} W_{it}(H_{it}) - \gamma_t S_{it} \\
&\quad + \frac{W_{it+1}(H_{it+1}) - S_{it+1} W_{it+1}(H_{it+1}) - \gamma_{t+1} S_{it+1}}{1 + \rho} \\
&= \beta_t H_{it}(1 - S_{it}) - \gamma_t S_{it} + \frac{\beta_{t+1} H_{it+1}(1 - S_{it+1}) - \gamma_{t+1} S_{it+1}}{1 + \rho}
\end{aligned}$$

$$(2.4)$$

where γ_t represents the direct cost of school attendance and ρ indicates the subjective rate of intertemporal discount. When perfect financial markets exist, ρ is replaced by the market interest rate.

There are various sources for the costs of acquiring education.

(i) *Direct monetary costs*, here represented by factor γ. They consist of tuition fees, book purchases, transport and living costs.

(ii) *Indirect monetary costs* (or *opportunity costs*) corresponding to forgone income due to school attendance. In equation (2.4) they are represented by the term $S_{it} W_{it}$: if the time fraction S_{it} is devoted to school attendance, it cannot be employed in the labour market; as a consequence, the student gives up a corresponding fraction of the income that would have been earned had the entire time-span been spent in the labour market. Opportunity costs are obviously related to labour market outcomes: while, for simplicity, we are assuming here full employment, one should keep in mind that higher (youth) unemployment reduces the costs of school attendance.

(iii) We ignore here *non-monetary costs*, which correspond to the effort put into education acquisition. If we consider that school levels become more and more selective the higher you go, we could imagine some sort of increasing non-monetary costs of schooling.

We are now in a position to establish some results about the demand for education from the optimal choice of investment in human capital. If we maximise utility (2.4) subject to constraints (2.1)–(2.3), including an existence interval $0 \le S_{ij} \le 1, i = 1, \ldots, n, j = t, t+1$, we obtain

$$\max_{S_{it}, S_{it+1}} V_i = \max_{S_{it}, S_{it+1}} \beta_t H_{it}(1 - S_{it}) - \gamma_t S_{it}$$

$$+ \frac{\beta_{t+1}[H_{it}(1 - \delta) + (A_i S_{it} E_{it} H_{it})^\alpha](1 - S_{it+1}) - \gamma_{t+1} S_{it+1}}{1 + \rho}$$

$$(2.5)$$

The first-order condition with respect to S_{it+1} easily shows that the optimal choice is $S_{it+1}^* = 0$. Given the simplified structure of the model, it does not pay to acquire education in the second period of life, because it augments the human capital to be sold in a hypothetical third period, when the individual will (presumably) be dead. This result is general: if an individual demands more education in order to increase his/her market value, it is better to do so in the early stages of life, in order to benefit from the increased earnings accruing from additional human capital for as long as possible. This proves true in spite of the declining value of the same capital at rate δ, which proxies both the scientific obsolescence of knowledge and the natural decay of the human brain.

When we take the first-order condition with respect to S_{it} (and supposing the existence of an internal solution) we get the following result:

$$\underbrace{\beta_t H_t + \gamma_t}_{\text{marginal cost}} = \underbrace{\frac{\beta_{t+1}}{1 + \rho} \frac{\alpha \Delta H_{it}}{S_{it}^*}}_{\text{marginal benefit}} \qquad (2.6)$$

Equation (2.6) tells us that each individual chooses to acquire education up to a point where the cost of acquisition (the left-hand side of expression (2.6), including direct and indirect monetary costs) equals the benefit of acquisition. The right-hand side of expression (2.6) represents the discounted value of the earnings increase due to human capital accumulation, taking into account the relative productivity of school attendance in generating new human capital. If we rearrange equation (2.6) in order to obtain the reduced form in terms of the optimal demand for education in the first period of life, we get

$$S_{it}^* = \left(\frac{\beta_{t+1}}{\beta_t(1+\rho)} \frac{\alpha(A_i E_{it} H_{it})^\alpha}{H_{it} + \gamma_t/\beta_t} \right)^{\frac{1}{1-\alpha}} = S\left(\underset{+}{A_i}, \underset{\mp}{H_{it}}, \underset{+}{\beta_{t+1}/\beta_t}, \underset{-}{\rho}, \underset{-}{\gamma_t}, \underset{+}{E_{it}} \right)$$

(2.7)

From equation (2.7) we obtain several conclusions.

(i) More talented people will demand more education, because their marginal return is higher. Equation (2.3) assumes that unobservable ability A_i raises the production of new human capital for any unit of time spent in school.

(ii) The demand for education is higher when future expected gain β_{t+1} is higher relative to current β_t. The former affects expected gains, the latter determines current (opportunity) costs. Thus, better employment conditions reduce the current demand for education.[21] In contrast, the expectation of higher returns in the future (for example, as a consequence of the generalised adoption of information technology) stimulates the current demand for education.

(iii) Future gains are discounted to the present in accordance with the subjective intertemporal discount rate. The higher the ρ parameter the more myopic the agent, the more he/she evaluates current costs in exchange for future gains and, consequently, the lower is his/her demand for education. When financial markets exist, the ρ parameter is replaced by the market interest rate, because the individual could borrow money to cover current costs (when young) and repay when future benefits start accruing (when adult). In this case, an increase in the market interest rate lowers the demand for education.[22]

(iv) The demand for education is more intense the lower the starting level of human capital H_{it}. However, this incentive declines with the accumulation of human capital, because of decreasing marginal productivity in the formation of new capital.[23]

(v) Finally, the demand for education declines if there is an increase in direct cost γ_t of school attendance, but increases if greater and

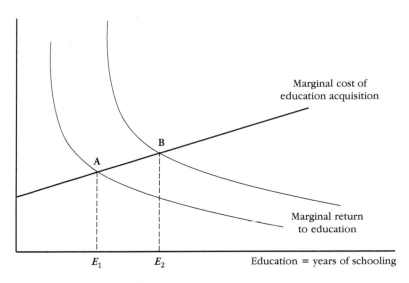

Figure 2.1 The model of human capital investment

better resources E_{it} are employed in the education production
function.

The working of this model can be visualised by making reference to
figure 2.1, depicting both sides of equation (2.6). Even if in equation
(2.4) we have assumed a constant cost γ_t, here the cost schedule is
drawn as upward-sloping, to account for the fact that higher levels of
education are typically associated with increasing costs (both monetary
and non-monetary – this is equivalent to a case where $\gamma = \gamma(S)$, $\gamma' >$
0). Conversely, the return schedule is downward-sloping to account for
the decreasing return on the production technology of new human capital. While, in the model, the choice variable S_{it} describes the amount
of time devoted to education in the first period of life, it can easily
be converted into years of education acquisition. How does the model
work? Suppose that an individual is optimally choosing the amount of
education E_1 corresponding to the intersection of marginal cost with
marginal benefit at point **A**. When he/she expects that in the next period
there will be an increase in the demand for skilled labour, the (perceived) relative return to education will rise (since β_{t+1}/β_t is expected
to be higher). This is represented as an outward shift of the marginal
return, provoking an increase in the demand for education up to
value E_2.

This figure may also help us understand why different individuals demand different amounts of education. Let us consider the role of unobservable ability ('talent' for short). We see from equation (2.7) that more talented individuals demand more education, and obtain higher human capital. This is due to the fact that they experience a higher marginal return for any portion of time invested in education. This can be seen by looking at earnings in the second period of life, as obtained by placing equations (2.3) and (2.2) into equation (2.1),

$$W_{it+1} = \beta_{t+1} H_{it+1} = \beta_{t+1}[H_{it}(1 - \delta) + \Delta H_{it}]$$
$$= \beta_{t+1}[H_{it}(1 - \delta) + (A_i S_{it} E_{it} H_{it})^\alpha] \tag{2.8}$$

and then taking the first derivative with respect to S_{it}

$$\frac{\partial W_{it+1}}{\partial S_{it}} = \beta_{t+1} \left[\frac{\alpha(A_i E_{it} H_{it})^\alpha}{S_{it}^{1-\alpha}} \right] \tag{2.9}$$

Equation (2.9) tells us that an additional year of schooling does not have the same impact on earnings for each individual. More talented people (higher A_i), as well as those attending better schools (greater E_{it}) expect a higher return because they 'accumulate' more human capital per unit of time, and therefore have an incentive to stay in school longer. In terms of condition (2.6), the right-hand side (marginal benefit) is higher for these people; in terms of figure 2.1, this is equivalent to the case where agents look at point **B** instead of point **A**.[24]

A second case of differentiated demand for education emerges when we consider the problem of financing educational choices. If we look at the first-period budget constraint implicit in equation (2.4), we notice that nothing ensures that $\beta_t H_{it}(1 - S_{it}^*) \geq \gamma_t S_{it}^* \Leftrightarrow \dfrac{\beta_t H_{it}}{\beta_t H_{it} + \gamma_t} \geq S_{it}^*$; i.e. the income obtained in the first period of life (when partially employed) exceeds the direct costs of optimally demanded schooling. If financial markets exist, any agent can borrow any required amount to finance educational expenditures, to be repaid in the second period when earning a higher income. In our simple model, where uncertainty about the future is absent and everything is perfectly observable, this seem a reasonable occurrence. But what about unobservable abilities? Investing in education is a risky investment, and the borrower has better information than the lender about the real chance of succeeding at school. He/she also has better knowledge about his/her prospective outcomes in the labour market, whereas a bank does not. In such a context, a

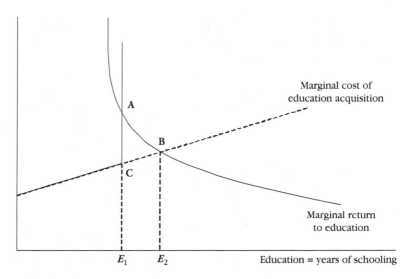

Figure 2.2 Human capital investment under liquidity constraints

bank (or any generic lender) will either require collateral or charge a higher interest rate, to protect against the default risk.

In both cases individuals are asymmetrically affected by this occurrence, since only individuals from poor families need to borrow in order to finance their schooling. When the bank requires collateral, the amount of education that an agent can demand is upwardly constrained by available wealth (which typically derive from family bequests). When the bank charges a higher interest rate, this reduces the optimal amount of education in accordance with equation (2.7). In both cases, people from poor families are discriminated against because of their lack of financial resources.[25] This situation can be visualised by looking at figure 2.2. The marginal rate of return to education is identical for all individuals, as in figure 2.1. If all agents had sufficient wealth and were not liquidity-constrained, they would all choose the optimal amount of education corresponding to point **B**. When some of them cannot entirely finance their demand for education up to point E_2, they are forced to limit their acquisition of education to point E_1. But this situation is inefficient, because there is a positive difference between the marginal return and the marginal cost of education (the distance between points **A** and **C**), leaving unexploited opportunities for human capital production. In such a context the state could fruitfully intervene, by taxing agents and using the proceeds to support poor families in financing their educational expenditures. This will increase the total amount of human capital investment in society.[26]

We can summarise what we have found so far. Human capital investment theory predicts that people will demand education up to the point where the marginal benefit is equal to the marginal cost. Marginal benefits depend on labour market conditions, on resources invested in education and on individual ability. Marginal costs depend on direct costs of schooling and, possibly, on individual ability. While, in principle, all individuals should demand the same amount of education, two factors contribute to differentiating educational attainment in the population. One is talent (be it 'pure intelligence' or 'better family background'), which boosts the human capital accumulation.[27] The other is family wealth, which can constrain poor families when financial markets are imperfect or absent. We now consider both arguments in more detail.

2.3 The role of individual talent

Observing different educational choices in the population, one may wonder about the underlying causes of these differences. The question is not trivial, because the two alternative explanations we have reviewed in the previous section have radically different policy implications. When different educational attainments derive from differences in talent endowment, there is no reason (at least on the grounds of efficiency) to intervene in order to facilitate the access to education of less endowed individuals. From an efficiency perspective, one should evaluate one additional unit of currency spent on educating the more endowed against spending the same amount for the less endowed. Equity reasons may render it advisable, but efficiency reasons may work in the opposite direction.[28] In contrast, if differential education is the outcome of wealth (or income) inequality, then we have already mentioned that redistributive policies are both equity- and efficiency-enhancing.

This explains why it is crucial in empirical analysis to distinguish between these two cases. In principle, one could divide the population into two (or more) groups and safely assume that the richest families are not liquidity-constrained. The remaining differences within this group could be attributed to differences in 'talent'.[29] But the concept of 'talent' is itself hard to grasp. When we look at educational attainment, it is difficult to distinguish whether a well-performing student is either a natural genius or the offspring of graduate parents. The problem arises from the fact that we do not possess good measures for factors such as 'intelligence', 'creativity', 'cleverness' and the like.

Some authors have polemically claimed that unobservable ability is not only genetically dependent but is also intergenerationally transmitted. Herrnstein and Murray (1994)[30] have put forward an explanation of income inequality and racial differences in the United States based on the following line of argument. There is positive evidence of correlation between talent (as measured by IQ test scores) and earnings. Likewise, there is positive correlation between talent measures across generations. If IQ test scores are a good proxy of unobservable ability, then earnings inequality is a 'natural' outcome, since nature distributes the genes of intelligence at random. Finding intergenerational correlation of IQ test scores can consequently be taken as evidence for the genetic transmittability of intelligence genes.[31]

While the theoretical argument (IQ proxying unobservable ability) may be questionable,[32] the policy implications were surprising. Recording a persistent income differential between whites and Afro-Americans in the United States, this differential is explained by referring to persistent IQ test score differentials, which repeat across generations. As a consequence, income inequality in the United States should be abandoned from the political agenda, being an obvious outcome of 'natural' differences: Afro-Americans are less endowed with unobservable ability, and therefore earn less. Since ability is transmitted across generations, Afro-Americans will keep on populating the bottom tail of income distribution. Any attempt to revise this result by adopting compensatory schooling is destined to fail.

These ideas were not new, at least in North American academia. As early as the 1960s the diffusion of IQ test measures had raised the issue of their correlation with family background, in particular with parental education.[33] The introduction of test scores in earnings regressions opened the discussion on whether their statistical significance was a correct measure of genuine unobservable ability or the result of spurious correlation with unobservable parental characteristics. The discussion proceeded along two lines. On the one hand, some authors were able to control for genetic ability by using particular samples (typically twins). An interesting attempt to decompose among different factors affecting educational attainment and labour earnings is provided by Mulvey, Miller and Martin (1997). They analyse an Australian sample of twins, either monozygotic (identical) or dizygotic (fraternal) ones. By regressing income differences for identical twins on educational differences, one is controlling for both family background and 'natural' unobservable ability. By repeating the same analysis for fraternal twins and comparing the results with the previous case one obtains an estimate of the relative role played by ability: '[H]ence the conclusion from the traditional twins model is that the estimated return to schooling for males of 7.1% is comprised of 2.3% due to the "true" returns to schooling, 4.2% due to the effects of family background and 0.7% due to the influence of genetic factors.'[34] On the other hand, the availability of a better data set allowed researchers to decompose the ability proxy by different subjects, in order to test which aspects were more relevant in shaping earning ability.[35]

Overall, the literature seems rather inconclusive on the role and measurement of unobservable ability. Some authors argue that education provides human capital, which in turn raises individual productivity. In this perspective, facilitating educational access by more disadvantaged individuals can attenuate income inequality. Some others argue against a causal interpretation, because individuals with higher ability receive more education and more income, but the correlation between the two is spurious. In the latter perspective, any corrective policy is, at best, uninfluential.[36]

2.4 Imperfect financial markets and the indivisibility of human capital investment

In section 2 we have seen that school attendance may be made impractical by a lack of financial resources. In principle, whenever a profitable investment is available, economic agents should take advantage of this opportunity by arbitraging between different sources of funds. Whenever any additional year of schooling has a marginal benefit exceeding its marginal cost (including interest repayment), it should be worth undertaking. Under decreasing marginal returns of time spent in schooling and the homogeneity of agents, we should observe the convergence of human capital (and therefore of earnings) in the population.[37]

However, actual financial markets do not work in this way, and do not offer an unlimited amount of lending to anyone. They typically ration the borrower by charging higher interest rates and/or require collateral in order to insure against default risks. Both stances hurt disproportionately families in the lower tail of income distribution, for they are unable to bear the opportunity costs of school attendance and need to borrow. But they typically need huge amounts (at least in relative terms) and do not have collateralisable ownerships. As a consequence, other things being equal, individuals from poorer families tend to acquire less education than individuals from richer families.

In the specific case of education financing, financial markets are very likely to work imperfectly (or even be absent), because of the impossibility of providing collateral (apart from the unrealistic case of slavery) and the existence of moral hazard incentives in education acquisition and labour market performance (since individual effort at school and at work is unobservable).[38] Without public intervention to correct this market failure, differential access to education persists across generations: poor families are unable to finance the education of their offspring, who in turn obtain less education, earn less and are themselves unable to finance the education of their own children. Thus imperfect financial markets could be responsible for persistent inequality, both in education and in income. However, from a theoretical point of view, the assumption of financial market imperfection is by itself insufficient to yield this result, and an additional condition is required: the indivisibility of human capital investment. In section 3 we have assumed that individual human capital H_{it} can be varied continuously, so that each individual can choose the exact amount of education to satisfy the optimality condition described by equation (2.7). However, the real world works differently, and educational certificates can be obtained at predetermined stages of career progression only. A university degree requires three years of university attendance, and attending only two of them may make an irrelevant impact on earnings ability.

In order to prove these propositions, we now move to the exposition of a simplified version of the Galor and Zeira (1993) model. It consists of an overlapping generation model, with a stationary population living for two periods. In the first period, when young, individuals can choose whether to work or study; in the second period, when adult, they work either as skilled (if they studied in the first period) or as unskilled (if they also worked in the first period). They also consume, give birth to offspring and die. The indivisibility of human capital investment is represented by a dichotomised choice: each agent can choose whether to pay a fixed cost γ for school attendance and obtain a degree, or work as an unskilled worker. The amount of human capital obtained by school attendance is fixed and identical across agents.[39] All agents are identical in terms of unobservable ability, but they can differ in terms of inherited family wealth. Combining an initial inequality with imperfect financial markets generates persistent inequality in education and income in the long run.

A crucial assumption requires that human capital investment always be profitable. If we indicate with W_t^n the market wage for a skilled worker at time t and with W_{t+1}^s the corresponding wage of a skilled worker (i.e. a person who paid the amount γ and forwent the income obtainable working as unskilled when young in order to become skilled when adult), the profitability condition (expressed in future values) requires that

$$W_{t+1}^s - \gamma(1 + R) > W_t^n + W_{t+1}^n(1 + R) = W^n(2 + R) \quad (2.10)$$

where R indicates the market interest rate.[40] W^n, W^s and R are exogenously given.[41] Under the condition expressed by equation (2.10) everyone would like to obtain education. Those who do not attend schools are prevented from doing so by the impossibility of paying the fixed cost of access γ.

The financial resources to fund education are derived either from inheritance from parents or from the financial intermediaries. If workers could gain access to foreign financial markets and debt repudiation could be safely excluded, all of them would borrow the amount required to finance education at the interest rate R, would attend school and become skilled, would repay the debt and would still obtain a profit (given the assumption (2.10)). In contrast, if debt default is an open possibility and access to international financial market is barred to workers, the financial intermediary bears a monitoring cost Z in order to minimise the probability of this event from the borrower. In a competitive financial sector, profits are driven to zero, and therefore the cost of fund collection (by assumption they are obtained on international financial markets) must equal their use. The monitoring cost will therefore be charged to the borrower according to the following relationship:

$$iD = RD + Z \quad (2.11)$$

where i is the lending interest rate and D is the amount of debt. Each borrower considering the possibility of defaulting on his/her debt takes into account the costs involved in prosecution avoidance by the lender; these costs are assumed to be proportional to its monitoring activity and are indicated by λZ, $\lambda > 1$. Knowing the set of incentives of the borrower, the lender will choose a level of monitoring activity that is proportional to the amount of debt, up to a point where the borrower is indifferent between debt repayment and debt repudiation:

$$D(1+i) = \lambda Z \tag{2.12}$$

Making use of equations (2.11) and (2.12), we can show that the borrowing rate exceeds the lending rate, determined on international financial markets.

$$i = \frac{1 + \lambda R}{\lambda - 1} \Leftrightarrow 1 + i = \frac{\lambda}{\lambda - 1}(1 + R) \Leftrightarrow i > R \tag{2.13}$$

The possibility of debt repudiation is the ultimate reason why poor families are discriminated against. Since they must borrow to finance their education, they face an opportunity cost of borrowing given by the interest rate i, which is higher than the opportunity cost R faced by rich families.[42]

Individuals are assumed to be altruistic, and therefore they care about the future welfare of their offspring by leaving a bequest X. Utility is defined over consumption in the second period of life and the bequest; when it takes a Cobb–Douglas formulation we get

$$U_t = \alpha \log C_{t+1} + (1 - \alpha) \log X_{t+1} \tag{2.14}$$

Each individual maximises his/her own utility for a given labour income and the inheritance received by his/her own parent. Given the fact that Cobb–Douglas utility functions are in the homothetic class, the optimal choice will be characterised by constant-income shares devoted to consumption and bequest. If I_{t+1} denotes total disposable income when adult, the optimal choice is

$$C^*_{t+1} = \alpha I_{t+1}, \quad X^*_{t+1} = (1 - \alpha) I_{t+1} \tag{2.15}$$

By replacing the optimal choice described by equation (2.15) in the utility function (2.14), we obtain the indirect utility function V_t

Table 2.2 *Possible life destinies*

Possible destinies	Lifetime disposable income	Bequest left to the offspring
(a) Individuals who do not acquire education	$(X_t + W^n)(1 + R) + W^n$	$X_{t+1} = (1 - \alpha)[(X_t + W^n)(1 + R) + W^n]$
(b) Individuals who need to borrow to acquire education $(X_t < \gamma)$	$W^s + (X_t - \gamma)(1 + i)$	$X_{t+1} = (1 - \alpha)[W^s + (X_t - \gamma)(1 + i)]$
(c) Individuals who do not need to borrow to invest in their own education $(X_t > \gamma)$	$W^s + (X_t - \gamma)(1 + R)$	$X_{t+1} = (1 - \alpha)[W^s + (X_t - \gamma)(1 + R)]$

characterising each generation t, which is loglinear in disposable income.

$$V_t = \alpha \log C^*_{t+1} + (1 - \alpha) \log X^*_{t+1}$$
$$= [\alpha \log \alpha + (1 - \alpha) \log(1 - \alpha)] + \log I_{t+1} \qquad (2.16)$$

Depending on the choice made with respect to education when young, we observe three possible destinies in the model (reported in table 2.2): (a) unskilled workers, who did not acquire education when young and worked as unskilled in both periods of life; (b) skilled workers from poor families, who did not receive an inheritance sufficient to finance their education, and therefore were forced to borrow in order to pay for it; and (c) skilled workers from rich families, who did not incur debt to get an education.

Under the assumption for profitability for the investment in education (see equation (2.11)), all individuals would like to become skilled. Those who inherit sufficient funds (e.g. exceeding the cost of accessing education γ) become skilled. Among the remaining population, there will be a fraction that is so poor that it will be unable to afford the debt required to obtain education: they will not invest in education, and remain unskilled. Given the absence of stochastic elements in the model, they will earn a low income and will leave a low bequest,

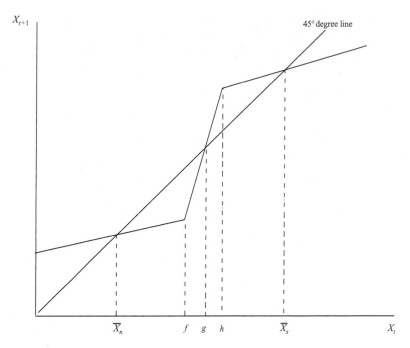

Figure 2.3 The dynamics of individual wealth

perpetuating the unskilled status in their dynasty. By equating cases (a) and (b) in table 2.2, we find the inheritance level at which it makes no difference whether an individual contracts a debt to become skilled or remains unskilled:

$$(X_t + W^n)(1 + R) + W^n = W^s + (X_t - \gamma)(1 + i)$$
$$\Updownarrow$$
$$\frac{W^n(2 + R) - W^s + \gamma(1 + i)}{i - R} = X_t = f \tag{2.17}$$

We have already seen in equation (2.15) that bequest are proportional to disposable income. Therefore, we can study the evolution of income distribution by means of the evolution of bequest distribution. And bequests evolve according to first-order difference equations reported in the third column of table 2.2, which are plotted in figure 2.3.[43]

All individuals inheriting an amount lower than f are better off not investing in education, and their income evolves according to case (a) in table 2.2, converging to $\frac{\overline{X}_n}{1-\alpha}$, where $\overline{X}_n$ is defined according to

$$\overline{X}_n = (1 - \alpha)[(1 + R)\overline{X}_n + W^n(2 + R)] \tag{2.18}$$

The individuals receiving an inheritance in the interval (f, g) will invest in education, but the debt burden exceeds their ability to pay, and they also converge to $\overline{X}_n$.[44] Finally, the 'happy few' who get a bequest greater than g experience a growing level of income across the generations, converging to $\frac{\overline{X}_s}{1-\alpha}$, where $\overline{X}_s$ satisfies

$$\overline{X}_s = (1 - \alpha)\{(1 + R)\overline{X}_s + [W^s - (1 + R)\gamma]\} > \overline{X}_n \qquad (2.19)$$

The speed of convergence rate will be lower for debtors (where $X_{t-1} < h$) than for people from rich families (where $X_{t-1} > h$), because of the different interest rate they pay to or receive from financial intermediaries. In the long run income distribution becomes bimodal, with a population share concentrated around $\frac{\overline{X}_n}{1-\alpha}$, and its complementary share concentrated around $\frac{\overline{X}_s}{1-\alpha}$. The mean income in the population is determined as weighted average, where weights depend on initial income distribution

$$\overline{X} = \frac{n(g)}{n}\overline{X}_n + \left(1 - \frac{n(g)}{n}\right)\overline{X}_s = \overline{X}_s - \frac{n(g)}{n}(\overline{X}_s - \overline{X}_n)$$
$$= \phi(n(g)), \quad \phi' < 0 \qquad (2.20)$$

where F is the cumulative distribution function at time zero, and $n(g) = \int_0^g dF(X)$ indicates the number of individuals with initial wealth smaller than or equal to g. Given the deterministic nature of the model, their descendants will in the long run achieve an income level equal to $\frac{\overline{X}_n}{1-\alpha}$. An egalitarian economy will be characterised by a low share $n(g)$ of (relatively) poor individuals, and will experience a higher average income in the long run. Income redistribution from rich to poor raises average income (or wealth) in the economy, but does not constitute a Paretian improvement, since the rich do not obtain any direct benefit from this move. In contrast, intertemporal redistribution achieved by means of fiscal policy (subsidising the education of the young by taxing their income when adult) solves the market failure, lowers the debt cost and is therefore Pareto superior.[45]

Appendix: Human capital investment in a continuous-time model

We present here a continuous-time version of the human capital investment model, drawing heavily on Ben-Porath (1967). The main advantage with respect to the model presented in section 2.2 is that we obtain in a multiperiod context a closed solution for the optimal path of investment. The basic assumptions of the model are:

(i) leisure does not enter the utility function; time can be devoted to either study or work;

(ii) perfect financial markets, so consumption smoothing is feasible; and

(iii) human capital has a constant rental rate β in the labour market, which ensures full employment.

While earnings potential is proportional to the current individual stock of human capital H_t, actual earnings W_t are given by

$$W_t = \beta H_t - S_t \beta H_t - \gamma B_t \tag{A2.1}$$

where S_t is the fraction of the available stock of human capital allocated to the production of human capital (capturing the opportunity cost of human capital investment), B_t represents other resources used in producing human capital (capturing the direct cost of schooling) and γ is the unitary cost of the additional resources employed in schooling.

The production function of newly added human capital is given by

$$Q_t = A(S_t H_t)^{\alpha_1}(B_t)^{\alpha_2}, \quad \alpha_1 + \alpha_2 < 1 \tag{A2.2}$$

where the shift parameter A is a proxy of individual talent.

The human capital is assumed to depreciate at a constant rate δ; its continuous-time variation is therefore given by

$$\frac{dH_t}{dt} = \dot{H}_t = Q_t - \delta H_t = A(S_t H_t)^{\alpha_1}(B_t)^{\alpha_2} - \delta H_t \tag{A2.3}$$

Cost minimisation in the production of new human capital yields an optimal choice between two factors, S_t and B_t, according to their relative cost and their relative impact. If we define our objective as the problem

$$\min_{S_t, B_t}(\beta S_t H_t + \gamma B_t) \quad s.t. \quad Q_t = A(S_t H_t)^{\alpha_1}(B_t)^{\alpha_2} \tag{A2.4}$$

by taking the ratio of the two first-order conditions, $\frac{\beta S_t H_t}{\gamma B_t} = \frac{\alpha_1}{\alpha_2}$, we obtain the cost function associated with the production of new human capital

$$C_t = \beta S_t H_t + \gamma B_t = \frac{\alpha_1 + \alpha_2}{\alpha_1} \beta S_t H_t$$

$$= \frac{\alpha_1 + \alpha_2}{\alpha_1} \beta \left(\frac{Q_t}{A}\right)^{\frac{1}{\alpha_1+\alpha_2}} \left(\frac{\alpha_1 \beta}{\alpha_2 \gamma}\right)^{\frac{\alpha_2}{\alpha_1+\alpha_2}} = C(Q_t) \qquad (A2.5)$$

Each agent maximises his/her human wealth, equivalent to the discounted value of disposable income over the lifespan, assumed to be finite with length T (known with certainty), net of the cost of accumulation described by equation (A2.5):

$$\max_{S_t} \int_t^T e^{-\rho v}(\beta H_v - C_v)dv = \max_{S_t} \int_t^T e^{-\rho v}(\beta(1 - S_v)H_v - \gamma B_v)dv$$

$$(A2.6)$$

subject to the accumulation equation (A2.3). By using the definition of equation (A2.5) the maximising behaviour can be expressed as

$$\max_{S_t} \int_t^T e^{-\rho v} \left(\beta H_v \left(1 - S_v \frac{\alpha_1 + \alpha_2}{\alpha_1}\right)\right) dv \quad s.t.$$

$$\dot{H} = A \left(\frac{\alpha_2 \beta}{\alpha_1 \gamma}\right)^{\alpha_2} (S_t H_t)^{\alpha_1+\alpha_2} - \delta H_t \qquad (A2.7)$$

or, using a more compact form,

$$\max_{S_t} \int_t^T e^{-\rho v} F(H_v, S_v) \quad s.t. \quad \dot{H} = g(H, S) \qquad (A2.8)$$

Problem (A2.8) can be solved using standard optimal control techniques.[46]

By replacing $A\left(\frac{\alpha_2 \beta}{\alpha_1 \gamma}\right)^{\alpha_2} = \eta$ for notational clarity, we write the Hamiltonian function as

$$\Omega = e^{-\rho t} \left(\beta H \left(1 - S \frac{\alpha_1 + \alpha_2}{\alpha_1}\right)\right) + \lambda(\eta(SH)^{\alpha_1+\alpha_2} - \delta H) \qquad (A2.9)$$

The necessary conditions associated with the Hamiltonian are

$$\frac{\partial \Omega}{\partial S} = -e^{-\rho t}\left(\beta H \frac{\alpha_1 + \alpha_2}{\alpha_1}\right) + \lambda \eta(\alpha_1 + \alpha_2)H(SH)^{\alpha_1 + \alpha_2 - 1} = 0 \quad (A2.10)$$

$$\frac{\partial \Omega}{\partial H} = -\dot{\lambda} \quad \Leftrightarrow \quad \dot{\lambda} = -e^{-\rho t}\beta\left(1 - S\frac{\alpha_1 + \alpha_2}{\alpha_1}\right)$$

$$+ \lambda \eta(\alpha_1 + \alpha_2)S(SH)^{\alpha_1 + \alpha_2 - 1} + \lambda\delta \quad (A2.11)$$

$$\frac{\partial \Omega}{\partial \lambda} = \dot{H} \quad \Leftrightarrow \quad \dot{H} = \eta(SH)^{\alpha_1 + \alpha_2} - \delta H \quad (A2.12)$$

The two addends in equation (A2.10) constitute the marginal cost and the marginal benefit, respectively, associated with human capital accumulation; this equation can be solved explicitly in terms of the optimal choice of schooling:

$$S^* = \frac{1}{H}\left(\frac{A\alpha_1\alpha_2^{\alpha_2}\mu}{(\alpha_1\gamma)^{\alpha_2}\beta^{1-\alpha_2}}\right)^{\frac{1}{1-\alpha_1-\alpha_2}} = S(\underset{-}{H}, \underset{+}{A}, \underset{-}{\gamma}, \underset{-}{\beta}, \underset{+}{\mu}) \quad (A2.13)$$

Equation (A2.13) is the continuous-time version of equation (2.7), and $\mu = \lambda e^{\rho t}$ represents the shadow (current) price on investment. Additional boundaries conditions $S^* \in [0, 1]$ are implicitly present. Finally, the transversality condition requires that $\lim_{t \to T} \mu(t)H(t) = 0$ be satisfied.

Using the result of equation (A2.13), equation (A2.11) can be rewritten it as $\dot{\lambda} = -e^{-\rho t}\beta + \delta\lambda$, or, re-expressing in terms of μ,

$$\dot{\mu} = -\beta + \mu(\delta + \rho) \quad (A2.14)$$

By the forward integration of equation (A2.14) we obtain[47]

$$\mu(t) = \frac{\beta}{\rho + \delta}\left(1 - e^{-(\rho+\delta)(T-t)}\right) \quad (A2.15)$$

Ben-Porath indicates the costate variable μ as the 'demand price' of human capital, since it corresponds to the marginal benefit of varying the stock of human capital.[48] By studying its dynamics we infer the properties of the optimal path of human capital accumulation.

Given the results that $\mu(0) > 0$ and $\mu(T) = 0$, we observe that along all the optimal path of investment $\dot{\mu} < 0$; as a consequence, $\dot{S}^* < 0$ and $\dot{Q} = Q(\dot{S}^*) < 0$ as well. The higher T is the higher is $\mu(0)$, and the higher is $S^*(0)$: the longer the life expectancy the higher the initial investment in human capital, since the time horizon for collecting education return is longer.

We devise three phases in the path of accumulation. In the initial phase, the existing stock of human capital, even when fully allocated to education, is insufficient to provide the flow of services demanded at the existing price. As a consequence, μ is high and the upper bound $S^* = 1$ is reached: the agent spends all his/her time in accumulating additional human capital, and no labour earnings materialise.

In the second phase of life, when the human capital stock becomes adequate, the marginal cost and the marginal benefit are equated, and $0 < S^* < 1$.[49] By placing the optimal solution (A2.13) into equation (A2.3), we get $\dot{H} = Q(S^*H) - \delta H$: since S^* declines steadily, the human capital stock reaches a maximum when $\dot{H} = 0$, and from then onwards declines. If we look at the dynamics of actual earnings defined in (A2.1), by making use of cost minimisation (A2.4) we get

$$W = \beta H \left(1 - S^* \frac{\alpha_1 + \alpha_2}{\alpha_1}\right) \quad \Rightarrow$$

$$\dot{W} = \beta \left(\dot{H}\left(1 - S^* \frac{\alpha_1 + \alpha_2}{\alpha_1}\right) - \dot{S}H\frac{\alpha_1 + \alpha_2}{\alpha_1}\right) \qquad \text{(A2.16)}$$

Since the second addend of (A2.16) is always positive (because a negative sign multiplies a negative term), actual earnings W start declining after H has peaked and has already started declining.

In the third and final part of life, the stock of human capital is excessive, such that disinvestment through depreciation is insufficient: the optimal investment becomes negligible, reaching zero in the final stage of life.

This model shows that the optimal investment path requires concentrating the phase of schooling in the initial part of life, even if human capital accumulation continues after full-time education. The stock of human capital increases up to a point when depreciation becomes dominant, then declines. Labour earnings follow a similar path, mimicking the empirical evidence on age–earning profiles that we reported in chapter 1.

Notes

1. See the discussion on the relationship between equality and heterogeneity in Roemer (1986).
2. The exposition of the differences between *functionings* and *capabilities* is found in Sen (1992). A typical example of what is meant by functioning is the following. Consider a free distribution of computers to children's families in a school. Does this represent equality in resource

distribution? The answer depends on the ability to use the computers to help the children do their homework. If some parents are illiterate, and are unable to operate a computer since they cannot read the instructions (that is, they have imperfections in their functionings), then resources are still unequally distributed (for they do not ensure equal capabilities in helping the children to learn), in spite of the formal equality in their distribution.

3. Helliwell and Putnam (1999) show that education (both at individual level and as community average) is the most important predictor of political and social engagement (where 'social trust' is measured either through objective indicators – such as participating in meetings – or through the subjective attitude towards other individuals – e.g. answering questions such as 'Do you agree/disagree with the proposition that "most people are honest"?').

4. Even in a Tiebout world (Tiebout, 1956), where people express their preferences with respect to expenditure and taxation by choosing the local community to live in, we could not be sure that a minimal provision of education would be achieved. For example, we could obtain a self-sorting of families into communities according to the relative significance attributed to the importance of children's education. And we would not be surprised to find local communities where girls' education is considered redundant with respect to boys' education.

5. In fact, the first instance of the introduction of compulsory education is attributed to Fredrick the Great, who introduced it in Prussia in 1763, followed ten years later by the Austrian Maria Theresa.

6. Eckstein and Zilcha (1994) present an overlapping generation model where parents randomly differ in the degree of altruism, and show that the introduction of free compulsory education (financed through taxation) constitutes a second-best policy, which is closer to the first-best chosen by a benevolent dictator. A related argument is offered by Appleton, Hoddinott and Knight (1996), who draw attention to the vertical integration nature of the educational process: reducing school attendance in the early stages reduces possible inputs at subsequent stages.

7. In fact, knowledge deprivation is in some ways a relative concept: in a population of illiterate persons one is not ashamed to be illiterate oneself, and therefore the inability to read does not represent bad functioning, creating a limitation in freedom.

8. The most recent one was called PISA (Programme for International Student Assessment), concluding in 2003. Previous researches were conducted by the IEA (International Association for the Evaluation of Educational Achievement). See OECD (2001), chapter F: 'Learning outcomes of education'.

9. 'The International Adult Literacy Survey (IALS) is the world's first international comparative assessment of adult literacy skills. The IALS study has combined household survey methods and educational assessment to provide comparable estimates of literacy skills for 24 countries. The survey tests representative samples of adults (aged 16–65) in their homes, asking them to undertake a range of common tasks using authentic materials from a wide range of social and cultural contexts. The IALS study is jointly sponsored by Statistics Canada, the US Center for Education Statistics and the Organisation for Economic Co-operation and Development (OECD). While traditional measures of literacy focus primarily on the ability to decode the printed word, the IALS study defines literacy as the ability to understand and use printed information in daily activities at home, at work and in the community. It compiled the cross-country data to ensure that the results are comparable across countries with different languages and cultures and that any known sources of bias are corrected' (UNDP 2001, p. 137). The UNDP report uses the percentage of adults lacking functional literacy skills, defined on the basis of prose literacy (i.e. the knowledge and skills needed to understand and use information from texts, including editorials, news stories, poems and fiction).

10. At this stage we are leaving to one side the question as to whether it is parents or children who undertake educational choices, and we will maintain the simplifying assumption that individuals are held responsible for their educational choices.

11. A variant of this approach is to regard education as providing higher social status, and therefore individuals demand education in order to increase the esteem they obtain from other people. Fershtman, Murphy and Weiss (1996) offer a model along this line.

12. Schultz (1963) proposes a tripartite description of the roles played by education: a present consumption component (say, the utility derived from the pleasure of knowing); a future consumption component (which takes into account the fact that education improves the ability to consume other goods in life – think of the improved health conditions or better-informed fertility choices associated with higher education); and an investment component (see below). For an attempt to disentangle the consumption and investment components, see Lazear (1977).

13. The term 'human capital' has nowadays become common in economic jargon, thanks to the pioneering works of Gary Becker (see Becker 1993).

14. In a more technical way, we can rephrase the same concept by saying that the investment in physical capital has an option value to waiting, while the corresponding value for investment in human capital is almost

zero (you cannot postpone going to school till you are older, waiting for better labour market conditions).

15. See the discussion in Piketty (1997).
16. This is because the rents associated with the ownership of physical capital are profits from productive activity, whereas the rents associated with the ownership of human capital are wages. For a critique along this line of argument see Bowles and Gintis (1975).
17. Suppose, for example, that self-consciousness favours the acquisition of education, and for similar reasons reduces absenteeism while working as dependent employee. Then firms will demand self-conscious workers because they are more productive (i.e. less absenteeist), and the workers themselves will also be more educated. See Weiss (1995) for additional examples.
18. This constitutes a two-period simplified version of the original model by Yoram Ben-Porath (see Ben-Porath, 1967). A continuous-time version is reported in the appendix to the present chapter.
19. Notice that here we are assuming an identical return rate on education across individuals who are differentiated in terms of ability; moreover, the same rate of return is independent of the amount of human capital employed in production (i.e. we disregard decreasing marginal productivity). Some of these assumptions will be relaxed later on (see chapter 6); see also the discussion in Card (1999).
20. We are not interested in going deeper into defining here what we mean by 'unobservable ability'. We find convincing the definition provided by Rubinstein and Tsiddon (1998): ability is 'everything that contributes to the child's income potential, is in the child at the time he takes his education decision, and cannot be purchased on the market' (p. 19).
21. There is evidence that the prohibition of child labour, by lowering the return to work for children, induces greater attendance at schools. See, for example, Dehejia and Gatti (2002).
22. This conclusion holds irrespective of whether the individual is actually borrowing in the financial market. In the event of an interest rate rise, even a rich person, who does not need to borrow money to cover the direct and indirect cost of schooling, may find it (economically) convenient to reduce his/her demand for education. By so doing he/she will obtain a higher current income, which – invested in the financial market – will yield a higher return tomorrow. Things are different if the imperfection of financial markets results in different interest rates being charged for different individuals. In such a case individuals from poorer families will face higher costs of borrowing, and, other things being constant, will demand less education.

23. Taking the first-order derivative of equation (2.7) it is easy to prove that $sign\left(\frac{\partial S_{it}^*}{\partial H_{it}}\right) = sign(\alpha - (1 - \alpha)\beta_t H_{it})$.

24. This case has been defined as 'elitist' by Becker (1993, chap. 3, p. 108), because only the elite amongst the ablest people choose the maximum amount of education.

25. Alternative formulations of financial market imperfection with respect to educational choices are analysed in Kodde and Ritzen (1985).

26. Becker (1993) calls this case 'egalitarian' because it provides a rationale for the public funding of educational expenditure. In this situation redistributive policies are Pareto improving, and there is no conflict between equality and efficiency. He also claims that, in principle, it is possible to distinguish between 'elitist' and 'egalitarian' cases by observing the positive (negative) correlation between return and years of schooling (Becker, 1993, pp. 128–30).

27. We could easily have introduced a cost-reducing assumption for talent: the brightest children (or children from educated parents) need less time to learn, thus facing lower opportunity costs. This corresponds to the case where $\gamma_i = \gamma(A_i)$, $\gamma' < 0$. The cost schedule in figure 2.1 would become flatter, whereas the return schedule would not shift, but the final outcome would be identical.

28. This is true only under first-best conditions, because otherwise granting equality of opportunity may raise output and the equality of outcomes at the same time: see Benabou (2000).

29. Becker and Tomes (1986) have proposed this strategy in order to estimate the intergenerational persistence of incomes dispensing for liquidity constraints. Shea (2000) proposes an alternative test, based on unexpected components of income affecting educational attainment. While positive correlation could be taken as evidence of liquidity constraints, he finds no effect when actual family income is instrumented with the unexpected component.

30. See also the critical book review by Goldberger and Manski (1995).

31. Feldman, Otto and Christiansen (2000) distinguish between 'genetic' heritability (genotypes) and 'environmental' heritability (phenotypes), and review the recent literature on IQ genetic transmittability: while, in the 1970s, the proportion of IQ that is genetically transmittable was held to be around 80 per cent, most recent work has reduced the estimate to as low as 30 per cent.

32. Flynn (2000) shows that IQ measures are unable to define a time-invariant standard for what can be termed 'normal intelligence', since, in many industrialised countries, each generation outscores the previous one.

33. See the account of this debate in Bowles and Nelson (1974) and in Bowles and Gintis (1976, chaps. 2 and 4).
34. Mulvey, Miller and Martin (1997, p. 130). Ashenfelter and Rouse (1998) pursue an alternative strategy by assuming the existence of a common unobservable variable called 'family ability', and study the correlation between this unobservable and the educational attainment of twins. Finding some evidence of negative correlation between family ability and the average wage in a couple of twins, they suggest that public education *could* act as a compensatory device. See the review of this line of research in Card (1999).
35. Murnane, Willet and Levy (1995) show that mathematical abilities were more relevant in wage regressions than any other measure based on test scores. Bowles and Gintis (2000) review several studies including controls for ability in earnings regressions, showing that the inclusion of ability does not reduce the explanatory power of schooling by more than 20 per cent: 'This suggests that a substantial portion of the returns to schooling are generated by effects of correlates of schooling substantially unrelated to the skills measured on the available tests' (p. 122).
36. More recently, an emerging literature on the so-called 'natural experiments' claims to be able to measure the real contribution of acquired education to earnings, irrespective of natural ability. Whenever an exogenous source of variation (a war, an educational reform or even the time of year of birth) induces people to attend more schooling, the unintended variation of education can be used to measure the additional earnings associated with education. See Angrist and Krueger (1999).
37. The convergence to identical incomes is a general property of the neoclassical growth model, due to decreasing marginal returns (see Stiglitz, 1969, and the counter-arguments in Bourguignon, 1981). See also the appendix to chapter 5 of the present volume. The intuition is that the poor experience a higher rate of return on their investment than the richer do, thus catching up in the long run. This result holds even in the presence of externalities from the accumulation of individual human capital (Tamura, 1991). Whenever agents differ along some characteristics (ability, family wealth, resources spent on education), we observe conditional convergence – i.e. the convergence of incomes for all individuals with identical characteristics (see Barro and Sala-i-Martin, 1992, for a discussion of σ-convergence).
38. This could even be exacerbated if the repayment is progressively related to earned income, as in the Australian experience: see Chapman (1997).
39. The indivisibility of human capital investment creates a non-convexity in the production of human capital, which sustains persistent inequality,

even in the long run. If the poor could acquire fractions of the degree by paying a fraction of its cost, in the long run they would achieve the same wealth as the rich.

40. An alternative formulation of equation (2.10) requires that the return to education, equal to $\frac{W^s - \gamma - 2W^n}{\gamma + W^n}$ (where the numerator is the income gain obtained through education, whereas the denominator collects the direct and indirect costs of educational choice), exceeds the market interest rate. When this does not create ambiguity, we will neglect temporal indices.

41. In order to sustain this assumption, Galor and Zeira (1993) consider a small economy producing a homogeneous good. In a small economy, R is given by international financial markets. While financial intermediaries can access these markets (which operate efficiently), workers are prevented from borrowing on these markets. If the production technology exhibits constant returns to scale in physical capital and skilled labour, then profit maximisation uniquely determines W^s for any given user cost of capital R. Let us suppose that production technology is $Y = L_s^\beta K^{1-\beta}$. Then the first-order condition for physical capital requires that $(1 - \beta)\left(\frac{L_s}{K}\right)^\beta - R \Leftrightarrow \frac{K}{L_s} = \left(\frac{1-\beta}{R}\right)^{\frac{1}{\beta}}$. By replacing this condition in the first-order condition for skilled labour L_s we obtain $W^s = \beta\left(\frac{K}{L_s}\right)^{1-\beta} = \beta\left(\frac{1-\beta}{R}\right)^{\frac{1-\beta}{\beta}}$, where the skilled labour wage is negatively related to the user cost of capital, via the substitutability of these two inputs. In an open economy the output price is determined on international markets, and for simplicity it is normalised to one. Finally, they assume the existence of a second type of technology, using unskilled labour only. In such a case W^n is equal to the average productivity in the sector using this last technology.

42. One may wonder why rich families do not lend directly to poor families, earning an interest rate falling somewhere between i and R. Acting this way, the rich family will bear the entire default risk from the borrower. But, even leaving aside the default risk, the equilibrium interest rate will depend on the relative supply of and demand for funds, which reflect the initial income (or wealth) distribution in the population. Thus, in a very unequal society there will be many borrowers and few lenders, and the equilibrium interest rate will be pushed up, further reducing the educational investment of the poor. See Piketty (1997) for a model along these lines.

43. Figure 2.3 is drawn under the assumption that $\overline{X}_n$ and $\overline{X}_s$ are stable equilibria, whereas g is an unstable equilibrium. This is equivalent to

assuming

$$\begin{cases} (1-\alpha)(1+R) < 1 \\ (1-\alpha)(1+i) = (1-\alpha)(1+R)\frac{\lambda}{\lambda-1} > 1 \end{cases}$$

which jointly imply that $\frac{\lambda-1}{\lambda} < (1-\alpha)(1+R) < 1$.

44. The g value corresponds to the unstable equilibrium satisfying $g = \overline{X} = (1-\alpha)(1+i)\overline{X} + (1-\alpha)[W^s - (1+i)\gamma]$.

45. Galor and Zeira (1993) also consider the case of an endogenous unskilled wage W^n. This reinforces a poverty trap, because a rising portion of the population converging to $\overline{X}_n$ lowers W^n, which translates into a further lowering of $\overline{X}_n$. In contrast, when $W^n > \frac{g}{1-\alpha}$ the economy converges to a unique long-run equilibrium, given by $\overline{X}_s$.

46. See, for example, Kamien and Schwartz (1981).

47. By multiplying both sides of (A2.14) by $e^{-(\rho+\delta)t}$, taking the integrals of both sides on the interval (t, T) and integrating by parts the left-hand side, we reach the following condition, $\mu(T)e^{-(\rho+\delta)T} - \mu(t)e^{-(\rho+\delta)t} = \frac{\beta}{\rho+\delta}(e^{-(\rho+\delta)T} - e^{-(\rho+\delta)t})$, from which equation (A2.15) is derived.

48. By rewriting the Hamiltonian (A2.9) as $\Omega = e^{-\rho t}(\beta H - C(Q)) - \lambda(Q - \delta H)$ and deriving it with respect to Q (namely, the optimal increase in human capital), we obtain $e^{-\rho t}\frac{dC}{dQ} - \lambda = 0 \Leftrightarrow \frac{dC}{dQ} = \lambda e^{\rho t} = \mu$.

49. 'The value at time t of acquiring an additional unit of human capital is the discounted value to that time of the additions to earnings that the undepreciated part of this unit will bring about' (Ben-Porath, 1967, p. 355).

3 | Liquidity constraints and access to education

The model presented in the previous chapter predicts that an initial position of income inequality reduces access to education and, as a consequence, future income distribution. It will be interesting to establish whether this prediction has any empirical validation in the real world.[1] In the present chapter we will review some macro-evidence providing support for this proposition. Starting from an optimal demand for education, where the years of education depend on family income among other things, we derive two testable predictions in the analysis of aggregate data on school enrolments: a negative (linear) dependence of enrolment rates on the Gini inequality measure on income distribution; and a positive dependence on public resources invested in education and/or on the skill premium in the labour market. On the one hand, optimal demand for schooling could be positively associated with unobservable ability; if ability is intergenerationally transmitted, we would get a positive correlation between family income and children's schooling. On the other hand, if liquidity constraints prevented school attendance by children from poor families, we would observe a correlation between educational choices and family incomes, at least in the lower tail of income distribution. We prove that, under the given assumptions, enrolment rates and measures of income inequality (namely the Gini index) should be negatively correlated. However, following the liquidity constraint explanation, the Gini coefficient should be negatively correlated whenever missing financial markets create a barrier preventing access to education by the poorest families. In contrast, if the intergenerational transmission of talent is a valid explanation, educational attainment and income distribution should be positively correlated at any stage of education. Since our empirical estimates prove a robust negative correlation at the secondary level for the whole population, and at the primary and tertiary levels for a gender component only, we believe that these results lend support to the view that poor families are prevented from accessing school by their low incomes. Thus, greater income inequality reduces access to school.

These predictions are tested on an (unbalanced) panel of 108 countries for the period 1960 to 1995. The main findings of this analysis are that, once we control for the degree of development with the (log of) per capita output, financial constraints seem relevant mainly in limiting the access to secondary education. However, when considering gender differences, there is evidence that female participation in education is more conditioned by family wealth, in some cases starting with primary education. Finally, there is weak evidence that public resources spent on education raise the enrolment rates.

3.1 Access to education and growth

In recent years there has been a revival of interest in studying the relationship between inequality and growth. After the work by Simon Kuznets in the 1950s (for example, Kuznets, 1955), in which the stages of growth were found to be shaping the degree of inequality in society, the issue was neglected for some thirty years, to reappear again at the beginning of the 1990s. Starting with the empirical finding of a negative relationship between income inequality and the growth of per capita income observed in different samples of countries over the last thirty years, several studies have proposed alternative explanations. Without any claim to completeness, one could group the existing explanations into two main lines of research.[2] The first one invokes political economy actions, in a context of asset market completeness. Greater inequality raises the demand for fiscal redistribution and introduces distortions that hamper private investment decisions.[3] An empirical variant of the same idea is that (wealth) inequality makes turmoil more likely (e.g. the lack of land reform), increases political instability, makes investors' horizons shakier and eventually reduces output growth.[4] In both cases it is the increasing threat of a reduction in the return on invested capital (or even the risk of expropriation) that reduces the agents' willingness to invest in physical capital, thus depressing the potential for growth.

The second line of research considers the borrowing constraints in financing access to education as the main explanation for the negative correlation between inequality and growth:[5] the poorest sections of the population do not possess adequate resources to access education and cannot find financial markets where they can borrow these funds to send their children to school; as a consequence, the investment in education is reduced at the aggregate level. In this case fiscal redistribution is efficient because it shifts resources from individuals with low rates of return to liquidity-constrained agents with very high rates of return.[6]

Empirical tests of these two lines of research are still inconclusive. Almost everyone accepts the idea of negative correlation,[7] but it is not yet clear through which variables it operates. The political economy explanation suffers from a lack of evidence regarding a negative relationship between redistribution and growth.[8] Alesina and Perotti (1996) find evidence of a negative relationship between inequality and growth via a variable measuring political instability (a first principal component extracted from the numbers of riots, assassinations, coups); but their analysis has no predictive power, and the ability to measure political instability is questionable.[9] It is more difficult to test the second line of research in the absence of information at the individual level about income and the educational choices facing the family. Using aggregate data, Perotti (1994) finds that a subjective qualitative measure of credit market rationing is statistically significant in explaining growth only when combined with income inequality. However, the most convincing piece of evidence in this respect comes from the comparison between Far Eastern and Latin American countries. The former are characterised by lower inequality and greater access to education, whereas the latter exhibit the reverse situation; possibly for these different patterns, the Far East experienced sustained growth during the 1970s and 1980s, while Latin America underwent stagnation.[10] Using household surveys for thirty-five countries, Filmer and Pritchett (1999) show that asset poverty (as measured by the first principal component extracted from information on the ownership of durable goods and the quality of the housing) reduces school attainment in the poorest 40 per cent of the population. Using aggregate data on secondary enrolment, Flug, Spilimbergo and Wachtenheim (1998) provide evidence that educational choices are limited by aggregate risk (as measured by volatility in output per capita) but are eased by financial development (as measured by the ratio of liquidity assets to domestic output). The following evidence provides additional support in the same vein, by widening the time-span, the number of countries and the set of regressors used to predict the enrolment rates for the three stages of educational attainment (primary, secondary and tertiary).

3.2 Individual demand for education and aggregate income distribution

In the previous chapter we obtained the optimal demand for schooling by equating decreasing marginal benefit (because lengthening school attendance reduces working life) and increasing marginal cost (because of the direct cost of higher stages of education and the opportunity cost of forgone incomes). The demand for schooling decreases with the intertemporal discount rate and with the direct costs of schooling, and increases with the return on education and the resources publicly invested in education (as long as they are effective in increasing the production of human capital). When agents are heterogeneous in ability, more talented children obtain more human capital (because they benefit more from schooling and they stay longer at school) and therefore earn more (Card, 1999). When agents are heterogeneous in family income and financial markets are imperfect, children from poor families obtain less education because they face higher costs, and earn less in the labour market. These two polar cases of heterogeneity, respectively named 'elitist' and 'egalitarian' by Becker (1993), rather then being mutually excluding usually coexist. Both heterogeneities can be intergenerationally transmitted. Inequality in family resources may prevent access to education, thus recreating inequality in incomes in the next generation. In contrast, when unobservable ability is correlated across generations, better-endowed parents are more likely to get endowed children. In both cases we empirically observe low intergenerational mobility in educational achievements and measures. Thus when we take a snapshot picture of income distribution, we are unable to distinguish whether the poor are so because they are less talented or because they are the descendants of poor families.[11] Unless one has access to individual data with reasonable proxies for unobservable ability for at least two generations, the two cases are observationally equivalent. The debate between supporters of a 'natural' explanation and defenders of the 'imperfect market' explanation of inequality has not yet reached a definite conclusion, given the lack of natural experiments to discriminate between the two, and we suspect it *never* will.[12]

Since individual data sets containing proxy variables for ability do not exist for a sufficient number of countries, we have to resort to indirect aggregate evidence. If educational achievements and family incomes are correlated across generations at individual levels (either for imperfect financial markets or for persistence in unobserved ability) then the distribution of income in one generation is correlated with educational access in the next one. The shape of this relationship is the object of our investigation.

Let us start with an overlapping generation model, analogous to the one we presented in the previous chapter. A standard human capital relationship between earned income and educational achievement can be summarised by

$$I_{it+1} = f(S_{it}, A_{it}) + \varepsilon_{it+1} \qquad (3.1)$$

The income I_{it+1} earned by individual i when adult depends on his/her educational achievement when young S_{it}, on his/her endowment of unobservable ability A_{it} and on good/bad luck in the labour market ε_{it+1}. If the individual maximises his/her expected income given a budget constraint (where the access to education can be limited by inherited family resources) and a 'production' technology for human capital, we obtain the optimal choice of schooling

$$S_{it} = g(A_{it}, X_{it}, \beta_t, E_t) \qquad (3.2)$$

The higher his/her unobservable ability A_{it} (because talented people have more success at school, drop out less and stay at school longer), the higher the family income X_{it} (since family income can limit access to education when financial markets are imperfect or even absent), the higher the expected return of education in the labour market β_t and the higher the public resources invested in education E_t (which may lower the access cost to education, provide better quality education and/or improve the cultural environment), the more education the individual will demand.

If unobserved ability is correlated across generations, the ability of current generation A_{it} depends on the ability endowment of parents in previous generation A_{it-1}:

$$A_{it} = h(A_{it-1}) \qquad (3.3)$$

By placing equation (3.3) into equation (3.2) we get

$$S_{it} = g(h(A_{it-1}), X_{it}, \beta_t, E_t)$$
$$\phantom{S_{it} = g(h(}+\phantom{(A_{it-1}),} +\phantom{X_{i}} + + \qquad (3.4)$$

By lagging equation (3.1) by one generation and inverting with respect to parent ability[13] we obtain

$$A_{it-1} = l(S_{it-1}, X_{it})$$
$$\phantom{A_{it-1} = l(}+\phantom{S_{it-1},} +\phantom{X_{it})} \qquad (3.5)$$

Finally, by inserting equation (3.5) into equation (3.4) we

$$S_{it} = g\left(h(l(S_{it-1}, X_{it})), X_{it}, \beta_{t+1}, E_t\right)$$
$$\phantom{S_{it} = g(h(l(}+\phantom{S_{it-1}, X_{it})),} +\phantom{X_{it},} +\phantom{\beta_{t+1},} + \qquad (3.6)$$

In this way we see that parent income is correlated with children's educational choices through two possible channels. The first (which we term 'ability') summarises the fact that brighter parents earn more and give birth to brighter children, who in turn achieve more education. The second (which we term 'liquidity constraint') indicates that, under imperfect financial markets, the poorest fraction of the population may be prevented from accessing school. If we loglinearise equation (3.6) and use lower-case letters to denote the logarithms of corresponding capital-letter variables, then

$$s_{it} = \alpha_0 + \alpha_1 s_{it-1} + \alpha_2 x_{it} + \alpha_3 x_{it} + \alpha_4 b_{t+1} + \alpha_5 e_t \qquad (3.7)$$

where $s_t = \log(S_t)$, $x_t = \log(X_t)$, $b_t = \log(\beta_t)$ and $e_t = \log(E_t)$. Case $\alpha_2 \neq 0$ suggests ability persistence, whereas $\alpha_3 \neq 0$ indicates liquidity constraints. In principle, the two cases could be empirically distinguished.[14] Since our theoretical expectations are $\alpha_2 > 0$ and $\alpha_3 \geq 0$ (zero being the limiting case of perfect financial markets), if we do not find evidence of correlation between children's educational choices and parents' incomes we can infer that both 'ability' and 'liquidity constraints' channels of persistence are absent. In contrast, finding positive correlation potentially allows for both explanations. However the 'ability' channel should operate at *all stages* of education (i.e. α_2 must be positive at all stages of educational choices), whereas the 'liquidity' channel could operate at *some stages* of education but not at others (typically, for non-compulsory and/or lower stages of education). But we cannot proceed any further without individual information about education and family background, and unfortunately these data sets exist mainly for developed countries and for recent years only.

If we wish to extend our analysis to a larger set of countries and years, we have to resort to aggregate information. We need, therefore, to develop the aggregate implications of the model described by equation (3.7). We introduce the assumption that incomes X are lognormally distributed – that is, $\log(X) = x \sim N(\mu_x, \sigma_x^2)$. As a consequence of the loglinearity of equation (3.7), educational choices will be normally distributed in the following generation, conditional on the 'ability' and/or the 'liquidity' channels being potentially operative. We will exploit the known properties of normal distributions to prove the following proposition.

Proposition 1: under the assumptions of the validity of model (3.7) and a lognormal distribution for incomes X, the enrolment rates for school (namely the proportion of the reference population attending school) are linearly related to specific inequality measures (such as the Gini concentration index) obtained from income distribution.

Proof: the enrolment rate P represents the fraction of the population aiming to achieve an amount of education exceeding the legal duration of a given stage of school. In symbols

$$
\begin{aligned}
P_1 &= \text{primary school enrolment} &&= \int_{n_1}^{\infty} f(S)dS \\
P_2 &= \text{secondary school enrolment} &&= \int_{n_2}^{\infty} f(S)dS \qquad (3.8)\\
P_3 &= \text{tertiary school enrolment} &&= \int_{n_3}^{\infty} f(S)dS
\end{aligned}
$$

where n_1, n_2 and n_3 are, respectively, the numbers of years required to complete the primary, secondary and tertiary level of education, and $f(S)$ is the density function of S. The Gini concentration index on income distribution can be represented as[15]

$$
G_X = \int_0^{\infty} 2[F(X) - Q(X)]g(X)dX, \quad Q(X) = \frac{1}{X}\int_0^X tg(t)dt \qquad (3.9)
$$

where $g(X)$ is the density function of X, $F(X)$ is the cumulative distribution function and the term in square brackets is the vertical distance between the Lorenz curve and the perfect equality relationship. Given the lognormality assumption, $\log(X) = x \sim N(\mu_x, \sigma_x^2)$ and its density function is given by

$$N(x; \mu_x, \sigma_x^2) = \frac{1}{\sigma_x \sqrt{2\pi}} \exp\left[-\frac{(x - \mu_x)^2}{2\sigma_x^2}\right] \tag{3.10}$$

The associated Gini index is

$$G_X = 2 \int_{-\infty}^{\frac{\sigma_x}{\sqrt{2}}} \frac{1}{\sqrt{2\pi}} \exp\left[-\frac{t^2}{2}\right] dt - 1$$

$$= 2 \int_{-\infty}^{\frac{\sigma_x^2}{\sqrt{2}} + \mu_x} \frac{1}{\sigma_x \sqrt{2\pi}} \exp\left[-\frac{(x - \mu_x)^2}{2\sigma_x^2}\right] dx - 1 \tag{3.11}$$

We can rewrite equation (3.7) in a more compact form as

$$s_{it} = \theta_0 + \theta_1 x_{it} \tag{3.12}$$

where θ_0 incorporates all shift parameters for the entire distribution. As a consequence of the linearity assumption, $s \sim N(\theta_0 + \theta_1\mu_x, \theta_1^2\sigma_x^2)$ and its density function is given by

$$N\left(s; \theta_0 + \theta_1\mu_x, \theta_1^2\sigma_x^2\right) = \frac{1}{\sqrt{2\pi\left(\theta_1^2\sigma_x^2\right)}} \exp\left[-\frac{(s - \theta_0 - \theta_1\mu_x)^2}{2\left(\theta_1^2\sigma_x^2\right)}\right]$$

$$= \frac{1}{\theta_1\sigma_x\sqrt{2\pi}} \exp\left[-\frac{(x - \mu_x)^2}{2\sigma_x^2}\right] \tag{3.13}$$

Enrolment rates can now be redefined as[16]

$$P_i = \int_{\log(n_i)}^{\infty} f(s)ds = 1 - \int_{-\infty}^{\log(n_i)} f(s)ds = 1 - \int_{-\infty}^{\frac{\log(n_i)-\theta_0}{\theta_1}} \frac{1}{\theta_1} f(x)\theta_1 dx$$

$$= 1 - \frac{1}{2}\left[2\int_{-\infty}^{\frac{\sigma_x^2}{\sqrt{2}} + \mu_x} f(x)dx + 2\int_{\frac{\sigma_x^2}{\sqrt{2}}+\mu_x}^{\frac{\log(n_i)-\theta_0}{\theta_1}} f(x)dx\right]$$

$$= \left[\frac{1}{2} - \int_{\frac{\sigma_x^2}{\sqrt{2}}+\mu_x}^{\frac{\log(n_i)-\theta_0}{\theta_1}} f(x)dx\right] - \frac{1}{2}\left[2\int_{-\infty}^{\frac{\sigma_x^2}{\sqrt{2}} + \mu_x} f(x)dx - 1\right]$$

$$= \lambda_j - \frac{1}{2}G_X, \; j = 1, 2, 3 \tag{3.14}$$

where λ_i corresponds to the first square brackets. Each enrolment rate is negatively related to the Gini index for income inequality, the relationship varying by a constant. QED

The intuition underlying this relationship can be grasped by observing figure 3.1. In the upper quadrant there are two normal density functions, the solid line corresponding to the case of $\mu_x = 0, \sigma_x^2 = 1$, and the dashed line to the case of $\mu_x = 0, \sigma_x^2 = 2$. This translates below into the corresponding cumulative distribution function (north-east quadrant). Assuming a linear combination of the type $s = 0.5 + 0.8 \cdot x$ (south-east quadrant), this maps the cumulative distribution function of $s \sim N(0.5, 0.64)$ or $s \sim N(0.5, 1.28)$ (south-west quadrant). In the last (north-west) quadrant we have reported the Lorenz curve corresponding to the distribution of X.[17] Now let us consider a mean preserving spread (i.e. the passage from the solid to the dashed line). This implies an increase in the population share with an income below any given value, and correspondingly an increase in the population share that is unable to achieve the income threshold that is necessary to access a fixed amount of education. At the same time the Gini concentration index for incomes increases. We find corroboration of the negative association of the Gini index for incomes and school participation rates. Figures 3.2 and 3.3 consider alternative scenarios where we have variations in the distribution of s irrespective of changes in income dispersion (as measured by the Gini concentration index). Figure 3.2 shows the case of an increase in mean income (from a mean equal to 0 – the solid line – to a mean equal to 1 – the dashed line) for a given variance ($\sigma_x^2 = 1$). We observe an increase in the access to education for any level of income, given a constant Gini index. Finally, figure 3.3 keeps income distribution constant and modifies the relationship between income and education (due to a change in the shift parameter θ_0 that reflects educational expenditure, technology, returns on schooling and the stage of development). The solid line corresponds to the case of $s = 0.5 + 0.8 \cdot x$, whereas the dashed line depicts the case $s = 1 + 0.8 \cdot x$. Once again, we obtain an increase in educational achievements for any given level of income.

Summing up, in the context of optimal demand for schooling with heterogeneous agents we have shown that educational attainment and family income are positively correlated. As long as it is possible to

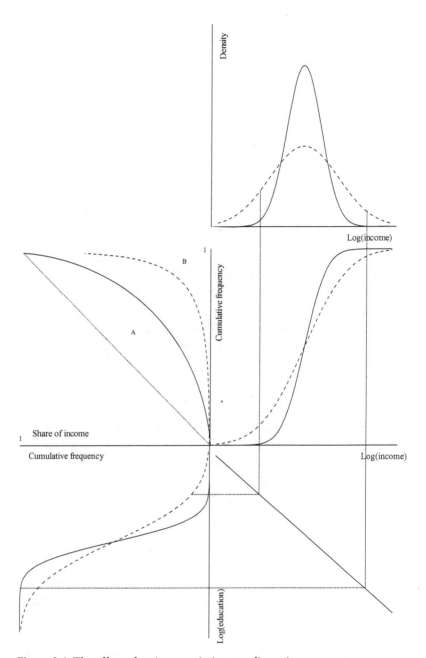

Figure 3.1 The effect of an increase in income dispersion

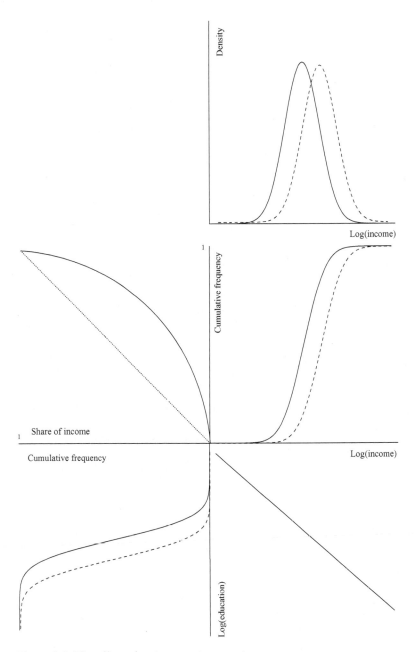

Figure 3.2 The effect of an increase in mean income

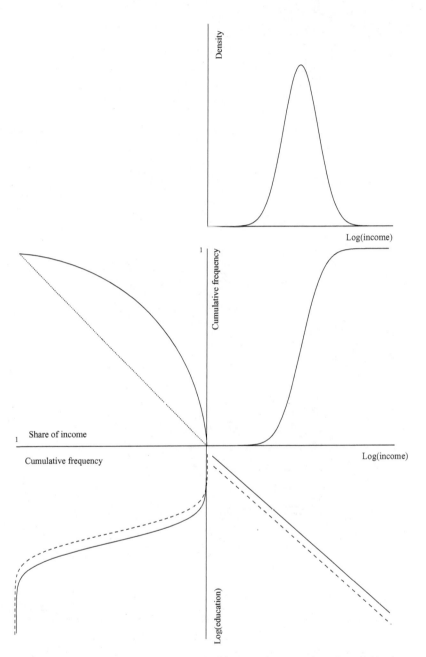

Figure 3.3 The effect of an increase in public spending on education and/or in the demand for skills

control for the mean income and other variables affecting the educational choice in the aggregate (cost of accessing the school, public resources devoted to education, wage premium for educated workers in the labour market and stage of development), we expect to find a negative relationship between the Gini concentration index on income distribution and enrolment rates at any level of education. In section 3.4 we find a negative relationship in existence either at the secondary level of education or for the female component only. These results are incompatible with a relationship between educational achievement and family income based on talent transmission. In fact, if the brightest students are the offspring of the richest families, we should observe the same relationship subsisting at any stage of education and for both male and female components of young cohorts. In contrast, finding that this relationship exists for specific educational choices (going beyond compulsory education or investing in a daughter's future) does not contradict the idea that there are liquidity constraints in the educational choices.

3.3 Data description

The data utilised in this analysis come from different sources: data on educational achievements and school quality are from Barro and Lee (1993, 1994, 1996, 2001);[18] data on income inequality are from Deininger and Squire (1996); data on physical capital stocks are from Nehru and Dhareshwar (1993); finally, data on female fertility, child mortality and population growth have been extracted from *World Bank Data on CD-ROM* (1998). In all cases the series have been updated to 1995, when available, using data from the World Bank (1998) and UNESCO (1998). The data refer to 108 countries for the period 1960 to 1995 and report information at quinquennial intervals: therefore, at best we have eight observations for each country. However, with a theoretical dimension of the data set equal to 864 observations (108 × 8), missing information (mainly on income distribution) reduces it by more than one-third, transforming it into an unbalanced panel. For the main variables (income inequality indices, enrolment rates, GNP and population) we rely on 470 observations (with an average of 4.3 observations per country), but in most cases when considering additional information this number has to be reduced even further. Descriptive statistics about these main variables are reported in table 3.1

Table 3.1 Descriptive statistics for the entire data set, 1960–1995

	Mean entire sample	Standard deviation	Restricted sample	Standard deviation	Mean year = 1960	Mean year = 1970	Mean year = 1980	Mean year = 1990
Gross enrolment rate in primary education	0.839 (812)	0.251	0.899 (470)	0.189	0.731 (101)	0.790 (103)	0.879 (102)	0.885 (101)
Gross enrolment rate in secondary education	0.424 (801)	0.313	0.482 (470)	0.290	0.226 (98)	0.342 (103)	0.467 (100)	0.547 (96)
Gross enrolment rate in higher education	0.114 (797)	0.136	0.134 (470)	0.135	0.036 (99)	0.070 (101)	0.120 (101)	0.181 (89)
Gini index of income distribution	0.414 (526)	0.105	0.422 (470)	0.101	0.456 (55)	0.428 (75)	0.396 (70)	0.402 (83)
Total population (thousands)	36,040 (831)	117,146	46,629 (470)	128,627	24,970 (102)	30,879 (102)	37,399 (102)	44,075 (107)
Real GDP per capita ($PPP, 1985 international prices)	3,916.4 (824)	4,003.0	4,524.9 (470)	4,061.0	2,453.8 (98)	3,336.7 (104)	4,417.1 (105)	5,115.2 (107)

NB: numbers in brackets report the number of non-missing observations in each sample (or sub-sample).

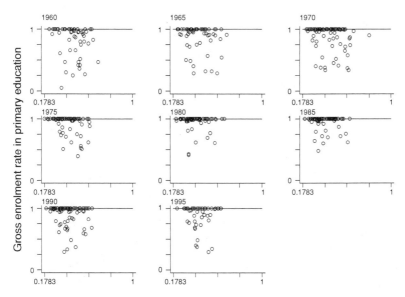

Figure 3.4 The Gini index of inequality for all countries by year: primary education

(the entire data set). On the whole, these data cover almost half of the 210 countries listed by the World Bank (1998), but account for 86.3 per cent of the world population (as measured in 1990).[19]

Looking at the descriptive statistics, we find evidence for well-known stylised facts. In the aggregate data, inequality in income distribution declined during the 1960s and 1970s, then showed an upward surge during the 1980s. However, when looking at the regions, we cannot find a uniform pattern, thus providing some support to the argument that inequality has not exhibited a specific trend since 1960.[20] Inequality is highest in sub-Saharan Africa and Latin America, and lower in industrialised countries and South Asia. Educational achievement rose quickly during the first two decades of the period, but this rise slowed down during the 1980s. By the beginning of the 1990s, many countries had all the population enrolled in primary education (OECD countries, Latin America, North Africa and East Asia), whereas only OECD countries had also reached near-complete saturation for secondary education. Graphical inspection of the association between school enrolment and income inequality confirms that most of the countries had achieved full participation in education at the primary level, thus reducing the potential variation in the former variable (figure 3.4). In contrast, at

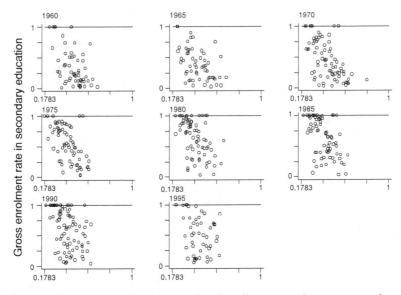

Figure 3.5 The Gini index of inequality for all countries by year: secondary education

the secondary and tertiary levels of education, a negative correlation emerges clearly (figures 3.5 and 3.6). However, at this stage we do not know whether this evidence is the result of spurious correlation (when, for example, inequality and school participation are both functions of the stage of development) or whether it represents a genuine effect. To ascertain the nature of this effect we have to move to multivariate regressions.

3.4 Empirical analysis

In this section we investigate the determinants of enrolment rates at different stages of education, and in particular we will concentrate on the effects of income distribution.[21] In line with the model introduced in section 3.2, the observed enrolment rate is a reduced form incorporating elements describing household behaviour (the demand for schooling) and government provision of this public service (the supply of schooling).[22] On the supply side, information about state spending, the number of teachers employed and the repetition rate is available; on the demand side, beyond information about income

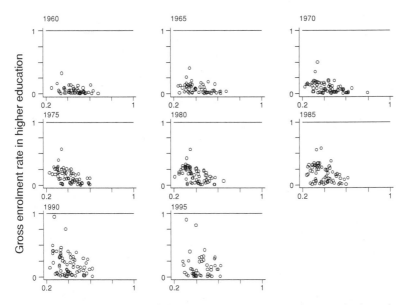

Figure 3.6 The Gini index of inequality for all countries by year: higher education

distribution, we will consider demographic factors (birth rates), family composition (fertility rates) and the sociocultural environment (proxied here by the mortality rates). Given that schooling is a stage-by-stage process (you cannot enrol at university unless you have completed secondary school), educational achievement at a certain stage is conditioned by the achievement obtained at the previous stage (what we term the 'ratchet effect'): given the absence of detailed information on schooling flows, we will proxy this effect with the average achievement of the entire population for that level of education.[23] Finally, we will control for the stage of development by conditioning on the level of real GNP per capita.

3.4.1 Primary education

Full enrolment for primary education has been almost completely achieved by all countries, especially in the most recent years. The public push towards making school attendance compulsory has lowered any cost barrier to accessing education, at least at this stage. We do not find evidence of any negative effect of income distribution (as measured by Gini indices) on gross enrolment for primary education.[24] However, since the Gini index does not provide a complete ordering of income distribution (because of the crossing of the corresponding Lorenz curves) we have also experimented with the income share accruing to the poorest segment of the population, the lowest quintile. In this case, the variable is weakly significant from a statistical point of view. Columns 1 to 4 of table 3.2 report the country fixed-ordinary least squares effect (OLS) regressions. However, a negative correlation still exists for the female component of the student population: column 4 of table 3.2 re-estimates column 1 by restricting itself to female primary enrolment, and again we find a weakly negative significant impact of income distribution. This could be taken as evidence that the expansion of compulsory education has mainly benefited boys, irrespective of the availability of financial resources from the family. Since we do not have good reason to believe that talent is unequally distributed according to gender, we consider this result as the first piece of evidence in favour of the borrowing constraints interpretation of the negative correlation between the Gini index and enrolment rates.[25] In other words, financial resources still preclude access to primary education by girls from poor families in some areas of the world. Why families might be more willing to afford educational expenditure for boys than for girls is closely intertwined with cultural habits.[26] Some additional effects of income distribution can be found looking at mortality rates. If we take child mortality as a proxy for extreme poverty, we find a significant negative impact on enrolment into primary education.[27]

The process of schooling (even at primary level) is, obviously, related to the stage of development of a country. If we measure this stage with (real) GDP per capita, we find effectively that primary enrolment is positively associated with its logarithm. But, exploiting a suggestion originally advanced by Sen (1976), and subsequently followed by international agencies as a starting point to measure the degree of human development,[28] we correct the level of per capita product Y with the contemporaneous Gini concentration index G, thus obtaining a measure of 'inequality-adjusted real income' Y_{adjust}:

$$Y_{adjust} = Y \cdot (1 - G) \tag{3.15}$$

Notice that, when using the logarithm of Y_{adjust}, a 1 per cent increase in Y is (approximately) equivalent to a one-point reduction in the Gini

Table 3.2 *Estimation of primary education enrolment: fixed effects, 1960–1995*

Gross enrolment rate in primary education	Total	Total	Total	Female
Gini index of income distribution	0.02 (0.33)	−0.20 (1.34)	–	−0.11 (1.35)
Income share of the lowest quintile in income distribution	–	−0.57 (1.06)	–	–
(Log of) real GDP per capita	0.04 (2.20)	0.05 (3.08)	–	0.04 (2.05)
(Log of) inequality-adjusted real GDP per capita	–	–	0.03 (1.86)	–
Child mortality rate in the first year (per 1,000 births)	−2.48 (8.05)	−2.13 (7.57)	−2.49 (8.09)	−3.14 (8.98)
Fertility rate (potential children per woman)	0.08 (7.30)	0.06 (6.21)	0.07 (7.24)	0.08 (7.29)
Crude birth rate (per 1,000 inhabitants)	−0.01 (5.78)	−0.01 (5.75)	−0.01 (5.76)	−0.01 (5.00)
Share of the corresponding population over 15 with some primary education	0.014 (0.29)	0.011 (0.24)	0.016 (0.32)	0.12 (2.14)
Student per teacher in primary education	0.002 (2.57)	0.003 (3.46)	0.002 (2.50)	0.001 (1.80)
Constant	0.59 (3.31)	0.60 (3.16)	0.71 (4.65)	0.55 (2.70)
Number of observations/ number of countries	436/92	303/84	436/92	424/92
Correlation between random component and individual explanatory variables	0.09	0.03	0.10	0.15
R^2 overall	0.54	0.50	0.52	0.62
R^2 within	0.43	0.51	0.43	0.46
F-test	36.34 (0.00)	28.10 (0.00)	42.11 (0.00)	40.69 (0.00)

NB: T-statistics in brackets.

index. The variable Y_{adjust} is significant, with a rather low semi-elasticity of 0.03 (column 3 of table 3.2); it implies that in order to obtain an increase in primary enrolment of 1 per cent one would require an increase in per capita income of 33 per cent, maintaining constant the inequality in income distribution. All the other variables keep their previous signs and significance.[29]

On the supply side, one finds evidence of a negative impact from population growth (as measured by the crude birth rate), because it necessarily implies a decline of per child resources. It is also true that, for many countries, the limited resources available may prevent school attendance.[30] This could constitute the explanation for the rather counter-intuitive result of the number of students per teacher exhibiting a significant and positive impact (instead of a negative one, as one would have expected, bearing in mind greater resources and better quality being associated with lower values of this variable). In other words, a greater number of students per teacher would indicate a country's effort to catch up with full attendance primary education.[31]

On the demand side, family background seems to account for some variation. If we take the fertility rate[32] as proportional to the average number of children in a family, we could expect either negative or positive effects: negative when resources are binding – the greater the number of children in a family the lower the resources per capita and the greater is the opportunity cost of school attendance; positive when supportive effects can be accounted for. In this case, the larger the number of siblings the higher the probability that someone else has already had some schooling experience, and therefore the greater is the chance of getting some help at home.[33] The relevance of the cultural environment (the so-called 'social capital') is also demonstrated by the positive effect played by the stock of people with some (but incomplete) primary education. The positive effect can be explained on two grounds. On the one hand, some of the population (older than fifteen years) with uncompleted primary education could re-enrol into primary education, thus raising the gross rate of enrolment. On the other hand, it may be correlated with the efforts of a country to overcome illiteracy, and therefore it describes the pressure put on children to enrol and complete primary education.[34]

We were unable to find strong effects from public resources invested in education on enrolment. Using a subset of countries for which educational resource information is available, a richer specification does not provide any improvement upon previous results. While income inequality remains insignificant, all the proxies used to capture different aspects of publicly invested resources tend to be insignificant. Additional resources invested in education can take different forms: fewer students per teacher, better-paid teachers, a greater ratio of governmental current expenditure on primary education per pupil on per capita GDP (or simply spending a greater share of GDP on education), a greater share of educational resources invested in buildings and equipment. Or we could even look at the amount of care being devoted to children attending school, negatively proxied by drop-out and repetition rates. In accordance with the previous model, we expect that an increase in public resources *ceteris paribus* should facilitate school attendance, and therefore increase school enrolment. In all these cases, with the exception of teachers' pay and drop-out rates, we do not find strong evidence of positive effects arising from more resources being allocated to primary enrolment. The case of the drop-out rate could be due to different regional patterns.[35] The case of teachers' pay is inconclusive: for a given level of resources, having better-paid teachers necessarily implies having fewer teachers, fewer or more crowded classes, and consequently less availability of the educational service. This is, for example, the explanation advanced by Ridker (1994) for the decline in primary enrolment in sub-Saharan Africa over the previous ten years.[36]

3.4.2 Secondary education

Moving on to secondary education, we find a strong correlation between income distribution and school enrolment. The Gini index is significantly negative: a 1 per cent decline in the index (more egalitarian distribution) implies a 0.25 per cent rise in secondary enrolment (column 1 of table 3.3). The same effect is obtained when considering inequality-adjusted real income Y_{adjust}, with a somewhat lower impact (column 3 of table 3.3). Also in this case we find additional evidence of possible discrimination against girls: a significant increase in inequality (say, a $\Delta Gini = +0.05$) reduces secondary school enrolment to 1 per cent for boys and 1.8 per cent for girls. Notice in addition that the coefficient measuring the impact of inequality for girls is bigger than in the case of primary school (-0.35 against -0.11), and this suggests that financial constraints are more relevant at this stage of education.

Table 3.3 *Estimation of secondary education enrolment: fixed effects, 1960–1995*

Gross enrolment rate in secondary education	Total	Total	Total	Female
Gini index of income distribution	−0.24	0.01	–	−0.35
	(2.68)	(0.06)		(3.73)
Income share of the lowest quintile in income distribution	–	0.69	–	–
		(0.88)		
(Log of) GDP per capita	0.14	0.15	–	0.15
	(6.37)	(6.03)		(6.37)
(Log of) inequality-adjusted real GDP per capita	–	–	0.13	–
			(7.17)	
Fertility rate (potential children per woman)	−0.05	−0.06	−0.05	−0.06
	(5.33)	(5.62)	(5.34)	(6.03)
Average years of completed primary education in the corresponding population over 15	0.06	0.04	0.06	0.06
	(6.15)	(3.42)	(6.10)	(5.20)
Ratio of physical capital stock to GDP (1987 local prices)	0.04	0.05	0.04	0.05
	(3.26)	(3.40)	(3.56)	(3.81)
Constant	−0.67	−0.82	−0.67	−0.65
	(3.31)	(3.05)	(3.93)	(3.07)
Number of observations/number of countries	386/76	264/69	386/76	369/76
Correlation between random component and individual explanatory variables	−0.65	−0.58	−0.64	−0.73
R^2 overall	0.79	0.76	0.79	0.82
R^2 within	0.65	0.68	0.65	0.69
F-test	115.1	67.27	143.3	127.7
	(0.00)	(0.00)	(0.00)	(0.00)

NB: T-statistics in brackets.

It is interesting to note also that liquidity constraints seem to affect the whole span of income distribution, since the coefficient of the income share of the lowest quintile is not significantly different from 0.[37]

On the demand side we find evidence of some effect deriving from the family composition, as proxied by the fertility rate. While this variable exhibits a positive effect at primary level (and was explained there as evidence of the effect of supportive effort within the family), in this case it presents a clearly negative impact, which can be interpreted as evidence of a family resource effect. If we consider that sending a child to a secondary school (which, in most countries, exceeds the threshold of compulsory education) is a more demanding task (at least on the financial side), an increase in family size implies a reduction in resources per child (in terms of both income, partially captured by the inequality and output per capita variables, and time devoted to child support by the parents).

On the supply side we find weak effects from resources invested in education; the number of pupils per teacher, the ratio of governmental current expenditure on secondary education per pupil on GDP per capita, the repetition rate, the aggregate expenditure on education (as a share of GDP) and its composition – all these variables exert a statistically insignificant effect (columns 2 and 5 in table 3.4).[38] However, when we interact data for public expenditure on education with the Gini index on income distribution, we find that their impact becomes significant: an increase in public resources devoted to current expenditure on education raises secondary enrolment, especially for countries with very unequal income distribution.[39] The Gini index remains negatively significant; in addition, when we take the total derivative of secondary enrolment with respect to the Gini index, from column 3 we get

$$\frac{\partial \text{ enrolment}}{\partial \text{ Gini index}} = -2.11 + 28.86 \cdot (\text{education.expenditure/GDP}) \\ + 2.33 \cdot (\text{capital expenditure/total expenditure})$$

(3.16)

which evaluated at sample means is equal to – 0.49. We take this result as a second piece of evidence in support of a liquidity constraint interpretation of the relationship between income distribution and school enrolment. Had this relationship been attributable to talent transmission, we would have expected an opposite result. Since more talented students take more advantage of greater resources invested in education,[40] we should find that an increase in public expenditure widens the dispersion of educational achievements and, other things being equal, strengthens the relationship between secondary enrolment

Table 3.4 *Estimation of secondary education enrolment using different variables for educational resources: fixed effects, 1960–1995*

Gross enrolment rate in secondary education	Total	Total	Total	Female	Female	Female
Gini index of income distribution	−0.38 (2.71)	−0.33 (2.18)	−2.11 (4.68)	−0.40 (2.66)	−0.35 (2.20)	−2.44 (5.17)
(Log of) GDP per capita	0.20 (5.44)	0.20 (5.00)	0.15 (4.13)	0.21 (5.13)	0.19 (4.44)	0.14 (3.37)
Fertility rate (potential children per woman)	−0.03 (2.27)	−0.03 (1.82)	−0.03 (1.87)	−0.03 (1.92)	−0.03 (1.65)	−0.03 (1.79)
Average years of completed primary education in the corresponding population over 15	0.07 (3.25)	0.07 (2.85)	0.10 (4.04)	0.09 (3.47)	0.09 (3.13)	0.13 (4.63)
Ratio of physical capital stock to GDP (1987 local prices)	0.04 (1.74)	0.04 (1.74)	0.04 (1.78)	0.04 (1.89)	0.04 (1.69)	0.03 (1.58)
Student per teacher in secondary education	–	0.001 (0.40)	0.002 (1.02)	–	0.0001 (0.03)	0.001 (0.73)
Repetition rate – secondary education	–	0.001 (0.68)	0.02 (1.42)	–	0.001 (0.75)	0.003 (1.59)
Per pupil government expenditure on secondary education/GDP per capita	–	−0.001 (1.19)	−0.001 (1.25)	–	−0.0007 (0.70)	−0.001 (0.77)
Government expenditure on education/GDP	–	−0.08 (0.09)	−10.70 (3.80)	–	0.28 (0.29)	−11.19 (3.80)
(Government expenditure on education/GDP) × Gini index	–	–	28.86 (4.00)	–	–	31.9 (4.22)
Capital expenditure/ total government expenditure on education	–	−0.23 (1.64)	−1.11 (2.28)	–	−0.30 (2.02)	−1.79 (3.48)

Table 3.4 *(cont.)*

(Capital expenditure/ total government expenditure on education) × Gini index	–	–	2.33 (1.99)	–	–	3.89 (3.13)
Constant	Yes	Yes	Yes	Yes	Yes	Yes
Number of observations/number of countries	133/50	133/50	133/50	130/49	130/49	130/49
Correlation between random component and individual explanatory variables	−0.75	−0.71	−0.71	−0.82	−0.80	−0.80
R^2 overall	0.77	0.77	0.78	0.83	0.82	0.82
R^2 within	0.76	0.77	0.82	0.77	0.79	0.84
F-test	49.0 (0.00)	25.1 (0.00)	26.7 (0.00)	52.9 (0.00)	27.2 (0.00)	31.1 (0.00)

NB: T-statistics in brackets.

and the Gini index of income distribution. In contrast, if the relationship is attributable to liquidity constraints, an increase in public expenditure lowers the barriers of access, and weakens the same relationship; this is what we infer from equation (3.16). In other words, public resources do not have a direct impact, but they are effective beacuse they ease family choices about letting their children proceed further with their education.

Another aspect related to the public supply of secondary education has to do with the 'vertical integration' of this process. If we consider that a student can enrol in a secondary school only if he/she has completed the primary level, it is evident that an increase in the completion of primary education provides additional inputs to the next stage of production. This 'ratchet' effect makes it rather implausible to observe enrolment rates at higher stages greater than those observed at lower stages. Effectively, we find that the average number of years of completed primary education in the population[41] has a significant positive effect; raising the sample mean (3.94 years) by an additional year should induce an increase in secondary enrolment in the order of four to six percentage points, depending on the chosen specification. Family choices also seem to respond to the existing situation on the labour market, probably via differential returns for education and/or the differential employment probability.[42] Under the assumption of complementarities between human and physical capital in production,[43] we can approximate the skill requirement in the economy with the existing capital intensity (the ratio of physical capital to output). In such a case, we observe that an increase in demand for skills in the labour market (i.e. an increase in the capital/output ratio) induces an increase in secondary school enrolment. However, the size of the effect is not very great; a 10 per cent increase in the capital/output ratio (from an average of 2.58 to 2.84) would raise secondary enrolment by just 0.4 per cent.[44]

3.4.3 Higher education

Coming finally to higher education, as in the case of primary education we find weak evidence for a direct impact of either income inequality or first quintile shares on higher education enrolment (columns 1 and 2 in table 3.5). Given the fact that many authors stress that the public financing of tertiary education has a regressive effect because the offspring of the middle classes are over-represented, we have also tested the possible existence of liquidity constraints within this group by using the income share of each quintile (taken either separately or jointly), but we could not detect any statistically significant effect. When we make use of the inequality-adjusted real income Y_{adjust}, the variable is significant but the result is driven mainly by the underlying effect of output per capita.[45] More surprising is the result that income inequality seems to affect male enrolment more than female enrolment. The differences in sample averages between the enrolment rates of the two genders are not very pronounced (16.2 per cent for men against 11.4 per cent for women), and therefore we cannot explain it with a composition effect. The talent transmission explanation cannot account for this difference, unless we pursue a self-selectivity explanation: males and females have different preferences, and the latter withdraw from the academic curriculum more frequently than the former. But we believe that a more

Table 3.5 *Estimation of higher education enrolment: fixed effects, 1960–1995*

Gross enrolment rate in higher education	Total	Total	Total	Female	Male
Gini index of income distribution	−0.07 (0.92)	0.14 (0.68)	–	−0.07 (1.05)	−0.13 (2.10)
Income share of the lowest quintile in income distribution	–	0.61 (0.83)	–	–	–
(Log of) real GDP per capita	0.08 (3.91)	0.14 (4.11)	–	0.04 (2.24)	0.08 (4.07)
(Log of) inequality-adjusted real GDP per capita	–	–	0.07 (3.97)	–	–
(Log of) government current expenditure in secondary education per pupil (PPP-adjusted 1985 international prices)	0.02 (2.13)	0.02 (1.51)	0.02 (2.52)	0.03 (2.87)	0.01 (0.77)
Average years of completed secondary education in the corresponding population over 15	0.07 (5.88)	0.04 (2.74)	0.07 (5.97)	0.08 (7.22)	0.05 (4.88)
Ratio of physical capital stock to GDP (1987 local prices)	0.01 (1.06)	0.02 (1.01)	0.01 (1.45)	0.01 (0.71)	0.02 (2.57)
Constant	−0.76 (5.08)	−1.39 (4.94)	−0.67 (5.83)	−0.51 (3.76)	−0.60 (4.51)
Number of observations/ number of countries	303/72	210/65	303/72	254/70	253/69
Correlation between random component and individual explanatory variables	−0.59	−0.68	−0.55	−0.59	−0.39
R^2 overall	0.63	0.57	0.63	0.59	0.60
R^2 within	0.57	0.57	0.57	0.60	0.61
F-test	60.22 (0.00)	31.47 (0.00)	74.9 (0.00)	54.63 (0.00)	55.51 (0.00)

NB: T-statistics in brackets.

realistic explanation lies in the fact that daughters from financially constrained families have already abandoned schools at earlier stages, and therefore the 11 per cent actually enrolled in school belong to rich families. In contrast, since financial constraints start to restrain male enrolment only at secondary level, the selection according to family resources has operated less strongly among them, and we can still find sons from middle-class families who are financially constrained when asked to afford enrolment at university. In our opinion, this is a third piece of evidence supporting the liquidity constraint line of interpretation

As far as the supply of higher education is concerned, there is evidence of a positive effect from public expenditure per pupil at the previous stage. If we take this variable as a proxy for the quality of education provided at secondary school, this evidence suggests that increasing the resources invested at one stage of education can be ineffective in directly raising student participation at that level, but can be beneficial in favouring the transition to the next stage (for example, by raising the self-confidence of the students). This impact is rather low; a 10 per cent increase in public expenditure per student enrolled in secondary school (equivalent to $103 measured at 1985 prices) induces an increase of 0.21 percentage points in higher education enrolment. The ratchet effect (namely the interdependence between sequential stages of education) also emerges, through the positive effect exerted by the average years of secondary education achieved in the population aged over fifteen years; an added year (from a sample average of 1.4 years) induces an increase of almost 50 per cent in higher education enrolment.[46] When considering alternative measures of educational resources, the effect of changing the total amount of public resources invested in education is significantly positive only with respect to higher education enrolment. Other direct measures of invested resources (such as students per teacher) do not provide direct information about the resources invested at this stage of education.[47]

On the demand side, the only evidence comes from the demand for skilled workers, as proxied by the capital/output ratio. Even if the coefficient is lower than in the case of secondary education, the elasticity is of comparable magnitude (see table 3.6). This might indicate that the productive sector requires technical training (mostly provided by secondary schools) rather than professional credentials provided by

Table 3.6 *Elasticities of enrolment at different educational levels*

	Primary	Secondary	Higher
Gini index of income distribution (column 1 in tables 3.2, 3.3 and 3.5)	−0.011	−0.211[b]	−0.185
(Log of) inequality-adjusted real GDP per capita (column 3 in tables 3.2, 3.3 and 3.5)	0.033[a]	0.281[b]	0.529[b]
Average years of completed education at previous stage (column 1 in tables 3.2, 3.3 and 3.5)	0.006[b]	0.520[b]	0.622[b]
Ratio of physical capital stock to GDP (column 1 in tables 3.2, 3.3 and 3.5)	–	0.215[b]	0.194
Female only			
Gini index of income distribution (column 4 in tables 3.2, 3.3 and 3.5)	−0.054	−0.311[b]	−0.260
Average years of completed education at previous stage (column 4 in tables 3.2, 3.3 and 3.5)	0.060[a]	0.467[b]	0.907[b]

[a] Statistically significant at 95 per cent.
[b] Statistically significant at 99 per cent.

universities. Notice, moreover, that the effect of this variable is significantly higher for men than for women.

3.5 Concluding remarks

In this chapter we have examined some empirical evidence in support of the negative correlation between inequality and growth. Starting from a general model of optimal demand for education, we have argued that the dependence on family income may derive either from talent transmission or from borrowing constraints with imperfect financial markets. In both cases, if family incomes are loglinearly distributed, we derive two testable predictions in the analysis of aggregate data on school enrolments: a negative (linear) dependence on the Gini concentration index on income distribution; and a positive dependence on public resources invested in education and/or on skill premiums in the labour market. These predictions have then been tested on an (unbalanced) panel of 108 countries for the period 1960 to 1995.

The main findings of this analysis are summarised in table 3.6. Once we control for the degree of development with the (log of) per capita output, income inequality seems relevant mainly in limiting the access to secondary education. However, when we consider gender differences, there is evidence that female participation in education is more strongly conditioned by family income, starting with primary education. In contrast, there is no clear evidence for a relevant impact of invested resources, except at the tertiary level. Some positive effect is also played by the labour demand for skilled workers, which tends to raise enrolment in post-primary education. Other conditioning variables, at primary and secondary level, are fertility rates and mortality rates, which tend to capture other aspects of social development. Finally, the data show that increasing education at one stage raises the odds for the following stages.

When we come to the interpretation of these results, we have argued that there is clear evidence in favour of a borrowing constraint interpretation as opposed to a talent transmission reading. First, we found differential effects from income inequality on male and female enrolment rates. While still compatible with a differences-in-preferences theory, we believe that this is the reflection of family behaviour: with scarce financial resources, families traditionally invest more readily in boys' than in girls' education. Second, we found that public resources affect secondary enrolment when interacted with income inequality. We take this as evidence of public expenditure on education alleviating family liquidity constraints. The opposite reading, where the brightest children are the offspring of the richest families, cannot account for these two facts.[48]

As long as our reading based on borrowing constraints is accepted, income redistribution should matter for educational goals. The size of the effect is not impressive: lowering the Gini index by five percentage points, a sizeable change at sample means, produces a total increase in school participation of almost two percentage points.[49] However, if one is willing to believe in these conclusions, when a country wants to raise the educational level of its population, rather than spending additional resources on building schools and hiring teachers (which, at best, have an indirect effect on secondary school enrolments) it should instead implement redistributive policies (via taxes and/or subsidies). As long as these policies are effective in reducing income inequalities within the population, they are also capable of relaxing the financial constraints faced by the poorest families, thereby promoting school enrolment. In the light of the statistical irrelevance of invested resources in promoting enrolment, any policy recommendation for expenditure reallocation (for example, from tertiary to primary, or vice versa) seems pointless, given the limited impact of resources on school enrolment.[50] But a similar argument applies to the idea of expanding a private provider of education. As long as school fees create an additional financial barrier to continuing education we expect a reduction in total enrolment, because it erects financial barriers for constrained families.[51]

Notes

1. We report here some of the empirical evidence analysed in Checchi (2003b), with the kind permission of the journal publisher.
2. A good survey of the recent literature is contained in Benabou (1996c).
3. See Alesina and Rodrik (1994), Persson and Tabellini (1994), Perotti (1993) and Bertola (1993).
4. An additional variant is found in Mauro (1995), in which inequality fosters corruption and depresses investment.
5. See Galor and Zeira (1993), Banerjee and Newman (1993), Torvik (1993) and Benabou (1996a, 1996b).
6. Redistributing incomes among agents is not the only way to increase efficiency. A scheme of education subsidies financed through the taxation of future incomes (intertemporal redistribution) recreates the missing market, and allows the achievement of the first-best. See Banerjee and Newman (1993).
7. Benabou (1996c) states that one standard deviation reduction in inequality increases GNP per capita by about 0.5 to 0.7 per cent. Perotti (1996) finds that a 1 per cent increase in middle incomes (proxied by the third and fourth quartile in income distribution) yields an increase in the GNP per capita growth rate in the order of 0.2 per cent. Persson and Tabellini (1994) provide a higher estimate (in the order of 0.7 per cent).
8. Which actually is positive and significant, as found in Perotti (1996). The same author, when acting as a discussant of Benabou (1996c), suggests a reverse causation: fast-growing economies have more resources available for redistribution. Alesina (1998) points out that most of the redistributive policies in developing countries benefit the middle class rather than the poorest people.

9. The relationship between inequality and political instability can be read in a reverse way: bitter social conflict (for example, during coups) may cause high numbers of killings and, if the coup is successful, the new regime may introduce regressive policies that increase income inequality (e.g. the Chilean case in the 1970s).

10. Bourguignon (1993) finds an overall negative relationship between inequality and growth in a sample of thirty-five developing countries of small to medium size. His results are mainly driven by the sub-sample of Asian countries, which experienced early land redistribution and more compressed income distribution, combined with government efforts to encourage higher education. He also points out that a positive relationship between inequality and growth could apply to Latin American countries, via the financing of investment (more inequality implies greater profits and therefore more financing opportunities for investment). Brandolini and Rossi (1998) make an effort to strengthen data comparability in a sample of seventeen countries, and do not find a consistent relationship between household income inequality and growth (even if they speak of *social institutions*, where the link could be either positive or negative depending on the country area).

11. Or any possible combination of the two cases. If, for example, expected future income is a positive function of talent, randomly distributed in each generation, poor individuals are the less talented children of both rich and poor families. See Chiu (1998).

12. See Ichino and Winter-Ebmer (1999) about the problems arising when trying to discriminate between the two explanations.

13. Becker and Tomes (1986) follow an analogous procedure.

14. For example, by looking at the significance of α_1, which derives from the inversion of equation (3.5), one can infer the potential existence of ability transmission. A similar strategy is used by Becker and Tomes (1986), in which they replace S_{t-1} with X_{t-1}, grandparents' income.

15. See, for example, Cowell (1995, pp. 141 ff.).

16. Whenever $\frac{\log(n_i)-\theta_0}{\theta_1} < \frac{\sigma_x^2}{\sqrt{2}} + \mu_x$ one has to consider the opposite of an integral with inverted extremes of integration.

17. It is known that the Gini concentration index corresponds to the ratio of the areas in the Lorenz graph: $G_X = \frac{A}{A+B}$.

18. Barro and Lee (1994) is, in turn based on Summers and Heston (1991).

19. Given the fact that this data set is reduced in scope in line with the patchy availability of income distribution data, one may suspect the possible introduction of sample bias. In order to check this possibility, using all the available information on a larger sample of 132 countries, we have run a panel probit regression predicting the availability of data

on income distribution (see table A3 in Checchi, 2003b). The results are reassuring, since there is evidence of easier data availability only for bigger countries (in terms of population) and for less recent years. In particular, the availability of information on income distribution seems unrelated to information on school enrolment at primary and secondary level, whereas it is positively correlated with higher education (since countries with a better-educated labour force have easier access to income data). Therefore, we think that this data set may provide a representative picture at world level of the determinants of schooling participation.

20. See, for example, Grilli (1994), Jones (1997) or Li, Squire and Zou (1998).

21. Deininger and Squire (1996) provide data of different quality, according to the coverage of the sample, the inclusion/exclusion of non-labour incomes and information about the recipients (individuals or families). Using what they define as 'high-quality' data reduces the available observations to 277 (which do not include data referring to 1995). However, the results are not very different when extended to include the 'low-quality' data, even if given their greater variability the estimates are less efficient. They also stress the different sources of information (income or expenditure), but controlling with a dummy on this aspect (either unconstrained or interacted with the Gini variable) does not lead to statistically significant results. Estimates on a restricted sample including only 'high-quality' data are available from the author. The original Deininger and Squire (1996) data set has been expanded using additional observations for 1995 from the World Bank (1998).

22. Information on the private provision of schooling is scattered, and therefore we cannot take into account information on the supply of private schooling. Arnove et al. (1997) report an impressive increase of private institutions providing education, especially at the university level, as a consequence of a decline in public expenditure in education in Latin America: the share of students enrolled in private universities rose from 5 per cent in 1970 to approximately 30 per cent in 1990.

23. In addition, remember that our model described by equation (3.7) predicts that the distribution of educational attainment in one generation depends, among other things, on the same distribution for the previous generation.

24. The insignificance of the estimated coefficient for the Gini index is robust against model misspecification (using the Huber–White estimator) and censoring of the dependent variable (random-effect tobit model estimation).

25. It is noteworthy that the same effect does not carry over to the random-effect estimation, or in cross-section: this could imply that there is something that is country-specific in this effect.

26. And social structures, at least in the case of castes in India. In this country primary education is not compulsory, and child labour is legal. The huge variation in literacy rates (which is 74 per cent among urban males and 20 per cent among rural females) is supposedly explained by the following factors: 'The central proposition of this study is that India's low per capita income and economic situation is less relevant as an explanation than the belief systems of the state bureaucracy . . . At the core of these beliefs are the Indian view of the social order, notions concerning the respective roles of upper and lower social strata, the role of education as a means of maintaining differentiations among social classes, and concerns that "excessive" and "inappropriate" education for the poor would disrupt existing social arrangements' (Weiner, 1991, p. 5). In effect, when we control for this possibility using random-effect estimation on regional sub-samples, we find that this result is mainly attributable to East Asian countries and, to a lesser extent, to Latin American countries.

27. Unfortunately, child mortality proxies too many effects that interplay with primary education. For example, child mortality is negatively correlated with maternal education and with health conditions (sanitation, the availability of doctors, etc.). For this reason we do not want to put excessive emphasis on an 'income distribution' interpretation. However, using household surveys, Filmer and Pritchett (1999) show that the first principal component extracted from information on the ownership of durable goods and the quality of housing is quite a good predictor of educational attainment.

28. See the *Human Development Report* for 1997 (UNDP, 1997) and other years.

29. Substantially, column 3 corresponds (approximately) to imposing a restriction on the coefficients of log Y and G in column 1, which is not rejected by the data. Imposing the restriction *coefficient*(log Y) = −*coefficient*(G) in column 1 of table 3.2 has an F-test(1,337) = 0.70 (p-value 0.40).

30. In the case of Tanzania, for example, where primary attendance was 0.34 in 1970, 0.93 in 1980 and 0.70 in 1990, class dimensions can vary between thirty and seventy-four pupils in rural areas. See Tibaijuka and Cormack (1998).

31. That the number of students per teacher does not represent a good proxy for school quality has already been pointed out (see, for example, Hanushek, 1995, 1996).

32. The fertility rate indicates the number of potential children that an 'average' woman – i.e. following the average behaviour of the country in terms of marriage age, frequency of pregnancies, etc. – is likely to give birth to during her fertility period. We also found a variable describing the 'number of persons per family' (source: World Bank – correlation coefficient with fertility rate = 0.73), but it has too few observations (211 in the whole sample) and therefore we had to discard it.

33. Similar results were obtained by Schultz (1988) on a sample of 155 countries over the period 1950 to 1980, when he found a positive effect from the relative size of school-aged population on enrolment rates for primary education.

34. Introducing the illiteracy rate as an explanatory variable is statistically significant with a negative sign, but the number of observations drops to 195 (corresponding to sixty-nine countries). In contrast, when using the number of daily newspapers or the number of radio sets per 1,000 inhabitants, one obtains negative but statistically insignificant coefficients.

35. Working on household surveys collected in thirty-five countries, Filmer and Pritchett (1999) show that '[v]ery low primary attainment by the poor is driven by two distinct patterns of enrolment and drop-out. There is a South Asian and Western/Central African pattern in which many of the poor never enrol in school. In these countries more than 40 per cent of poor children never complete even grade 1 and typically only one in four complete grade 5. In contrast there is a Latin American pattern in which enrolment in grade 1 is (nearly) universal but drop-out is the key problem' (p. 3). However, their conclusion does not contradict present results: 'These data cast some doubts on the notion that physical availability of school facilities at the primary or secondary level is the key issue in many countries' (p. 4).

36. He notices that the lack of locally trained manpower attracts expatriates, who have higher reservation wages and are often remunerated with grant aids, thus crowding out local competences even further. Schultz (1988) also finds a negative effect from teacher's wages on primary and secondary enrolment.

37. It renders the Gini coefficient insignificant as well, but it remains significant in random-effect estimation using robust estimators. The Gini coefficient also remains significant when analysing yearly cross-sections, whereas at regional level its significance seems more attributable to North African and South Asian countries.

38. Given the reduction in the number of countries/years for which information is available, we could introduce sample selection biases. However, when we compare the full sample estimates (column 1 of table 3.3) with

the reduced sample (column 1 of table 3.4), we notice that the size and significance of the coefficients are not modified.

39. From column 3 of table 3.4, taking the total derivative of secondary enrolment with respect to government expenditure on education over GDP yields positive values for the Gini index above 0.37.

40. As in the case of the model presented in section 2 of chapter 2.

41. The variable 'average years of primary education' (sample mean referring to the population over fifteen is 3.94 years) is obtained by multiplying the variable 'share of the population with completed and uncompleted primary education' (sample mean referring to the population over 15 is 0.632) with the variable 'years of duration of primary education' (sample mean referring to 1965 is 6.31). Therefore, an increase of one year in the average duration of primary education can be obtained by increasing the primary attendance in the population by 0.158 (obtained as result of 1/6.31).

42. These two channels cannot be directly tested because of the lack of appropriate data. Estimates of returns on schooling for several countries (but limited to a very few years) are reported in Psacharopoulos (1994). Unemployment rates with respect to educational attainment do not exist over such a long time-span and for so many countries.

43. A rather plausible assumption: see Benabou (1996b, 1996c).

44. This evidence is confirmed by including another variable, the 'ratio of total worker to population', which Barro and Lee (1994) report as drawn from Summer and Heston (1991), and extends up to 1985. We have been unable to update this variable in a consistent way. However, if we re-estimate the model reported in column 1 of table 3.3 over the period 1960 to 1985 including this variable, it is significant with coefficient equal to 0.491 (1.96). This implies that an increase in the employment rate of 10 per cent calls for an increase in secondary enrolment of almost 5 per cent. This seems unrelated to the type of secondary education that is available: a variable measuring the share of vocational education in secondary education is statistically insignificant.

45. Here, again, the data (using the specification of column 1 in table 3.5) do not reject the restriction: $coefficient(\log Y) = -coefficient(G)$: F-test(1,226) = 0.03 (p-value 0.86).

46. One could envisage the possibility that education at a later stage could influence enrolment at earlier stages (think of the case of limited access to university reducing the enrolment to secondary school). While being valid in principle, this objection neglects the fact that it is always possible to create a private supply of the rationed service.

47. We would also have expected a negative correlation between the share of students enrolled in vocational secondary schools and enrolment in

university (since students from generalist secondary schools are inputs to higher education), but this does not arise in our data.

48. An alternative explanation of the same evidence is put forward by Bourguignon and Verdier (2000). They present a model where an oligarchic class decides upon the optimal number of the poor to be educated. Since the franchise is one to one with education, the latter variable feeds back into taxation and redistribution, decided upon by majority voting. Thus, when inequality is high, majority voting is likely to produce strong redistribution, and therefore the oligarchy has an incentive to restrict access to education. However, their explanation is valid as long as democratic participation is positively correlated with educational achievements. Since the former variable is hard to define, this constitutes a focus for future research.

49. This incorporates the direct effect (row 1 of table 3.6) and the indirect effect (row 1 × row 3, lowered by one level).

50. These pieces of policy advice are typically based on the comparison between private and social returns on education. Since the usual ranking of returns is primary > secondary > tertiary, there should be grounds to claim an expenditure reallocation in favour of the primary level. See Birdsall and James (1993) and Psacharopoulos (1994).

51. For this reason the following conclusion does not seem to be warranted: '[P]reliminary evidence suggests that the second pattern – restricted public sector capacity and a large private sector – is superior with respect to access, providing much higher overall enrolment ratios and thus higher rates of participation by lower-income groups' (Birdsall and James, 1993, p. 344).

4 | *The supply of education*

4.1 Human capital formation

In the second chapter we derived an optimal demand for schooling under the constraint of a given technology in human capital formation, which is reproduced in implicit form in equation (4.1) for ease.

$$\Delta H_{it} = f(A_i, S_{it}, E_{it}, H_{it}) \qquad (4.1)$$

The variable A_i indicates individual (unobservable) ability, S_{it} the fraction of time devoted to schooling by individual i, E_{it} the per-capita resources used in schooling (teachers, libraries). In an intergenerational framework, H_{it} can be taken as a proxy of the family background (including the social capital that is relevant for acquiring an education); we can consider the effect of peers (namely the effect of the average quality of classmates on individual performance) as a special case of it.[1] The same set of variables affects the optimal demand for schooling (see equation (2.7)) and the marginal return to education (see equation (2.10)).

Equation (4.1) is known in economic literature as the *educational production function* (Lazear, 2001; Pritchett and Filmer, 1999), since it relates some inputs (student abilities, schooling resources, cultural environment) to the output of human capital formation. However, this production function has the peculiarity of considering student activity (here denoted by S_{it}) as inputs and outputs at the same time. In fact, more resources employed in schooling (higher E_{it}) induce longer school attendance (higher S_{it}), and presumably higher educational attainment; at the same time, longer attendance in schools favours greater formation of new human capital (higher ΔH_{it}). This describes a sort of multiplicative effect of educational resources: there is a direct impact on the current production of new human capital (given by $\frac{\partial(\Delta H_{it})}{\partial E_{it}}$), and an indirect effect via the optimal plan revision induced by newly added resources (given by $\frac{\partial(\Delta H_{it})}{\partial S_{it}^*} \cdot \frac{\partial S_{it}^*}{\partial E_{it}}$). To take an example, think of the opening of a new library within a school: the direct impact on children's education is given by the newly added opportunities of browsing through new volumes and learning about new subjects. At the same time, a new library makes the school more attractive to families and children, who are now encouraged to remain longer at school in order to take greater advantage of it. Both effects strengthen the formation of new human capital.

When students are inputs in the production process, it becomes crucial to consider their individual abilities and the overall ability of the group of students. Educationists have made clear that it is much easier (and more rewarding) to teach bright students: they understand better and more quickly, raise clever questions and are typically more motivated in studying. But the converse is also true: students are brighter when teachers are better qualified and more motivated.[2]

This is only one side of the coin, since unobservable ability is positively correlated with family background (mainly with parental education). Thus, in most cases the brightest students are the offspring of educated parents, and this creates an incentive for teachers to teach in schools where there is a greater proportion of better-endowed students. The reverse is also true: knowing that better teachers are crucial in producing more human capital, parents of abler students have a greater incentive to hunt for better schools. As a consequence, treating students as educational input is intimately related to the problem of self-sorting in schools (and classes within schools).

While individual ability may be important when interacting with teacher quality, it could also become relevant at the aggregate level of the class (or of the school). Everyone wants to be in a class with good teachers, but everyone wants good classmates too, because it is common knowledge that the 'speed of learning' in a class is the average speed, which is positively correlated to the average ability. But this cannot always be the case: being in a class of geniuses may have depressing effects on average students, whereas a middle- to bottom-quality class may encourage the performance of average-ability students. The overall effect of average ability in a class (*peer effect*) depends on the hypothesised effect of the social interaction, which can be either of the 'complement' variety (human capital formation improves only when there is a generalised increase in the quality of all students) or of the 'substitute' variety (the ability of a better-endowed student can – at least partially – compensate for the low performance of a less endowed student).

By varying student qualities (whenever schools can sort students according to their observable abilities, as in the admission to some private schools and/or to most high schools) and class size, school managers can vary the potential for human capital formation in each class. Since families choose schools according to their expectations with respect to admission and class formation policies, actual human capital formation emerges as the equilibrium result of supply and demand for school quality. Let us now discuss the issue of class formation in greater detail.

4.2 Class formation and peer effects

There are three main problems in defining optimal class formation: the selection of students according to their ability, the class composition (i.e. mixing students of different ability in the same class or creating ability-homogeneous classes) and the class size. The first two issues arise whenever students are differently endowed with abilities that are relevant in educational achievement (attentiveness, brightness, cooperativeness). Otherwise, only the third issue remains relevant.

The problem of screening students arises from the unobservable nature of individual ability. A large part of schooling activity is devoted to testing students in order to obtain indirect measures of these unobservables. Test scores are, in turn, used as screening devices for admission to further education. On the whole, one could state that one by-product of schooling activity is information about students' quality.[3] This view supports the idea of educational certificates as signals for prospective employers: the longer a student remains at school the more extensive the selection that has been passed, and the greater must be his/her unobservable ability.[4]

While testing is the only alternative in the case of imperfect symmetric information (neither the student, his/her family nor the teachers know his/her ability in advance), whenever students and families have an informational advantage on unobservable ability, charging tuition fees can be an alternative to screening students. Suppose one intends to create an elite school by admitting only the best students, in a context where families have superior information about students' abilities (imperfect asymmetric information). All families would like to gain access to the exclusive elite school, because this will grant higher returns to education in the future, thanks to the better human capital formation. There are two alternative ways to find the best students: either through submitting all applicants to specific examination, or by selecting them in accordance with their willingness to pay.

The main drawback of the allocation mechanism based on testing is that it wastes resources: students spend time to prepare for the admission tests, families spend money in order to provide extra tutoring for the same aim and schools have to pay teachers (or external examining agencies) to mark exams. In addition, student performance is very often correlated to family background, and therefore the final result does not always identify 'pure' ability in the students.[5] The market mechanism (selecting students by means of admission fees that increase with perceived school quality) is in principle more efficient: by ordering people according to the maximum fees they are willing to pay, they indirectly reveal their hidden abilities. Seen from this perspective, in order to obtain the best students it is sufficient to raise fees adequately. Under the maintained assumption that private schools provide better-quality education, the empirical counterpart is that we should observe better-ability students in private schools, because only for high-ability children is it rational to pay more for better education.[6]

However, the market allocation mechanism works properly only when financial markets operate perfectly – that is, when families can borrow money to pay high fees on the expectation of high-ability children. Otherwise, if markets for education financing do not exist, poor parents of high-ability children will be outspent by rich parents of lower-ability children. Since financial markets for education financing typically either do not exist or are heavily subsidised by the state, meritocratic selection is in general Pareto-superior as an allocative device in class formation. Better students could still be prevented from participating in higher education by high opportunity costs. For this reason, the combination of meritocratic selection and publicly financed scholarships contingent on family income can yield the most efficient matching of students to schools.[7]

The problem of sorting students in order to obtain an appropriate match between students and schools arises not only in schools of different qualities. If learning activity in class is affected by the ability and behaviour of classmates, families are not indifferent to the class assignments of their children. Whenever other people's features affect current behaviour we speak of the *peer effect*, indicating the externality created by each individual on other people. Peer effects can take different forms: conformity, competition, envy, and so on. School classes are a typical example where peer effects reveal themselves. Consider, for example, the case where student abilities are technical complements.[8] In such a case each student benefits from being in a class of bright students, because he/she gets more insights in class discussion, feels more pressure to compete and, in general, obtains additional stimuli by being associated with intellectually rich classmates.

While the empirical relevance of peer effects is far from being ascertained on empirical grounds,[9] it has strong implications with respect to class formation and class size. Lazear (1999) has proposed an interesting model that shows the importance of interaction between students' abilities. If student ability is correlated with attending classes without disrupting other people's learning activities, one can empirically measure it by the fraction of time during which a student pays attention to the teacher; let us define it as p_i, $0 \leq p_i \leq 1$, $\forall i$. As a consequence, teaching is possible only when all students in a class pay attention – that is, for a fraction of time equal to $\prod_{i=1}^{n} p_i$, where n is the class size.

When all students in a class are of equal quality, then the teaching activity is possible for a fraction p^n of time: in such a context teaching and learning directly depend positively on students' quality and negatively on class size (since $p_i \leq 1$).[10] In order to grasp the extent of this effect, let us consider the case in which each student is able to pay attention for 98 per cent of his/her class time; then teaching and learning activities in a class of twenty-five similar students will be possible only for 60 per cent of time (as a result of $0.98^{25} = 0.60$). If student quality declines, paying attention only 94 per cent of the time, learning and teaching become possible only for 21 per cent of the time, and it would be necessary to reach a class size of just eight students in order to restore the ability to teach the 60 per cent of the time.

Even though this example may seem extreme, it makes it clear that schools themselves have incentives to attract better students. In order to analyse this aspect, let us consider a case in which a given number of identical schools exist. Each school is able to accommodate the same number of students, but the students are different in terms of ability. When peer effects matter, each school has an incentive to attract better students, because this will improve the quality of its teaching.[11] Whenever a pre-assigned school order exists, the first school will choose the best students. Since being admitted to the best school can be priced (either directly through admission fees, or indirectly through the price of housing whenever proximity to the school is a necessary requirement for admission), the school can use either exams or market mechanisms. Then the second school chooses the second-best students, and so on. The final outcome is perfect segregation of students according to their abilities and of schools according to the average quality of admitted students,[12] irrespective of whether sorting occurs either through tests or through market channels.

However, a stratified educational system does not necessarily represent the most efficient allocation of students. If the peer effect linearly affects the educational production function then exchanging students between schools does not alter the overall production of human capital.[13] In contrast, when the educational production function exhibits increasing marginal returns in terms of the peer effect, then perfect segregation is effectively the most efficient allocation of students. However, whenever we observe a decreasing marginal productivity of average ability, mixing students of different abilities may prove superior in terms of human capital production.[14]

4.3 Integration or segregation?

In order to show how the previously introduced elements interact in the process of class formation, we now propose a simplified version of a model that was originally proposed by Roland Benabou (1996a) to analyse territorial segregation (i.e. the endogenous formation of rich and poor neighbourhoods) but that can easily be adapted in terms of class formation.[15] The model focuses on the relevant concept of *social capital*, which summarises all the relevant factors of the environment that affect individual behaviour: thus it extends from the average (unobservable) ability of classmates, to incomes and the wealth of their families (which become relevant when schools are locally financed), up to social networking (which may become relevant when entering the labour market). The model predicts social integration or segregation as an endogenous result of optimising agents according to the role played by social capital in human capital formation. As a consequence, school choice will shape the distribution of human capital in the society, and is strictly related to income inequality.

We start by considering an overlapping generation model in which agents live for two periods. Each agent attends the school chosen by his/her parents in the first period of his/her life. School attendance provides newly formed human capital, which depends on family background (summarised by parent human capital) and by the quality of the school attended. The quality of the school is determined by a peer effect (here proxied by the average human capital possessed by parents of schoolmates) and by a resource effect (the amount of resources available from local taxation). Then the agent earns an income that is proportional to the newly formed human capital, becomes a parent and chooses a school for his/her child's education. Given the fact that schools gather students from local neighbourhoods, school choice and residential choice coincide; it is therefore plausible that the agent gets indebted in order to finance the school/residence choice. Labour earnings are used for consumption and payment for school/residence sunk costs in the first period of life. In the second period of life the agent works, consumes, repays the possible debts and dies. In the meantime, the child starts attending the school chosen by his/her parent.

Given this basic structure of the model, we assume for simplicity that only two schools serve the whole society (be it a district or a metropolitan area), indexed by index j, $j = 1, 2$; each of them can host one-half of the student population. The schools have access to the same teaching technology and therefore, *ex ante*, they are identical. Again for simplicity, we assume that there exist only two possible levels of human capital: H_A corresponds to the case of high-education type (call it 'college graduate' or 'skilled worker' type), while H_B corresponds to low-education type. By definition, $H_A > H_B$ holds. The population is assumed constant and normalised to unity. When n indicates the high-educated fraction in the population, the average human capital in the society is given by

$$\overline{H} = nH_A + (1 - n)H_B \tag{4.2}$$

We denote with n^j the fraction of students from high-educated parents in each school. We also take as convention the first school to be the 'best' school in terms of social capital, given the assumption of $n^1 > n^2$.

Altruistic individual preferences are defined over individuals' own consumption in the two periods of life (where C_t^t and C_{t+1}^t indicate the consumption of generation t when young and when old, respectively) and over the human capital accumulated by the child H_{t+1}. Each agent chooses the school in which to enrol his/her child E^j, $j = 1, 2$, by maximising his/her indirect utility function, which corresponds to the solution of the following problem,

$$U^j(H_t) = \max_{D_t} U\left(C_t^t, C_{t+1}^t, H_{t+1}\right)$$
$$= \max_{D_t} [\log C_t^t + \log C_{t+1}^t + \log H_{t+1}] \qquad (4.3)$$

subject to the following constraints:

$$C_t^t + B^j = H_t(1 - \tau) + D_t \qquad (4.4)$$

$$C_{t+1}^t + D_t(1 + R(D_t, H_t)) = H_t \qquad (4.5)$$

$$H_{t+1} = f(H_t, L^j, E^j) \qquad (4.6)$$

The budget constraint (4.4) specifies that consumption when young plus enrolment fees B^j for sending one's child to school E^j can be financed either through labour income (for simplicity, equal to the endowment of human capital), net of taxes, τ (to be used to finance local schools), or through borrowing an amount D_t. Similarly, the budget constraint (4.5) for the second period indicates that consumption when old and debt repayment (where financial market imperfections make the borrowing rate R dependent on earning capability and the extent of the loan) must balance second-period earnings (which, for simplicity, are not taxed). Finally, the constraint (4.6) corresponds to the educational production function, where the newly produced human capital depends on parents' human capital H_t, on the quality of the school attended L^j (the peer effect) and on the resources available to the same school E^j.

To characterise the effect of social capital, it is crucial to define whether heterogeneity of family backgrounds within the same school is beneficial or detrimental to human capital formation. To formalise this idea, we assume that school environment quality L^j takes the form

$$L^j = L(n^j; H_A, H_B) = \left(n^j H_A^\sigma + (1 - n^j)H_B^\sigma\right)^{1/\sigma} = L(n^j), \quad L' > 0 \qquad (4.7)$$

When $\sigma < 1$, the heterogeneity is detrimental because the two individual types are complements in 'producing' the quality of social capital:

to see this, it is easy to prove that $L^j < \overline{H}$ for $n^j \neq 0$ and $n^j \neq 1$.[16] Vice versa, when $\sigma > 1$, heterogeneity is beneficial because the two types are (technical) substitutes, and L is concave in n^j (and therefore $L^j > \overline{H}$).

Educational attainment also depends on the local neighbourhood through the channel of funding, obtained through local taxation. If, for simplicity, we do not take into account the effect of differing tax rates in each area, we may say that educational expenditure per student E^j is financed by admission fees that are made progressive by a lump sum payment B^j plus an additional component that is proportional to family income. In the absence of the central redistribution of funds between schools, a balanced budget constraint requires that

$$E^j = B^j + \tau(n^j H_A + (1 - n^j)H_B) = E(n^j), \quad E' > 0 \quad (4.8)$$

As a consequence, schools attended by students from educated parents receive more financial resources.[17]

By making use of equations (4.4)–(4.8), the maximand of equation (4.3) can be re-expressed as

$$U^j(H_t) = \max_{D_t}[\log(H_t(1-\tau) + D_t - B^j) + \log(H_t - D_t(1 + R(D_t, H_t)))$$
$$+ \log(f(H_t, L(n^j), E(n^j)))] \quad (4.9)$$

Equating the marginal rate of intertemporal substitution to the market interest rate identifies the optimal level of borrowing:

$$\frac{\dfrac{\partial U}{\partial C_t^t}}{\dfrac{\partial U}{\partial C_{t+1}^t}} = \frac{C_{t+1}^t}{C_t^t} = \left(1 + R(D_t, H_t) + D_t \frac{\partial R}{\partial D_t}\right) \quad (4.10)$$

While the optimal consumption path is defined by equation (4.10), we still need to define the optimal school choice. Given its nature of discrete choice (choose the 'good' school 1 or the 'bad' school 2), each agent will consider the cost of school enrolment $(B^j + \tau H_i)$ and the benefit provided by the presence of n^j children from educated families (i.e. type H_A parents). The benefit can be higher or lower according to whether family backgrounds are technical substitutes or complements in producing the social capital (as made clear by equation (4.7)). In addition, having classmates from richer families increases the local funds available for the school (in accordance with equation (4.8)). Each

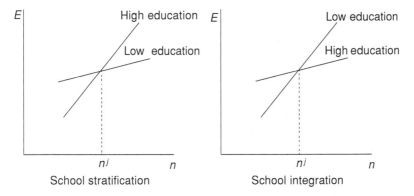

Figure 4.1 Alternative configurations of iso-utilities

agent will choose the combination (E^j, n^j), $j = 1, 2$, granting him/her the highest utility level.

In order to study this choice, let us consider the slope of indifference curves in the (E, n) space, given the optimal choice described by equation (4.10). By means of the implicit function theorem,[18] it is possible to show that such a curve will slope as

$$\frac{dE}{dn} = -\frac{\frac{\partial U}{\partial H_{t+1}} \left(f_L \frac{dL}{dn} + f_E \frac{dE}{dn} \right)}{-\frac{\partial U}{\partial C_t^t}}$$

$$= \frac{C_{t+1}^t}{H_{t+1}} \cdot \frac{\left(f_L \frac{dL}{dn} + f_E \frac{dE}{dn} \right)}{\left(1 + R(D_t, H_t) + D_t \frac{\partial R}{\partial D_t} \right)} \qquad (4.11)$$

Equation (4.11) represents a marginal rate of substitution between costs (the denominator) and benefits (the numerator) of attending a given school. If this rate of substitution is increasing in the parent's human capital, this implies that educated parents (type H_A) exhibit steeper iso-utility curves (the left panel of figure 4.1) than less educated parents. In such a case a stratified equilibrium will take place, because more educated (and richer) parents obtain greater benefit from school quality, are more willing to spend, and therefore outspend poorer parents. Similarly, reducing the quality of social capital implies less harm being done to low-education parents when compared to high-education ones, which makes them less inclined to pay for a better school environment. The symmetric equilibrium (where $n^1 = n^2 = n$, i.e. the two schools have identical composition) is unstable, because it is sufficient for just one rich family expressing its greater preparedness to pay to fuel a cumulative rise of admission fees for the better school, up to the point where all highly educated parents would like to send their children there.

The opposite is the case if the marginal rate of substitution $\dfrac{dE}{dn}$ is negatively correlated with family education (income); then the only stable equilibrium will be perfect integration in both schools (the right panel of figure 4.1).[19] It is therefore clear that, whenever stratification conditions apply, all H_A-type parents will spontaneously opt for the better school 1, whereas all H_B-type parents will prefer the worse school 2.[20]

School stratification has intergenerational implications, because all children from good family backgrounds obtain better social capital from their school environment, attend schools with more financial resources and get H_A units of human capital. School stratification converts into social stratification. Vice versa, when school integration prevails, all human capital levels (incomes) converge to the same level, and an egalitarian society should emerge.

While integration may seem socially desirable, nevertheless the spontaneous allocation of students could go in the opposite direction. In such a case, only public intervention to force such an integration (a typical example being desegregation policies in the United States) can lead to more efficient outcomes in terms of human capital formation. This may provide a rationale for a widely diffused practice of reserving quotas for various minorities.[21]

4.4 Class size

A final aspect related to class formation is the problem of optimal class size. If the educational outcome of a school can be identified and priced easily, then profit maximisation could identify the optimal class size. Going back to the educational production function (4.1) and amending it by taking into account the fact that per capita resources E_{it} are increasing in the number of teachers m, while peer effect H_{it}

dissipates with an increase in class size, we can formalise this problem for a given number of student n as follows:

$$\max_m \left[\sum_{i=1}^{n} \beta \Delta H_{it} - wm \right]$$

$$= \max_m \left[\sum_{i=1}^{n} \beta f\left(A_i, S_{it}, \underset{+}{E(m)}, \underset{-}{H\left(\frac{n}{m}\right)} \right) - wm \right] \quad (4.12)$$

where β is the market price of an additional unit of human capital and w is the salary of a teacher. Maximisation (4.12) can be simplified by considering that S_{it} is endogenously selected by students on the basis of their individual ability, family background and expected return in the labour market (the β coefficient). By taking the first-order condition associated with this problem, we obtain

$$\beta \sum_{i=1}^{n} f_E(A_i, E, H) \cdot E_m - \beta \left(\frac{n}{m^2}\right) \sum_{i=1}^{n} f_H(A_i, E, H) \cdot H_m - w = 0$$

$$(4.13)$$

or, rearranging terms,

$$\frac{n}{m} = \sqrt{\frac{n\left(\frac{w}{\beta} - \sum_{i=1}^{n} f_E \cdot E_m\right)}{-\sum_{i=1}^{n} f_H \cdot H_m}} \Leftrightarrow m = \sqrt{\frac{n\left(-\sum_{i=1}^{n} f_H \cdot H_m\right)}{\frac{w}{\beta} - \sum_{i=1}^{n} f_E \cdot E_m}} \quad (4.14)$$

Equation (4.14) suggests that a profit-maximising school (i.e. a private school) will optimally choose greater class sizes the bigger the student pool, the higher the teacher salary and the lower the average effect of school resources (or peer effect) on individual human capital formation. Symmetrically, a private school will hire more teachers the bigger the student pool, the lower the teacher salary and the higher the average effect of school resources (or peer effect) on individual human capital formation. Notice that a higher return to education (a bigger β) would suggest smaller classes and/or more teachers, because families would be available to pay the monetary cost of additional resources on the expectation of greater rewards in the labour market.

In order to derive optimal size prescription, it is necessary for the educational production function to be affected in practice by class size in empirical data, as predicted in equation (4.12). However, in this respect the empirical evidence is mixed. Krueger (1999) analyses the available evidence on the STAR (Student/Teacher Achievement Ratio) experiment run in Tennessee in the period 1985 to 1989, when 11,600 students in their first four years of school were randomly assigned to classes of different sizes.[22] Krueger found that, after controlling for observable characteristics of the student and his/her family background, 'in all grades, the average student in small classes performed better on this summary [the achieved percentile in the distribution of test scores] than did those in regular and regular/aide classes'. In a subsequent paper, Krueger and Whitmore (2001) merge the experiment sample with the records of college entrance exams (SAT (Scholastic Aptitude Test) and ACT (American College Test) tests), and they are able to show that students assigned to smaller classes were more likely to apply for college; this effect was more pronounced among Afro-Americans than among white students. In addition, students from small classes outperformed those in regular classes by a small amount in test scores.[23]

Instead of reviewing a randomised experiment, Hoxby (2002a) exploits natural variations in the population size of a long panel of Connecticut elementary schools, finding that class size variation (due to age cohort size) does not have a statistically significant effect on student achievements (as measured by test scores in grade 4-6-8). Similarly Woessman and West (2002) analyse a larger sample from the TIMSS (Third International Mathematics and Science Study), conducted during the academic year 1994/95 by the IEA across forty countries. Their paper discusses in detail the problem of the self-sorting of students in smaller classes, either for school policies (as in the case of remedial programmes for children from a poor background) or for parental effort (in order to secure better learning environments for their children). By taking differences between adjacent classes they eliminate the self-sorting within schools, and then control for the endogeneity of class size by using an instrumental variable estimator, where the school-average class size is used as the instrument. They find evidence for a negative effect of class size on thirteen-year-old students in four cases out of thirty-six, leading to the conclusion that 'in the vast majority of cases . . . the estimated coefficient is not statistically significantly different from zero'.

Therefore, while in principle we could identify an optimal class size by equating marginal costs to marginal benefits, in practice the benefit can be hardly detected, given the high variability of the estimated impact of class size on student performance.

4.5 Resource effectiveness

The uncertain effects of class size on student performance do not constitute an exceptional case. Many other indicators of school resources (such as the student/teacher ratio, teachers' salaries, teacher education, school size, the availability of books and/or libraries) have been found to have ambiguous effects by those trying to estimate educational production function in the vein of equation (4.1). Eric Hanushek has repeatedly provided reviews of this literature.[24] The general puzzle to be addressed is that 'the constantly rising cost and "quality" of the inputs of schools appear to be unmatched by improvement in the performance of students'.[25] Family and neighbourhood are generally found to exert a greater impact on school achievement than aggregate indicators of school resources. While early studies directly tested the potential \ impact of school resources on test score achievement, more recent ones have focused on the acquisition of cognitive abilities as the main output of the educational production function. While the effect of school resources is uncertain with respect to student achievement, stronger effects are found through continuation in school.[26]

There are two main issues in measuring the effect of school resources on educational achievements:

(i) sample selection; and
(ii) data aggregation.

The first problem is given by the potential endogeneity of school resources, which could be correlated with the unobservable abilities of students through their self-sorting. If we take a linearised version of equation (4.1)

$$T_{it} = \eta_0 + \eta_1 A_i + \eta_2 E_{it} + \eta_3 H_{it} + \varepsilon_{it} \qquad (4.15)$$

where T_{it} is a generic measure of educational attainment (be it test scores, cognitive ability or years of education). Any OLS estimation of η_2 will be biased if $Cov(A_i, E_{it}) \neq 0$, which can occur either because better students choose schools endowed with better resources (or even the opposite: better teachers want to teach in schools where students are better – $Cov(A_i, E_{it}) > 0$),[27] or because schools devote extra resources to less brilliant students ($Cov(A_i, E_{it}) < 0$). To minimise the problem, it is possible to resort to first differences (a value-added formulation):

$$\Delta T_{it} = \eta_2 \Delta E_{it} + \eta_3 \Delta H_{it} + (\varepsilon_{it+1} - \varepsilon_{it}) \qquad (4.16)$$

The formulation (4.16) is possible only when panel information on students is available, and when school resources vary from one year to another. If, for example, E_{it} refers to a teacher input characteristic (such as stipend, education or hours of work), it is not likely to change over the years and it cannot therefore be identified. In principle, it would be possible to identify the relative contribution of each single teacher, using a two-step procedure. Possessing information on a wide sample of students who have changed teachers in their school careers, the contribution of each single teacher could be identified by a specific dummy (as long as there have been students changing classes and teachers). In the second step, individual teacher dummies could be regressed on the observable characteristics of teachers in order to identify which variables could account for the relative contribution to students' achievements. However, the amount of data required is enormous, and this explains why this or similar procedures have rarely been attempted. In fact, the reverse applies: the same strategy has been implemented by using aggregate data based on schools or district areas. This reduces the amount of information required (because individual-level data on resources are replaced by school or area averages), but may introduce aggregation biases that could create more problems than they are able to solve.

The aggregation procedure is correct under the assumption of independent disturbances across the group structure, otherwise it leads to downward-biased least square estimates of standard errors (Moulton, 1990). But schools or districts can share observable and unobservable characteristics, which should be controlled for (either by imposing a clustered structure for the errors distribution or by using two-stage procedures). Still, even in the case of aggregate data, the effect of local school resources is identifiable only by students changing location, because otherwise group averages would be observable.[28]

If only group averages are used (as in cross-country analysis) then, typically, positive and significant effects are found in the literature. Lee and Barro (2001) take test scores on internationally comparable tests

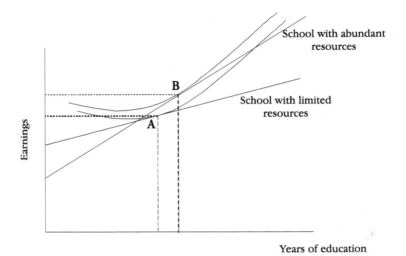

Figure 4.2 – Educational choice under different endowments of school resources

(taken at the age of nine and fourteen) as measures of educational achievement and regress them on proxies for family resources (output per capita and average years of education) and for school resources (pupils per teacher, average expenditure per student, average salary per teacher and average length of academic year). Using information for fifty-eight countries over the period 1960 to 1990 they find significantly positive effects for school resource variables.

Similar results are obtained when school effectiveness is tested with respect to labour market outcomes. Card and Krueger, in various studies (1992, 1996a, 1996b), have argued that an abundance of school resources is reflected in longer stays at school and higher returns on education. The basic idea is described by figure 4.2. Individuals differ in terms of ability, whereas schools differ in terms of resource endowments. If school resources are inputs in the educational production function then student self-sorting gathers better students in schools with more abundant resources (because they have a lower cost of school attendance and/or expect a higher return per invested unit of school resources). This corresponds to point **B** in figure 4.2. The remaining low-ability students will choose less education and will experience lower earnings (point **A**). By estimating a regression line for each sub-sample, a researcher would expect two different slopes, the 'high resource' schedule being characterised by lower intercept (a high-talent individual choosing not to acquire education will be penalised in the labour market) and higher slope (student attending better schools will experience higher returns on education). Thus, this model yields three theoretical predictions: greater school resources are positively correlated with longer stays at school, higher returns to education and lower intercepts in the earning–education function.[29] Card and Krueger (1992) test this approach by using census data for the US population born between 1920 and 1949 and by attributing to each individual the school quality information associated with the area where the person was born, finding significant effects from the student/teacher ratios experienced in the birth area and the subsequent labour market experience (even when controlling for birth region, residence region and cohort effects).[30] Card and Krueger (1996a) follow a natural experiment approach by comparing individuals born (and supposedly educated) in North Carolina (where race-segregated schools were absent) and in South Carolina (where school desegregation took place more recently). They find evidence of a persistent difference in wages for Afro-Americans born in North Carolina and white people born in South Carolina,[31] and they attribute this permanent difference to the difference in educational systems (different class sizes being a crucial aspect of it). Finally, Card and Krueger (1996b) review related literature (twenty-four articles), confirming that on average a 10 per cent increase in educational expenditure per student is associated with a 1 to 2 per cent increase in these students' subsequent annual earnings.

How do we reconcile these two sets of contradictory results? On the one hand, we find that educational resources are scarcely related to school performance (as measured by test scores and/or literacy tests); nor do test scores have any impact on subsequent earnings.[32] On the other hand, we find that district-average educational resources per student affect educational attainment and subsequent labour market earnings. These results cannot be easily reconciled from a human capital perspective, where earnings mirror acquired competences. However, schools perform screening activity as one of their additional joint products, and test scores are crucial in this prospect. They implicitly indicate the likelihood that teachers place on the pursuit of studies beyond a specific level. In an earning function, when we already control for educational attainment, these scores are, instead, likely to play a limited effect (the so-called *sheepskin effect*, since people with identical educational credentials look similar to potential employers).

But school resources can still be effective in extending school attendance. If mass scholarisation takes 'low-quality' students in schools (i.e. students from a poor background, who require increasing inputs for identical outputs), we would observe constant (or even declining) school productivity (as measured by test scores), but increased educational attainment in the population. Extended attendance can explain the positive correlation between school resources and earnings, but we still lack a convincing (and testable) explanation for the correlation with marginal return rates of education.

4.6 Resource efficiency

A recurrent explanation for the finding that the effectiveness of educational resources is absent when estimating educational production functions makes reference to inefficient use of the same resources (Hanushek, 1986; Pritchett and Filmer, 1999; Gundlach, Woessman and Gmelin, 2001). The basic idea is simple: with decreasing marginal productivity of inputs, an intensive use of one input can reduce the impact of its productivity to a negligible level (statistically indistinguishable from zero). Extensive use is not justifiable under cost minimisation. In fact, we can define a cost function linked to an aggregate educational production function (equivalent to the sum across individuals of equation (4.1)) as

$$\min_{\overline{E}} \sum_{j=1}^{m} p_j E_j \quad \text{subject to } \Delta H = f(E_1, E_2, \ldots, E_m) \qquad (4.17)$$

where E_j represents a generic input (say teachers, books, libraries, and so on) linked to a market price p_j. Considering the first-order conditions associated with problem (4.17) and taking their ratio we get

$$\frac{p_j}{p_k} = \frac{f_{E_j}(E_1, E_2, \ldots, E_m)}{f_{E_k}(E_1, E_2, \ldots, E_m)} \qquad (4.18)$$

which can also be re-expressed as

$$\frac{f_{E_j}(E_1, E_2, \ldots, E_m)}{p_j} = \frac{f_{E_k}(E_1, E_2, \ldots, E_m)}{p_k} \qquad (4.19)$$

Equation (4.19) defines cost effectiveness, corresponding to the condition that achievement gains per unit of currency spent have to be equalised across inputs. As Pritchett and Filmer (1999) convincingly demonstrate, the vast majority of studies on educational production function are inconsistent with condition (4.19).[33] In a similar vein, using aggregate data on educational expenditure, Gundlach, Woessman and Gmelin (2001) find that the educational sector in OECD countries has exhibited a productivity decline in the order of two to four percentage points a year over the period 1970 to 1994.[34]

How can we account for this evidence of technical inefficiency? Several explanations are at hand. The easiest one is that the educational production function is a multi-output technology. Schools aim to improve competences of students (often proxied by test scores), but they are also expected to foster civic attitudes, self-control, an aesthetic sense, the ability to cooperate with fellows, and so on.[35] As long as educational resources are relevant in fostering these attributes, we cannot satisfy condition (4.19) and still be on the efficiency frontier. The problem is that these other outcomes are hardly measurable, and therefore this claim goes unchecked.

An alternative explanation invokes the lobbying activity of teachers and families.[36] If school resources are chosen under teachers' influence (i.e. in accordance with teachers' welfare) then we will observe an excessive use of the resources that are more relevant in this utility function. Indirect evidence of this proposition exists. Hoxby (1996a) finds that the unionisation of teachers[37] can account for a greater use of educational inputs; this evidence is consistent either with teachers having better information about the educational production function (*efficiency-enhancing*) or with teachers' unions being rent seekers. In addition to educational budget expansion, teachers' unions may also be able to change budget allocation in favour of inputs that reduce teachers' workload (such as reducing class size and/or teaching load per teacher) or increase teachers' salaries. Pritchett and Filmer (1999) review several articles estimating educational production functions in less developed countries, and show that statistical significance is greater for inputs that are not a direct concern of teachers (such as books, libraries, class homework), whereas other inputs (pupil/teacher ratios or teachers' salaries) tend to prove insignificant. Additional evidence is obtained from the comparison between private and public schools, since the former are less under the control of teachers.

An alternative interpretation has been proposed by Woessman (2003) reviewing the TIMMS survey covering thirty-nine countries. His starting point is that 'public schooling systems still differ substantially across countries in their institutional structure of educational decision-making processes. They give different amounts of decision-making power to the different agents involved in educational production, which creates different incentives for their behaviour. These differences in institutions and incentives will affect the agents' decisions on resource allocation and thereby the effectiveness of resource use in the education sector, which should impact on the educational performance of the students' (p. 119). After controlling for family backgrounds and educational resources, he is able to prove that the degree of school autonomy has a positive bearing on student performance; institutional features such as external examinations and a competitive environment set by a large private schooling sector have statistically significant positive effects on student performance in mathematics and science. His interpretation is given in terms of the agency problem: greater autonomy for schools implies more effective monitoring of teachers by parents concerned about students' learning, thereby being conducive to better student performance. Conversely, greater influence by teachers' unions in the education process leads to lower performance levels.[38]

The role of external competition is also stressed by Hoxby (2000c). In order to evaluate her contribution, we must refer to the concept of Tiebout choice. In his original paper, Charles Tiebout (1956) argues that the underprovision of public goods when individual preferences are unobservable could be solved by decentralised expenditure (and taxation). By moving to the location closer to the preferred combination of tax rate and public supply, each individual reveals his/her true preferences: conditional on externalities being limited to community size, spatial mobility is a way to reveal hidden preferences and to levy taxes up to the desired amount. The idea of 'voting with your feet' can be applied to the quasi-market for education. By increasing their opportunity set (i.e. by raising the number of alternatives in school choice), families can obtain the desired amount of education for their children, in terms of resources, peer effect and social capital. This increase in self-sorting according to preferences with regard to schooling raises *private allocative efficiency*, whereas the effect on *social allocative efficiency* depends on the shape of the educational production function (see section 4.3 above). Increased parental choice calls for better scrutiny of the available alternatives, yielding stricter monitoring of existing schools. As in any agency problem, stricter monitoring leads to improved performance and/or to a more efficient use of existing resources, thus reducing the unitary cost of delivering education.

Using data on 6,523 US metropolitan districts, Hoxby (2000c) measures the extent of available parental choice with concentration indices built on enrolment rates.[39] This measure exerts a positive impact on student achievement and a negative impact on both spending per student and the enrolment share in private schools. The author takes this evidence as confirming that increased competition among public schools (i.e. greater availability of choices) can be beneficial for both students and taxpayers. Her results are robust despite the increased sorting of households by districts, because increased homogeneity among district families has little net effect on achievement, on spending per pupil or on productivity (constructed as the ratio between achievement and spending, as in equation (4.19)).

Analogous conclusions were reached by Fiske and Ladd (2000), who review the large-scale school reform undertaken in New Zealand between 1989 (under a Labour government) and 1991 (a Nationalist government). The state system of compulsory education was fully decentralised; administrative responsibility was passed to locally elected boards of trustees; charter schools (combining central funding and accountability with management autonomy) were also introduced. Oversubscribed schools had the right to designate criteria of admission (thus shifting the system from 'increased parental choice' to 'increased school choice'). According to the evidence collected by the authors, better-educated parents mainly exploited the increased availability of choice. Five years after the reform, they noticed an increased polarisation of enrolment by ethnic and/or socio-economic groups. They also report an increased polarisation among schools: most popular schools attracted most of the students oriented to a university career, better teachers and wealthier families. A still unsolved question had to do with low-performing schools, typically located in culturally (and economically) deprived areas. The reform left this issue unresolved, leading the authors to suggest that the new mechanism did not provide any formal way to balance the narrow interests of a particular group of parents against the legitimate needs of broader communities: 'The bottom line is that it is impossible to sustain a system in which all parents are completely free to select the school their child will attend. Some mechanism must be devised for rationing places in popular schools, and this inevitably involves constraints on choice. The challenge is to keep the constraints from falling disproportionately on students from disadvantaged families . . .' (Fiske and Ladd, 2000, p. 287).

Summing up, while there is strong evidence that public schools do not act in line with the principle of profit maximisation, it is not yet clear why this occurs. It has been argued that it has to do with teachers' influence (including rent seeking); if so, the implication would be that more competition between schools should reduce rents and improve both the productive efficiency of resources (for a given level of demand for education) and the (private) allocative efficiency of students and teachers (for a given supply of schools). However, this discussion shows that increasing the freedom of choice at the margin is rather different from increasing it as a whole.[40] The crucial fact that education is compulsory, at least at the initial stages, requires it to be delivered sufficiently close to families in order to enact the legal or constitutional obligation. While in competitive markets unprofitable firms will be driven out of the market by the (prospective) losses incurred by their owners, in the quasi-market for education less efficient schools need to be retained in order to supply a minimum of education to some pupils. While, in principle, it would be possible to disentangle family background, unobservable ability, peer effect and the (in)efficient use of resources in the educational production function, in practice it becomes impossible to isolate cases of inefficient use of resources from cases of low-quality inputs, since students self-sort in accordance with alternative features (parental status, parental education, family income and wealth, ethnicity, religious beliefs).

4.7 Efficiency versus equity

This discussion on the legal obligation to provide at least some education to all citizens, irrespective of the attained level of efficiency, leads us to the potential trade-off existing between efficiency and equity in education provision.

In modern societies, increasing access to education has advanced hand in hand with the extension of voting rights.[41] Publicly funded education has also exerted redistributive effects.[42] In addition, the free provision of equal amounts of education to all students should produce intertemporal equalising effects on income distribution.[43] On the whole, one may argue that educational expenditure has an intrinsic equalising content, which can be strengthened if it is decided to allocate these resources in a compensatory manner (namely by favouring individuals from poor backgrounds).

On the other hand, in previous sections we have seen that compensatory allocation can prove ineffective and/or inefficient, depending on the configuration of the educational production function. In fact, there can be plausible cases where a society as a whole produces more human capital by concentrating resources on the best students; equality can be achieved by the subsequent redistributive taxation of labour incomes. As in other spheres of public economics, the public provision of education faces a trade-off between equity and efficiency, with the result that a society can improve in one dimension only at the expense of a worsening in the other.[44]

Some authors have tried to escape from the trade-off. Hoxby (1996b) recasts the equity–efficiency trade-off in terms of centralised–decentralised school financing. In her view, local financing is able to achieve allocative efficiency (each individual invests his/her desired amount of resources in education) and productive efficiency (each unit of human capital is obtained at the lower cost of delivery) at the same time. The goal of equity is to apply this standard of optimality to everyone, regardless of family background or income. Since optimal investment can be prevented by an imperfect financial market, moral hazard behaviour and/or the imperfect recognition of externalities, there is scope for public intervention to relieve inequality of opportunity. This can be done with means-tested school vouchers or with categorical aid,[45] but the former is more effective in strengthening competition among schools. However, these prescriptions ignore other aspects that prevent educational investment: culturally poor families value education less (especially when living in poor neighbourhoods, where role models seem to confirm their judgement); economically poor families are more risk-averse, at least with respect to educational investment; schools are not evenly distributed in the territory, and mobility costs can be high; and educational systems can be based on early tracking (as in the case of Germany and Italy, for example), thus making past choices irreversible. Under these circumstances, efficient use of educational resources may conflict with equity goals taking the form of compensatory additional resources to be spent on disadvantaged individuals.

By focusing on higher education, Arrow (1993) also tries to avoid the notion of a potential trade-off between equity and efficiency (to be understood as 'excellence' in his framework). Since private returns on higher education are greater than social ones by far, students applying for university should pay (almost) the entire cost of their education: why should society subsidise individuals who, by nature, are destined to earn more? In his perspective, the equity–efficiency trade-off is misplaced at the university level, given that the existing demand for skilled labour covers only a fraction of the entire labour force. But this 'natural' outcome can be revealed as inefficient whenever the brightest children from poor families are given no opportunity to enter university. Arrow's conclusion holds only under the conditions of the perfect screening of natural abilities by the preceding levels of schooling and perfect information on families. Otherwise, subsidising university education to ensure greater equality of opportunity makes sense. But this somehow reduces the selectivity of access to the best universities, recreating the trade-off with efficient outcomes.

In my opinion, the trade-off between equity and efficiency persists in educational markets, since it is practically impossible to correct for all existing obstacles to educational investments. Improvements in the efficient use of resources can certainly be achieved by means of appropriate incentive schemes for schools and teachers, but as long as parents' education remains one of the most significant predictors of children's schooling there is scope for compensatory action by public authorities, in order to improve on the equity side. This is especially true when families have incentives to differentiate through their educational investment, as is explained more fully in the next chapter.

Notes

1. The effect of social environment can be accounted for either by introducing the crucial variables in the utility function (think of the case of peer esteem) or by taking into account its contribution to individual formation. While Becker and Murphy (2000) follow the first route, most of the literature in the economics of education seems to prefer the alternative strategy.
2. In formal terms, this corresponds to the case where the cross-partial derivatives $\frac{\partial^2 f}{\partial E \partial A} = \frac{\partial^2 f}{\partial A \partial E}$ are positive.
3. Bertola and Coen Pirani (1998) propose a model in which schooling is described as a screening activity (they term it 'allocative education'), the precision of which depends on the amount of resources invested.

4. For a signalling interpretation of educational achievement, see Spence (1973).

5. In addition, the incentive to undergo an exam declines when students do not have an informational advantage on their own ability. Stiglitz (1975) discusses this case, in the context of a general theory of screening.

6. Fernandez (1998) studies the case of allocating students of different abilities across schools of different quality. She shows that under perfect capital markets two allocative mechanisms (admission fees and test scores) yield efficient outcomes (in terms of human capital production). Under borrowing constraints, exams dominate market mechanism in terms of matching efficiency (allocating better students to better schools). A crucial assumption for this result is the complementarity between ability and school quality.

7. Fernandez and Gali (1999) propose a model where meritocratic selection (in relative terms, like a tournament) reaches matching efficiency, associating better students to better schools in the absence of financial markets. Here the crucial assumption relates to the assumed negative correlation between unobservable ability and the cost signalling, thus allowing the best students to emerge irrespective of their social origin.

8. In formal terms, let us consider a simplified version of equation (4.1), where the only relevant inputs are given by student abilities in a class. To make the complement/substitute issue clear, we assume that the f function is in the CES (constant elasticity of substitution) class – as, for example, $\Delta H_i = \left[\sum_{k=i}^{n} A_k^\sigma\right]^{\frac{1}{\sigma}}$, where n is the class size. The education production function is symmetrical for simplicity, but a more complicated version could in principle be considered. Since the elasticity of substitution between two students is equal to $-\frac{1}{\sigma-1}$, whenever $\sigma > 1$ students' qualities are technical substitutes and human capital production is enhanced by mixing students of different qualities (*integration*). On the contrary, if $\sigma < 1$ it is more productive to form classes with students of equivalent levels (*segregation*) in order to obtain the highest production of human capital.

9. As in many other cases in labour economics, detecting the existence of peer effects requires the existence of control cases, which are not easy to identify unless in the case of random class assignment. Hoxby (2000b), using a difference-in-difference approach, has considered gender and race class differences in order to investigate whether different class composition affects average class performance, finding only a limited impact.

10. Given this specification of teaching technology, students' abilities are technical complements, and the segregation of students into classes of identical quality is efficient from a production point of view.

11. Robertson and Symons (1996) and Fernandez and Gali (1999) offer similar models. Both papers assume students differentiated in terms of

quality. In the first paper schools are different in equilibrium, due to peer effect; therefore, they compete to attract better students (*cream-skimming*). In the second paper, schools are assumed different, and they accept students passively, depending on their willingness to pay.

12. This is the main result obtained by Robertson and Symons (1996), where *ex ante* schools start identical and differ in the order they follow in admitting students; *ex post* they are different in the average ability of their students, and therefore are forced to charge different fees.

13. This is straightforward, because exchanging a good student for a bad student reduces the average ability in the good-type school and raises the average ability in the bad-type school. Given an identical educational production function, the reduced production of human capital in good schools is matched exactly by the increase in bad schools. See Hoxby (2000b).

14. Continuing the example introduced in the previous note, when we exchange students between high-ability schools and low-ability schools under decreasing marginal productivity of the average ability (*peer effect*) the human capital loss in the first type of school is overcompensated for by the gain in the second type of school.

15. We reproduce here a modified version of the basic model presented in Benabou (1996a); a more concise version of the same model can be found in Benabou (1994). The original model describes the endogenous formation of a city composed of two distinct zones, where self-selection works through the ability to pay the settling cost and the quality of local schools depends on the average 'quality' of local inhabitants. In addition, schools are financed through taxation on real estate (as is typically the case in the United States), thus providing greater economic resources to schools located in richer environments.

16. The elasticity of substitution in equation (4.7) is equal to $-\frac{1}{\sigma-1}$, which is positive for $\sigma < 1$. It is also easy to check that $L(1) = H_A$ and $L(0) = H_B$.

17. In Benabou (1996a; see also 1996b) it is shown that, when we endogenise the decision over the optimal level of taxation, richer communities vote for lower tax rates and, despite this, local schools obtain more funds in absolute terms.

18. In deriving equation (4.11), we have replaced the tuition cost B_j with the average resources obtained by each student E_j, disregarding the redistributive implication of changing the composition of school bodies (i.e. the derivative $\frac{dE_j}{dn_j}$).

19. By taking specific functional forms for utility and financial market imperfections, Benabou (1996a) is able to show that three conditions can disjointly be responsible for the emergence of stratification: technical complementarity between family background and social capital (that is,

$\frac{\partial f_L}{\partial H_t} > 0$); strong financial market imperfections, rendering the borrowing rate a negative function of family income (that is, $\frac{\partial R}{\partial H} + D\frac{\partial^2 R}{\partial H \partial D} < 0$); and wealth effects in the intertemporal distribution of resources.

20. If $n < 1/2$ some H_B-type parents will be forced to send their children to school 1 because they do not get admission to school 2, since all available positions have already been taken. The opposite applies for H_A-type parents in the case where $n > 1/2$. We assume a random selection of these families who do not get their first-choice accommodation.

21. De Fraja (2005) provides an alternative justification of quotas on efficiency grounds, modelling a situation of positive discrimination that favours disadvantaged groups (i.e. groups with very few high-potential individuals).

22. There were three types of classes: small classes (thirteen to seventeen students), regular classes (twenty-two to twenty-five students) and regular classes with a teacher aide (an additional teacher to help with handicapped/disadvantaged pupils). At the end of the four-year experiment all participating students were returned to regular-size classes.

23. In a European context, using NCDS data (the National Child Development Survey, a longitudinal analysis following a single cohort of individuals born in 1958), Dustmann, Rajah and van Soest (2003) find that the pupil/teacher ratio affects negatively and significantly both test scores and the probability of proceeding further along the educational path at the age of sixteen. On the same data set, Dearden, Ferri and Meghir (2002) show that the explanatory power of school resources variables declines with the introduction of family- and social-capital-related regressors.

24. See, for example, Hanushek (1986, 1996, 2002). For another review, see Burtless (1996).

25. Hanushek (1986, p. 1148). Making reference to US data, Hanushek (1996) puts forward the fact that spending per student has steadily increased by 3.5 per cent a year (due to a decline in the pupil/teacher ratio and increasing teacher stipends), whereas student performance has remained constant, if not declining.

26. 'An additional part of the return to school quality comes through continuation in school. There is substantial evidence that students who do better in school (either through grades or scores on standardised achievement tests) tend to go further in school' (Hanushek, 2002, p. 13).

27. 'If a researcher does not control for family background, then when analysing a data set in which children from wealthier families attend schools with smaller class sizes and better-paid teachers, the researcher will find a positive correlation between student outcomes and school

resources. But that correlation may simply mean that students from wealthier families are primed to do better in school. Conversely, to the extent that students from poor families are more likely to be assigned to remedial classes with higher resources per student, an incautious researcher who does not control for family background would conclude that greater school resources reduce school outcomes' (Blau, 1996, p. 6). In addition, self-selected samples (such as those constituted by students taking the SAT tests) provide estimates of school resources that are biased when applied to the entire population (see Hedges and Greenwald, 1996).

28. However, this makes it impossible to control for social environment, which is a crucial determinant of educational attainment. When samples are restricted to 'immobile' students (i.e. children from non-moving families), most of the resource effects are found negative (Hanushek, 2002).

29. We cannot take these correlations as causal, as Card and Krueger (1996a) make clear with the following example. Let us suppose that students from wealthier families tend to stay in school longer; in addition, the very same persons will earn more because of the social networking of their families. In addition, suppose that wealthier families demand smaller class sizes, even though class size is uninfluential on learning. We would observe positive correlations between school resources and both educational attainment and earnings, but both correlations would be spurious, merely reflecting the failure to account for the independent effect of family wealth.

30. Heckman, Layne-Ferrar and Todd (1997) have repeated the same type of analysis extending the sample to younger cohorts, controlling for the potential endogeneity of migration and allowing for the non-linearity of the relationship between education and log-earnings, but they find even stronger effects (see also Heckman, Layne-Ferrar and Todd, 1996).

31. 'For blacks, the estimated payoff to a year of education in 1980 was 2.1 for those born in South Carolina and 4.0 per cent for those born in North Carolina; while for the whites the order of the returns was reversed: 6.6 per cent for South Carolina and 6.0 for North Carolina' (Card and Krueger, 1996a).

32. See, for example, Altonji and Dunn (1996) or Murnane, Willet and Levy (1995).

33. Pritchett and Filmer (1999) openly recognise that educational production function estimation is blurred by the ignorance of the degree of utilisation of each factor: '[T]here is a crucial distinction between testing whether inputs have low productivity at their current rate of application versus testing whether they are "inputs" at all' (p. 224).

34. Gundlach, Woessman and Gmelin (2001) consider a two-sector model in which educational service is stagnant whereas the residual sector grows at a constant rate. Assuming that prices are determined in competitive markets (which is a rather strong assumption for education, given its public-sector nature in most of the countries in the sample), we should observe an increase in the relative price of education at the same growth as that of productivity in the residual sector. The difference between the two is taken as a proxy of the productivity decline in the educational sector.

35. Edwards (1977) shows that test scores in schools (and wages in workplaces) are highly correlated with personal traits that teachers (and job supervisors) seem to appreciate: 'Rule' (rule orientation), 'Depend' (the habit of predictability and dependability) and 'Internalise' (personal identification with enterprise/school goals). As long as these traits can be induced in students, these are outputs of the educational system.

36. 'Class size reductions are enacted often because they are popular with nearly every constituency interested in schools. Parents like smaller classes because their personal experience suggests that they themselves give more to each child when they have fewer children to handle . . . Teachers may like smaller classes because they reduce the effort that they must expend in order to deliver instruction. Teachers' unions may like class size reductions because they increase the demand for teachers. Administrators may like class size reductions because they increase the size of their domain' (Hoxby, 2000a, pp. 1239–40).

37. A school district is defined as being 'unionised' if three conditions are contemporaneously met: the presence of collective bargaining; the existence of a collective agreement; and the presence of a union claiming more than 50 per cent of district teachers among its members.

38. However, this paper suffers from different degrees of variable aggregation, since the dependent variable (individual student performance) is regressed onto family characteristics, class or teacher information and country variables.

39. She computes Herfindahl indices on enrolment shares for each district within a metropolitan area, and takes it as a proxy of choice availability. Since this variable is potentially endogenous, she instruments it with a variable measuring the extent of natural barriers created by existing rivers.

40. Even in the New Zealand case, parents' freedom to choose has been limited by the reimposition of residential zoning as the basis for enrolment policy.

41. Gradstein and Justman (1999) propose a model that replicates Kuznets' curve through the extension of franchise. During a process of growth,

there is an increase in the population share with income beyond the threshold required to gain voting rights. As a consequence, the income of the median voter declines, and more resources are devoted to public education financing.

42. It has been argued that education financing through general taxation can be regressive so long as the offspring of richer families have a higher propensity to proceed with an the academic career. However, other aspects have to be taken into account in making these types of calculation: most fiscal systems are progressive (i.e. the rich pay a higher percentage of taxes on their incomes), and the number of children may vary according to family income. With respect to a representative sample of Italian families surveyed in 1995, 53.0 per cent of families in the lowest quartile of incomes had a child aged between six and twenty-five cohabiting, while in the top quartile 68.8 per cent did so. Even taking into account a potential bias due to the fact that poorer families give birth to children earlier, only 8.3 per cent of families in the lowest quartile had a child enrolled at university, whereas the corresponding figure for the top quartile was 22.5 per cent; as a consequence, the bottom quartile received only 10.6 per cent of the benefit from the public funding of Italian universities, while the top quartile received 40.5 per cent. However, according to the fiscal law applying to the same year, the bottom quartile was contributing only 7.9 per cent of the revenues from income and consumption taxation, while the top quartile was contributing 49.4 per cent. In this respect, the public funding of Italian universities still exerts a redistributive effect. For the details, see Flabbi (1999).

43. Checchi (2004) studies the relationship between income inequality and education inequality (measured by Gini indices obtained from years of education), finding evidence of a non-linear relationship between the two.

44. A famous book on the argument is that by Arthur Okun (1975).

45. '[C]ategorical aid should be financed by taxes, such as statewide income taxes, that have no marginal price effect on the spending decisions of individual school districts' (Hoxby, 1996b, p. 66).

5 | Education financing

5.1 Introduction

When Milton Friedman published his famous contribution on *Capitalism and Freedom* in 1962, he devoted an entire chapter to the role of government in education. He made a careful distinction between the public and private financing of education and its public (or private) provision, arguing that public financing could be justified on the grounds of neighbourhood effects (positive or negative externalities on other people)[1] and/or paternalistic attitudes (concern for children of irresponsible parents), but that it would not carry over to vocational education, where private returns on increased skills would accrue to the individual. However, nothing could justify what he termed the 'nationalisation' of education provision, because this would reduce the parental freedom of choice. In his view, the role of government would be reduced to administering the allocation of publicly financed vouchers to families and to checking the existence of minimum requirements in approved schools.[2]

While Friedman's analysis is stringent in its market perspective, it seems to neglect some aspects of education provision that we have already highlighted in previous chapters, in particular the existence of differences in abilities and/or in family backgrounds. Friedman viewed access to education as identical (or randomly different) individuals facing an investment opportunity, and objected to the public subsidisation of choices providing private returns. However, when individuals differ in several respects (family incomes, unobservable abilities, neighbourhood effects, and so on), there is no guarantee that market allocation would automatically provide the equality of opportunity outcome, not to say the most efficient outcome. The problem is even exacerbated when there is intergenerational persistence of family choices.

The underlying logic of Friedman's argument is typical of neoclassical models of growth, characterised by the decreasing marginal productivity of inputs.[3] Even if individuals are characterised by differences in the distribution of an accumulable asset (such as family wealth or human capital), under the condition of perfect financial markets poor individuals will face a higher marginal return than rich individuals, and therefore will experience a stronger incentive to invest. As a consequence, in the long run the returns will be equalised, and a perfectly egalitarian distribution will arise.

If long-run equalisation were the most likely outcome, one would be encourged to abstain from any policy intervention that might distort the incentive structure and induce delays in the convergence process. But two inequalities are often encountered in the field of educational investments: financial markets for education financing are imperfect (or even non-existent), and individuals are differently endowed with abilities. A further complication is given by the intergenerational transmission of differences in ability endowment. In the next section, we will explore the consequence of market solutions whenever these aspects are taken into account, and we will discuss how alternative forms of education financing may solve or exacerbate the problem. Each case will be considered in two respects: equality of opportunities (each individual, conditional on effort, faces the same set of choices) and productive efficiency (for a given set of available resources – including individual abilities – the total output is maximised).

5.2 The demand for education when agents differ in abilities and family incomes

A general framework for the analysis can be sketched as follows.[4] Consider an overlapping generation model, in which individuals acquire education in the first period of life, while in the second period of life they have a child, work, consume, leave an inheritance and die. Individuals are born different in terms of unobservable ability, an input that cannot be purchased in any market, but that can be publicly observed at no cost. Individuals are distributed according to their ability $A_i \in [\underline{A}, \overline{A}]$ according to $F(A)$, with density $f(A) = F'(A)$. Ability can matter either in education acquisition or in the subsequent labour market career. We summarise these two cases into the following functional form, where labour market income is characterised by

$$W_{it} = W(E_{it}, A_{it}), \quad W'_E > 0, \quad W'_A > 0, \quad W''_{EE} < 0,$$
$$W''_{AA} < 0, \quad W''_{EA} > 0 \tag{5.1}$$

Equation (5.1) states that labour market income W_{it} of individual i born in generation t depends positively on the amount of education he/she received and on his/her endowment of ability; both inputs exhibit the usual decreasing marginal productivity property. A crucial assumption is that education increases earnings more for abler individuals (alternatively, ability and education are complements in generating earning capability). Thus abler individuals obtain a higher return on education, and therefore face a stronger incentive for its acquisition. This assumption also has distributive implications: according to it, given two equally educated individuals, a marginal increase in the education of the brighter increases his/her future income more than the same increase would if assigned to the less bright. As a consequence, given the observability of talent, a benevolent planner will never allocate the same amount of education to two differently endowed individuals.[5]

Altruistic parents care about their own consumption and their children's total income Y_{it+1}, which they can affect by financing their education or through direct monetary transfer:

$$U_{it} = U(C_{it}, \quad Y_{it+1}), \quad U'_C > 0, U'_Y > 0 \tag{5.2}$$

The way in which parents contribute to education financing depends on the institutional context, whether through taxation and the public provision of an identical amount to everyone, or through access to private schooling. While these aspects will be discussed in the next section, we will be content with assuming that each unit of education has a (relative) price p_E to the family, independently of public or private provision (for example, think of the opportunity cost of attending one additional year of schooling). Thus each family budget constraint is given by

$$Y_{it} = C_{it} + p_E E_{it+1} + X_{it+1} \tag{5.3}$$

where E_{it+1} is the educational expenditure a member of generation t on behalf of his/her child born in the next generation $t + 1$, while

X_{it+1} is a financial bequest to the same child. The model is closed by the definition of total income

$$Y_{it} = W_{it} + r X_{it} \tag{5.4}$$

By inserting equations (5.1), (5.3) and (5.4) into (5.2) and then maximising with respect to the educational expenditure E_{it+1} and financial bequest X_{it+1}, we obtain the result that parents will finance the education of their child up to the point where the marginal return to education equals its relative price.[6]

$$W'_E(E^*_{it+1}, A_{it+1}) = \frac{r}{p_E} \tag{5.5}$$

Using the implicit function theorem, it is straightforward[7] to show that

$$E^*_{it+1} = E(A_{it+1}), \quad E' > 0 \tag{5.6}$$

which implies that abler children obtain more education because it is more profitable to invest in their education. However, equation (5.5) applies only under the assumption of perfect financial markets, when parents can borrow against the future income of their child, because X_{it+1} can take either positive or negative values. When we impose the further constraint of $X^*_{it+1} \geq 0 \Leftrightarrow p_E E^*_{it+1} \leq Y_{it}$, we require educational expenditure to be financed out of current parental income, which can prove insufficient, especially in the case of high-ability children.[8]

When a parent is liquidity-constrained, the educational investment becomes conditioned by available resources, and equation (5.6) has to be replaced by[9]

$$E^*_{it+1} = E(A_{it+1}, Y_{it}), \quad E'_A > 0, \quad E'_Y \geq 0 \tag{5.7}$$

Given a specific educational attainment (for example, college attendance), equation (5.7) depicts a locus in the (Y_t, A_{t+1}) space, as described by figure 5.1. All families aiming at $E^*_{it+1} \geq \overline{E}$ (and capable of financing it) will invest in education, whereas all remaining families will refrain from further progress in education. The implication of this behaviour is that the proportion of children from richer families rises with the level of educational attainment. While children from poor families will attend the highest level of schooling only if their ability exceeds the threshold given by the implicit cost for a parent to give up

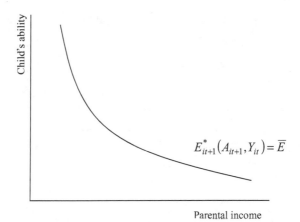

Figure 5.1 The combination of ability and family income attaining a specific $\overline{E}$

his/her current consumption, less able children from richer families will nevertheless attain the educational certificate, since parental resources overcompensate for their lack of ability.[10]

There are cases where different levels of attainable education are available. One case is given by the stratification of the educational system, between generalist academic-oriented secondary tracks and more vocationally oriented ones (especially at the secondary level: typical examples are the German gymnasium, the French *lycée* and the Italian *liceo*). A second case may be given by the presence of better-quality private schools.[11] In the presence of peer effects, this can be the simple consequence of the self-sorting of students according to their abilities (as we have already seen in the previous chapter): every parent wants to see his/her child in a class of brilliant students, and is willing to pay a price for it.[12]

Whatever the case, the existence of different educational levels creates the possibility of sorting students according to ability and family incomes. Suppose two levels of educational resources are available, E_1 and E_2, with $E_1 > E_2$. This corresponds to two loci in the (Y_t, A_{t+1}) space, where the former dominates the latter. In such a case, we should observe students from better backgrounds (namely higher family income and/or better talent) choosing the highest-quality school, whereas students of intermediate quality attend the second-best school and low-ability children from poor families will not attend school (or will go to public schools if freely available).

The general conclusion of this family of models (see also the next chapter) is that children from richer families are over-represented in the highest levels of education. Do we find confirming evidence of this behaviour? The next section will provide some supportive evidence of these theoretical predictions.

5.3 An application: the choice between private and public university in Italy

The model presented in the previous section suggests that more talented students from richer families tend to self-sort into private schools whenever:

(i) private schools (or universities) are available, or

(ii) private schools provide better-quality education.

Unfortunately, the second assumption is hard to verify, since school quality should be ascertained against future labour market prospects. However, conditional to the assumption that there is a positive premium in attending a private institution, we may wonder whether this induces student stratification.[13]

In this section we make use of the entire population of students attending an undergraduate course in economics in the city of Milan during the academic year 1996/97.[14] When we compare our population with representative samples of the nationwide population, by using unconditional means we observe that students attending a private university come from richer families.[15] In addition, students attending these faculties seem to have obtained better scores in secondary school attendance (see table 5.1).

Prima facie, it seems that there is some corroborating evidence in favour of the previous considerations: better students (as captured by the marks obtained at the end of secondary school, which reflect both parental education and unobservable ability) self-sort into university attendance.[16] In addition, as long as family incomes allow the financing, and the students pass an entry test, they enrol at a private university. Private university attendance is significantly more expensive than public. In our reference academic year 1996/97, entry fees for a public university ranged between €687 and €1,885, depending on the family

Table 5.1 *Descriptive statistics for students attending a faculty of economics: Italy, 1996/97*

	Italian population	Students attending public university	Students attending private university
Gross family income (lire, millions)			
Mean family income	64.642	69.824	119.430
Median family income	56.537	61.572	96.173
Standard deviation income	33.882	41.543	70.150
Marks at end of secondary school (out of 60)			
Average marks	44.85	47.18	51.41
Standard deviation marks	6.88	6.68	7.00

income. The corresponding figures for a private university ranged between €601 and €5,847.[17]

When we analyse the distribution of students according to (log) family income and talent, we find evidence of negative correlation (see figure 5.2).[18] We proxy individual talent by normalising the marks at the exit of secondary school by type of secondary school, in order to account for differences in grading policies of different school types. The regression lines are negatively sloped and do not intersect, providing additional support to the idea that families invest in further education for their children provided that they reach a sufficient level of talent. While we do not directly observe children who do not enrol in university, we would expect to find them in the bottom left portion of the same graph.

These considerations can be made more rigorous by analysing the choice between public and private university attendance, conditional on having already chosen to attend a faculty of economics at university.[19] In table 5.2 we estimate a probit model for the choice of attending a private university. This table shows that families are more likely to send children to a private institution the better performance they have exhibited during their secondary school (as captured by the 'Talent' variable) and the richer they are. They are also marginally more inclined to send boys than girls to a private university, possibly

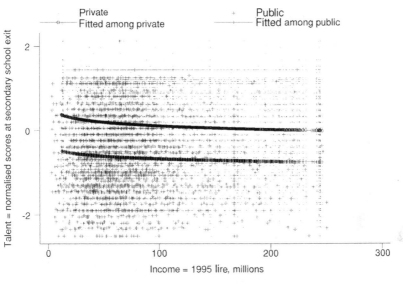

Figure 5.2 The distribution of ability and family income

reflecting a typical southern European country attitude to invest more in male than female children. The second column of the same table hints that sorting has already begun at earlier stages, when students choose the secondary school type: the brightest students have been directed towards academic-oriented tracks, whereas less gifted ones have been oriented towards vocational schools.[20]

While finding evidence of sorting according to family income does not contradict previous theoretical assumptions (altruistic parents, complementarity between acquired education and ability, financial market imperfections), it is also observationally equivalent to many other explanations.

One explanation refers to the screening role of private institutions. Irrespective of the quality of teaching and learning within a specific university (which should be correlated with the quality of newly formed human capital), whenever a firm knows in advance that students are sorted according to their talent between private and public institutions, it will pay a positive premium to students graduating from private institutions. In such a case, private school attendance operates as a signal that is purchased in the market at a price exceeding the price of public institutions. Private education will then be demanded as long as its cost falls short of expected income gains.

Table 5.2 *A maximum likelihood probit estimation of private university attendance of a faculty of economics: Italy, 1996/97*

Number of observations	Without secondary school controls	With secondary school controls
Talent	0.006	0.007
	(23.45)	(28.78)
Log (inc)	0.099	0.071
	(34.51)	(27.48)
Male	0.045	0.030
	(11.09)	(8.52)
Classical high school		0.066
		(14.89)
Scientific high school		0.091
		(18.11)
Technical secondary school		–0.001
		(–0.03)
Foreign secondary school		0.057
		(10.60)
Constant	yes	yes
Residence	yes	yes
Pseudo-R^2	0.231	0.290

NB: Number of observations: 16,750; t-statistics in parentheses.

A second explanation concerns status acquisition. Whenever a degree from a private institution is perceived as an 'admission ticket' to becoming a member of the ruling elite, thanks to social networking during an academic career, then it can be sold at a positive price in a market where public education is freely accessible.[21] When we compare the social composition of students from a private university with that of the entire population (as is done in table 5.3), we notice that the occupations constituting the sociological concept of *elite* (entrepreneurs, professionals, firms' owners, managers) make up 12.8 per cent of the entire population, whereas they account for 47.2 per cent of the social background found in the private university. Seen in this perspective, having access to a private university is equivalent to gaining admission to a private club, and families are willing to spend money for the 'exclusiveness' granted by the club itself, irrespctive of the quality content of the training received there.[22]

Table 5.3 *Occupational composition in Italy, 1993*

	Entire population	Parents of students attending a private university
Blue-collar worker (or similar)	33.26	9.16
Office worker	28.02	7.00
Junior manager/cadre	5.21	15.55
Manager, senior official, principal, headmaster, university teacher, magistrate	3.16	21.62
Self-employed	12.99	15.04
Member of the arts or professions	3.21	15.37
Teacher	3.32	5.26
Entrepreneur	6.42	10.20
Owner or member of a family business	4.41	0.80

NB: The composition of the Italian population is obtained from the Bank of Italy survey conducted in 1993; for comparability reasons, the student population is restricted to those who were enrolled in the same year. Figures are percentages.

5.4 The collective choice over public or private schooling

The preceding discussion has shown us that, when individuals differ in terms of ability and income, the educational choices can magnify these differences whenever altruistic parents invest in the education of their children.[23] An additional complication has to do with the fact that most educational choices are collective ones, and as such they often ignore the externalities associated with individual choices. This has to do with the peculiar nature of education. In fact, it cannot be taken as a pure public good, since it does not possess the requirements of non-rivalry or non-excludability.[24] Opening access to school to additional students implies additional costs (in terms of classes, teachers, libraries), and it is always possible to exclude students from access (using admission fees, admission tests or a combination of the two). For a publicly provided private good[25] it is not easy to determine the optimal amount of public provision.

When individuals are heterogeneous, any process of collective choice will leave at least some individual dissatisfied with the amount of educational resources chosen by the majority. In addition, unless there exists some possibility of internalising the spillover effects, the collective choice does not constitute the first-best that would be chosen by a benevolent planner maximising a social welfare function. Finally, the uniform provision of education to all individuals prevents talented individuals from fully exploiting their endowment. All these aspects can be grasped by the following simple model inspired by Joseph Stiglitz (1974).

Let us consider a two-period model, in which in the first period of life agents invest in education, while in the second they obtain an income from work (positively correlated to individual talent and to the education acquired in the first period), consume and bequeath to their offspring. Equation (5.8) describes the educational production function in its simplest form,

$$H_{it} = E_{it} \tag{5.8}$$

where H_{it} is the human capital stock achieved by individual i born in generation t that is equal to the resources E_{it} invested in his/her education. Labour earnings W_{it+1} are assumed to depend on both talent endowment A_{it} and human capital H_{it}, with decreasing marginal returns for both factors.

$$W_{it+1} = A_{it}^{\gamma} H_{it}^{\beta}, \quad 0 < \gamma \leq 1, \quad 0 < \beta < 1 \tag{5.9}$$

We assume that the child chooses his/her education on the basis of the financial inheritance obtained from his/her parents and his/her own talent, which is freely observable. Finally individual preferences are defined over second-period consumption C_{it+1} and the inheritance to be left to the offspring X_{it+1}. Using homothetic preferences in the Cobb–Douglas class we can write

$$U_{it} = C_{it+1}^{\alpha} X_{it+1}^{1-\alpha} \tag{5.10}$$

whereas the budget constraint is given by

$$Y_{it+1} = C_{it+1} + X_{it+1} \tag{5.11}$$

where Y_{it+1} indicates total income and the price is set equal to one for simplicity. By maximising equation (5.10) under the constraint (5.11), we get the indirect utility function V_{it} as a linear function of total income:

$$V_{it} = \alpha^{\alpha}(1-\alpha)^{1-\alpha} \cdot Y_{it+1} = a Y_{it+1}, \quad a = \alpha^{\alpha}(1-\alpha)^{1-\alpha} \tag{5.12}$$

We now consider alternative configurations of education financing, in order to recognise its implications for individual utilities.

5.4.1 Private schooling

As a benchmark, we start by considering the absence of public schooling. Any individual can freely choose in the market a private school providing exactly the desired amount of education. He/she chooses to invest in education up to the point where the marginal cost of resources equals the marginal benefit in terms of earnings. By denoting with R the market interest rate and assuming perfect financial markets, we express available resources as

$$Y_{it+1} = (X_{it} - E_{it}) \cdot R + W_{it+1} = (X_{it} - E_{it}) \cdot R + A_{it}^{\gamma} E_{it}^{\beta} \qquad (5.13)$$

The agent chooses the optimal amount of education by maximising his/her indirect utility under the budget constraint given by equation (5.13):

$$\max_{E_{it}}(a Y_{it+1}) = \max_{E_{it}} \left(a \left[(X_{it} - E_{it}) \cdot R + A_{it}^{\gamma} E_{it}^{\beta} \right] \right) \qquad (5.14)$$

Thus we obtain the optimal demand for education under private schooling:

$$E_{it}^{priv} = \left[\frac{\beta A_{it}^{\gamma}}{R} \right]^{\frac{1}{1-\beta}} \qquad (5.15)$$

In accordance with what we have already derived in chapter 2, abler individuals demand more education. In addition, the higher the return to education (coefficient β) and the lower the market interest rate R, the higher the demand for education.[26]

5.4.2 Public schooling

We now consider the opposite case, where education is freely and uniformly provided and is financed through wealth taxation. From the government budget constraint

$$E_{it}^{pub} = \frac{\tau_t \cdot \sum_{i=1}^{n} X_{it}}{n} = \tau_t \cdot \overline{X}_t \qquad (5.16)$$

where τ_t indicates the tax rate chosen by generation t,[27] n is the population size and $\overline{X}_t$ is the average inheritance. Individual income is redefined accordingly as

$$Y_{it+1} = R \cdot X_{it} \cdot (1 - \tau_t) + W_{it+1} = R \cdot X_{it} \cdot (1 - \tau_t) + A_{it}^{\gamma} E_{it}^{\beta}$$
$$= R \cdot X_{it} \cdot (1 - \tau_t) + A_{it}^{\gamma}(\tau_t \cdot \overline{X}_t)^{\beta} \tag{5.17}$$

Each individual has a preferred tax rate that will depend on initial wealth and talent endowment. If we maximise the indirect utility in order to derive the preferred tax rate

$$\max_{\tau_{ti}}(a Y_{it+1}) = \max_{\tau_{ti}} \left(a[R \cdot X_{it} \cdot (1 - \tau_{ti}) + A_{it}^{\gamma}(\tau_{ti} \cdot \overline{X}_t)^{\beta}]\right) \tag{5.18}$$

we reach the following result:

$$\tau_{it} = \frac{1}{\overline{X}_t} \cdot \left(\frac{\beta A_{it}^{\gamma}}{R} \cdot \frac{\overline{X}_t}{X_{it}}\right)^{\frac{1}{1-\beta}} \tag{5.19}$$

As in the case of private schooling, abler individuals prefer higher taxes as a way to obtain more resources invested in their education. In contrast, the preferred tax rate declines with increasing family wealth, since rich individuals do not want to contribute to the redistribution implied by the public financing of schools. In order to grasp the implication of public schooling on educational investment, we need to know how talent and wealth are jointly distributed in the population. For two particular cases we can better characterise the solution given by equation (5.19).

5.4.2.1 Identical endowment of talent: $A_{it} = A, \ \forall i, \forall t$
In such a case, the optimal tax rate given by equation (5.19) becomes

$$\tau_{it} = \frac{1}{\overline{X}_t} \cdot \left(\frac{\beta A^{\gamma}}{R} \cdot \frac{\overline{X}_t}{X_{it}}\right)^{\frac{1}{1-\beta}} \tag{5.20}$$

Since preferences are now single-peaked,[28] we can define the outcome of democratic choice under majority voting. Among all available proposals, the proposal from the individual with median wealth is the only one able to defeat all other proposals in pair-wise comparisons:

$$\tau_t^* = \frac{1}{\overline{X}_t} \cdot \left(\frac{\beta A^{\gamma}}{R} \cdot \frac{\overline{X}_t}{X_t^{median}}\right)^{\frac{1}{1-\beta}} \tag{5.21}$$

In contrast, if a benevolent planner maximising a social welfare function (as, for example, the sum of individual utility functions) undertook the choice of the optimal tax rate, the tax rate would appear as

$$\tau_t^{planner} = \frac{1}{\overline{X}_t} \cdot \left(\frac{\beta A^\gamma}{R} \right)^{\frac{1}{1-\beta}} \tag{5.22}$$

By comparing equations (5.21) and (5.22), we can notice that whenever $X^{median} < \overline{X}$ (which corresponds to the majority of empirically observed wealth distributions, which are typically positively skewed) the optimal level of taxation chosen under democratic voting is higher than the Pareto optimal level chosen by a planner. As a consequence, there is 'excessive' investment in education, because people at the bottom of the wealth distribution aim to manipulate taxation in order to increase their income opportunities through educational investments. The alternative case is given next.

5.4.2.2 Identical wealth endowment: $X_{it} = X_t = \overline{X}_t$

If individuals are identical in terms of family wealth, they differ in terms of talent endowment only. Once again, preferences are single-peaked with respect to desired taxation, and we can apply the median voter theorem to determine the tax rate chosen under majority voting:

$$\tau_t = \frac{1}{\overline{X}_t} \cdot \left(\frac{\beta \left(A_t^{median} \right)^\gamma}{R} \right)^{\frac{1}{1-\beta}} \tag{5.23}$$

A benevolent planner would choose

$$\tau_t^{planner} = \frac{1}{\overline{X}_t} \cdot \left(\frac{\beta \widehat{A}_t^\gamma}{R} \right)^{\frac{1}{1-\beta}} , \quad \widehat{A}_t^\gamma = \frac{\sum_{i=1}^{n} A_{it}^\gamma}{n} \tag{5.24}$$

where $\widehat{A}_t$ represents a non-linear combination of individual talent endowments. In the limiting case where $\gamma \to 1$, $\widehat{A} \to \overline{A}$, if the talent distribution is not symmetrical and positively skewed (placing more weight on below-average values) then a democratic choice of taxation leads to lower taxation and lower educational investment than the socially optimal level. This result is explained by the fact that abler individuals do not want to subsidise less able individuals, at the cost of reducing their earnings potential.

Joint consideration of these two cases suggests that democratic choice of educational investment through tax financing is very likely to lead to under- or over-investment in education, it being impossible to achieve Pareto optimal levels of investment.

5.4.3 Mixed system (public and private) schooling

We now allow the coexistence of public schooling with a private supply of education, addressed to either richer or abler individuals who want to invest additional resources in education beyond the universal provision to all students. As an illustration of the possible outcomes, we retain the previous assumption of individuals who are identical with respect to family wealth but are different in terms of talent. The optimal level of taxation chosen under democratic conditions is

$$E_t^{pub} = \left(\frac{\beta \left(A_t^{median} \right)^\gamma}{R} \right)^{\frac{1}{1-\beta}} \tag{5.25}$$

and the indirect utility associated with the i-th individual is equal to

$$V_{it}^{pub} = a \left[R \cdot \left(X_t - E_t^{pub} \right) + A_{it}^\gamma E_t^{pub^\beta} \right] \tag{5.26}$$

Notice that the indirect utility (5.26) increases in individual talent. Let us now consider an individual considering the possibility of turning to the private sector, while continuing to finance the public sector because taxes cannot be waived. To obtain his/her optimal amount of education, he/she has to solve a problem identical to (5.14), where wealth is now net of taxation. His/her optimal choice is analogous to equation (5.15), and the indirect utility function is given by

$$V_{it}^{mix} = a \left[R \cdot \left(X_t - E_t^{pub} \right) - R \cdot E_{it}^{mix} + A_{it}^\gamma E_t^{mix^\beta} \right]$$

$$= a \left[R \cdot \left(X_t - E_t^{pub} \right) - R \cdot \left(\frac{\beta A_{it}^\gamma}{R} \right)^{\frac{1}{1-\beta}} + A_{it}^\gamma \left(\frac{\beta A_{it}^\gamma}{R} \right)^{\frac{\beta}{1-\beta}} \right] \tag{5.27}$$

where E_{it}^{mix} is the optimal demand for education by the private sector by individuals who still pay the cost of the public sector (since they cannot avoid taxation). By equations (5.26) and (5.27) we identify a marginal type (call him/her the κ-th individual) who makes no distinction between attending public schools or private ones:

$$A_{\kappa t}^{\gamma} E_t^{pub^{\beta}} = A_{\kappa t}^{\gamma} \left(\frac{\beta A_{\kappa t}^{\gamma}}{R} \right)^{\frac{\beta}{1-\beta}} - R \cdot \left(\frac{\beta A_{\kappa t}^{\gamma}}{R} \right)^{\frac{1}{1-\beta}} \tag{5.28}$$

By solving equation (5.28) in terms of $A_{\kappa t}$ we can identify the marginal type:

$$A_{\kappa t} = \left[\frac{R}{\beta} \cdot \frac{E_t^{pub^{(1-\beta)}}}{(1-\beta)^{(1-\beta)/\beta}} \right]^{\frac{1}{\gamma}} \tag{5.29}$$

It is easy to show that all individuals with a talent endowment greater than $A_{\kappa t}$ will obtain a higher prospective income (and utility) by turning to the private sector. This leads to the presumption that private schools are better-quality because better-talented people self-sort there.[29]

Let us note that the marginal κ-th individual changes with the quantity of educational resources invested in the public sector. As a consequence, the population share of private schools declines with the educational investment in the public sector.[30] From a formal point of view, this renders it hard to provide a closed solution to the determination of the optimal rate of taxation. The outflow of the ablest students towards the private sector raises the resources per-student for the remaining population in the public sector. This implies an improvement in the quality of the public sector that may call for a reduction in the optimal tax rate chosen under democratic voting. However, the improvement of educational investment in the private sector calls people back from the private sector. In this perspective, preferences lose the property of single-peakedness, and multiple equilibria become endemic.[31]

5.5 Growth and inequality under public and private schooling

The preceding model has shown us that families may have an incentive to under-invest in education in order to escape the redistributive nature of public schooling financed through general taxation. The existence of these disincentives yields macroeconomic implications, both in terms of growth and of inequality persistence. Intuitively, the greater the possibility for each family to get closer to the desired amount of education for their children without incurring the implicit cost of subsidising poorer families, the greater will be the overall investment in education. As a consequence, the larger the variation between schools (either through a well-established private sector or thanks to a decentralised educational system) the higher should be the observed educational attainment. As long as the investment in human capital has a positive impact on the growth rate of the economy, we should expect greater growth in countries (or regions) where there is a wider array of alternative schooling. There is (almost) always a drawback. Stronger growth trades off with greater income inequality, since greater variation of educational attainment should be correlated with greater dispersion in incomes.[32]

To prove these claims more formally, we will proceed with an overlapping generations structure, where individuals live for two periods. We now take into account the potential disincentive effect of income taxation by including a choice over effort in the initial period of life. Therefore, when young all individuals choose their spare time allocation between leisure and study. Newly formed human capital will depend upon available resources and effort, and in turn will affect labour income earned during the second period of life. Consumption and bequest are the only two alternative destinations of labour income.[33]

5.5.1 *Private schooling*

We start our exposition by considering a simplified educational system, in which only private schools are available, such that each agent may choose the desired amount of education. Given the intrinsic difficulties in studying the evolving distribution of talents and incomes, we simplify the problem by assuming that individuals are identical in all respects but family incomes. Under the drastic assumption of an absence of financial markets, human capital investment in one's own child is the only available asset to transfer resources across generations. This can be represented by the following relationship:

$$W_{t+1} = H_{t+1} = S_t^\theta X_t^\gamma H_t^\beta \tag{5.30}$$

Equation (5.30) tells us that labour income W_{t+1} earned in the second period of life $(t+1)$ by an individual born in generation t is proportional (for simplicity equal) to human capital H_{t+1} acquired during the first period of life.[34] Human capital formation is the outcome of three contributing elements: *individual effort*, as measured by the amount of leisure T_t waived in favour of school attendance $S_t = 1 - T_t$ (where the endowment of time available $\overline{T}$ has been normalised to unity); the amount of *financial resources* X_t inherited from the family and devoted to education financing;[35] and *family background*, as proxied by the level of parental human capital H_t, in order to take into account both 'nature and nurture' channels in intertemporal persistence.

Altruistic preferences (as in equation (5.2)) take into account leisure consumption when young ($T_t = 1 - S_t$) and commodity consumption C_{t+1} plus bequeathing X_{t+1} when old:[36]

$$U(T_t, C_{t+1}, X_{t+1}) = \log(1 - S_t) + \log C_{t+1} + \log X_{t+1} \quad (5.31)$$

whereas the budget constraint is represented by

$$W_{t+1} = C_{t+1} + X_{t+1} \tag{5.32}$$

Using the human capital production technology described by equation (5.30), and exploiting the homoteticity property for preferences, it is easy to derive the optimal choices:[37]

$$C_{t+1}^* = \frac{W_{t+1}}{2} = \frac{H_{t+1}}{2} \tag{5.33}$$

$$X_{t+1}^* = \frac{W_{t+1}}{2} = \frac{H_{t+1}}{2} \tag{5.34}$$

$$S_t^* = \frac{2\theta}{2\theta + 1} \tag{5.35}$$

Given the fact that individuals remain identical across generations, we can plug the optimal choices (5.34) and (5.35) undertaken by parents into equation (5.30), which describes the human capital formation of the child. As a consequence, we get the intertemporal dynamics of human capital and/or income (given the one-to-one correspondence between the two):

$$H_{t+1} = \left(\frac{2\theta}{2\theta + 1}\right)^\theta \left(\frac{H_t}{2}\right)^\gamma H_t^\beta = \left[\frac{1}{2^\gamma}\left(\frac{\theta}{1/2 + \theta}\right)^\theta\right] H_t^{\gamma + \beta} = \Theta H_t^{\gamma + \beta}$$

$$\tag{5.36}$$

Re-expressing using logarithms (denoted by reversing the letter case),

$$\log H_{t+1} = h_{t+1} = \log \Theta + (\gamma + \beta) h_t \tag{5.37}$$

Equation (5.37) represents the law of motion in both human capital (and income). Intergenerational persistence is due to education financing based on family wealth (the γ parameter) and cultural background (the β parameter). Since $(\gamma + \beta) > \beta$, the present model is consistent with the idea that intergenerational persistence is higher in the absence of suitable financial markets for education financing.

If we now make the additional assumption that income W_t (or human capital H_t, since the two are by assumption identical) are lognormally distributed within each generation (with generation-specific mean μ_t and variance σ_t^2), we obtain the evolution of income distribution across generations[38]

$$\mu_t = \log \Theta + (\gamma + \beta)\mu_{t-1} \tag{5.38}$$

$$\sigma_t^2 = (\gamma + \beta)^2 \sigma_{t-1}^2 \tag{5.39}$$

We now observe that the higher the γ and β parameters the higher will be the growth rate of the economy, as described by the mean income (or mean human capital). Notice that financial wealth is also proportional to human capital, and therefore evolves with the same law of motion (see equation (5.34)). Since individual incomes follow the same dynamics (given by equation (5.37)), the entire economy expands at the same growth rate.

In accordance with growth models in the neoclassical tradition (see the appendix), this dynamics possesses a long-run equilibrium (which is identical for all agents, irrespective of the initial conditions), given by

$$\overline{\mu}_{private} = \frac{\log \Theta}{1 - \gamma - \beta} \tag{5.40}$$

Such equilibrium is stable whenever $(\gamma + \beta) < 1$.[39]

5.5.2 *Publicly financed schooling*

We now consider the possibility of a public intervention that offers identical quantities of education irrespective of family wealth. Public subsidies to poor families are financed through general taxation. The tax rate is chosen under majority voting, and applies to the next generation. We will term this case a *public system*. Under this case, the production technology for human capital is re-expressed as

$$W_{t+1} = H_{t+1} = S_t^\theta E_t^\gamma H_t^\beta \tag{5.41}$$

where E_t represents the amount of educational resources chosen by the parent generation for the schooling of the child generation, which is distributed identically to all individuals. The altruistic component of preferences is expressed in terms of parental 'pleasure' for greater resources devoted to child education:

$$U(T_t, C_{t+1}, E_{t+1}) = \log(1 - S_t) + \log C_{t+1} + \log E_{t+1} \quad (5.42)$$

The budget constraint takes into account the tax rate τ_t, which is chosen by the parent generation to sustain education in the next generation:

$$C_{t+1} = (1 - \tau_t) W_{t+1} = (1 - \tau_t) H_{t+1} \quad (5.43)$$

The quantity of educational resources available per student depends on the overall resources collected through taxation:

$$E_t = \tau_t \cdot \frac{\sum_{i=1}^{n} H_{t,i}}{n} = \tau_t \cdot E[H_t] \quad (5.44)$$

Placing equations (5.44), (5.43) and (5.41) into (5.42) and solving for the optimal choices in time allocation and preferred taxation, we get

$$S_t^* = \frac{\theta}{1 + \theta} \quad (5.45)$$

$$\tau_t^* = \frac{1}{2} \quad \Leftrightarrow \quad C_{t+1} = \frac{W_{t+1}}{2} \quad (5.46)$$

It is easy to see that this specific utility function leads parents to allocate half of their income to consumption, as was also the case under the private financing of education (see equation (5.33)). In addition, equation (5.46) indicates that the preferred tax rate does not vary across individuals, and thus we can claim it will be selected independently of the voting system. By comparing equations (5.35) and (5.45), we observe that the time optimally allocated to studying is less than the time allocated under private financing (which we will denote as the *private system* for short). This can be explained by the appropriability of the yield of individual effort. In a private system greater effort implies greater income, more consumption and higher-value bequests to descendants; in a public system greater effort still leads to greater consumption, but it spills over to *all* other individuals through taxation. In this way the public financing of education works as a redistributive policy, reducing the extent of the liquidity constraint by lowering at the same time the incentive to individual investment.

Placing equations (5.44), (5.45) and (5.46) into (5.41) we get

$$H_{t+1} = \left(\frac{\theta}{1+\theta}\right)^{\theta} \left(\frac{E[H_t]}{2}\right)^{\gamma} H_t^{\beta} = \left[\frac{1}{2^{\gamma}} \left(\frac{\theta}{1+\theta}\right)^{\theta}\right] (E[H_t])^{\gamma} H_t^{\beta}$$

$$= \Phi \cdot (E[H_t])^{\gamma} H_t^{\beta}, \quad \Phi < \Theta \tag{5.47}$$

If we maintain the assumption of the lognormal distribution of H_t we obtain

$$E[H_t] = \exp\left[\mu_t + \frac{\sigma_t^2}{2}\right] \tag{5.48}$$

Under such a case, income distribution evolves according to

$$\mu_{t+1} = \log \Phi + \gamma \log(E[H_{t-1}]) + \beta \mu_t$$

$$= \log \Phi + (\gamma + \beta)\mu_t + \frac{\gamma \sigma_t^2}{2} \tag{5.49}$$

$$\sigma_t^2 = \beta^2 \sigma_{t-1}^2 \tag{5.50}$$

Maintaining the assumption of stability (i.e. $(\gamma + \beta) < 1$), the mean income (or, equivalently, the mean human capital) converges to

$$\overline{\mu}_{public} = \frac{\Phi}{1 - \gamma - \beta} < \overline{\mu}_{private} = \frac{\Theta}{1 - \gamma - \beta} \tag{5.51}$$

By comparing the dynamic evolution of incomes and wealth under the two regimes, we advance the following considerations.

(i) Both a private and a public system provide analogous growth, but the former achieves a higher long-run equilibrium than the latter (see equation (5.51)). As a consequence, individuals obtain a higher level of indirect utility under a private system.[40]

(ii) In a public system income inequality (as measured by σ_t^2) declines more rapidly than under a private system (as can easily be checked by comparing equations (5.39) and (5.50)). In the non-generic case of $(\gamma + \beta) = 1$, income inequality persists unaltered in a private system, while it progressively disappears under a public system.

(iii) In a public system, the higher the mean income the more egalitarian the initial distribution of income.[41]

(iv) if we ask the population to select the educational system (whether private or public) under which they prefer to live, the old generation would always select a public system under majority voting. The reason lies in the fact that a public system ensures greater human capital accumulation for all children from families with below-average incomes. For any left-skewed income distribution (such as the lognormal one), the median income voter always lies below the mean income family. As a consequence, a public system will always be selected.

5.6 Education financing and school stratification

The models presented so far assume public education consisting of an equal supply of resources to all students. But in the previous chapter we have argued that there can be efficiency reasons to sort students according to their abilities (either through tests or by their willingness to pay). This raises the issue of ability tracking within the public sector. Once schools of excellence are introduced in the public sector, there is no reason why educational resources cannot be diversified across schools, either in a compensatory manner (more resources to less talented people) or in an efficiency-enhancing perspective (providing resources in accordance with the individual marginal benefit). This reproduces the above-mentioned trade-off between equity and efficiency, which is inescapable in the public supply of education.

In principle, tracking students according to their ability should have the advantage of allocating resources efficiently (i.e. output-maximising) to each individual.[42] But the main objection to ability tracking comes from the impossibility of disentangling measured ability from family background. Especially in countries in which the educational systems are characterised by (early) ability tracking, students are sorted according to measured abilities into different types of schools, which subsequently open to different labour market positions.[43] Since measured ability during the fifth grade reflects both innate ability and family background, it is not surprising to find that children of educated parents are over-represented in academic-oriented tracks (such as Gymnasium establishments). As a consequence, students with high ability but poor background may end up trapped in schooling and working careers where their talents are not fully exploited, whereas low-ability students from educated parents can achieve a university degree and access highly ranked positions.[44] Pupils with a less privileged socio-economic background face inequalities of educational

opportunities and have to display better test scores than their counter-
parts with better backgrounds in order to be admitted to most academic
tracks.[45]

More generally, we could argue that any school system has to find
its 'optimal degree of stratification'. In fact, school organisation can be
read in three dimensions: *comprehensive* versus *stratified*, *public* versus *private* and *centrally financed* versus *locally financed*. The distinction between comprehensive and stratified educational systems usually
emerges at the stage of secondary school: the former system offers
to all students the same type of educational track, usually based on
general competences (typical examples are the English and the North
American school systems); the latter system sorts students according to
their intended labour market position, since students and their families
can choose from vocational training or academic-oriented preparation
(the German system is an archetype of this organisation). While the first
dimension concerns the possibility of market segmentation (in a generalist school system all customers obtain the same commodity, whereas
in a stratified system customers can choose between different goods),
the second one has to do with the amount of resources available. In
a public system financed through general taxation all students receive
identical treatment (i.e. different students obtain the same amount of
resources when they enrol in the same type of school), whereas in a
private system families can choose the preferred amount of resources
invested in the education of their offspring. As a consequence, the
amount of resources available to students depends on family wealth
(i.e. identical students from different families obtain different amounts
of resources). The third divide partially overlaps with the second, as
long as there are local differences in people's preferences and families
are territorially mobile. In a decentralised system schools characterised
by high and low levels of spending on students may coexist. If families
are sufficiently mobile, they will 'vote with their feet' – i.e. they will
(optimally) choose their residence so as to adhere as closely as possible
to their preferred spending.

Following Tiebout (1956), let us imagine a society formed by local
communities that are self-administered – i.e. each community chooses
its preferred tax rate, to be used to finance the production of a local
public good (for example, the provision of education through the local
public school). Under the further assumptions of the territorial mobility of the population (due to low mobility costs) and the optimisation

of residential choices (each individual opts for the community associated with the highest indirect utility), the communities will stratify according to the preferred amount of public good. Individuals less interested in education provision will go for low-taxation communities, whereas people concerned about education will concentrate in different communities.[46] From a theoretical point of view, there are significant analogies between local financing and private financing.[47] As a consequence, a centrally financed educational system should reduce educational inequality (since it provides the same amount of educational resources to everyone) at the cost of reduced investment in human capital, since it lessens private incentives to invest more in better-endowed children.[48] Some empirical evidence seems not to contradict this theoretical expectation. As an example, in California in the 1970s a bill was passed prompting greater centralisation of education financing, in order to reduce the educational inequality, which was especially high among immigrants. The consequences were a reduction of educational disparities and an increase in the average standard of education provision across the state, though these were, however, accompanied by an overall reduction (in the order of ten percentage points) of the resources publicly and privately invested in education.[49] More generally, between 1975 and 1991 several North American states revised their financing systems in a more centralised and equalising direction. Nevertheless, there is scant evidence of improved school achievement, as measured by SAT scores.[50] The overall effect on residential segregation is difficult to ascertain.[51]

These three dimensions (the degree of curriculum stratification, the private share in education provision and local financing) can be combined in alternative ways, also depending on the schooling levels. A stratified, mainly public and centrally financed educational system (as in Italy) and a generalist, mixed public-private and locally financed educational system (as in the United States) are both possible. Empirically, it is straightforward to obtain information on the source of financing, but the other aspects are harder to measure. Table 5.4 provides some aggregate evidence on the fact that private sources of funding rise with pre-compulsory and post-compulsory education: in the first case, it pays either for insufficient public provision and/or for possible amenities such as extended timetables, improved facilities, and so on; in the second case, the private return on education favours the partial transfer of costs onto the final earners of educational benefits.[52]

Table 5.4 *Cross-country comparison of the proportion of public and private expenditure on educational institutions, 1999*

	Pre-primary		Primary and secondary		Tertiary	
	Public	Private	Public	Private	Public	Private
France	95.8	4.2	92.8	7.2	84.3	15.7
Germany	62.2	37.8	75.6	24.4	91.5	8.5
Italy	98.7	1.3	98.3	1.7	80.3	19.7
Japan	48.6	51.4	91.8	8.2	44.5	55.5
Switzerland	99.9	0.1	87.7	12.3	96.7	3.3
United Kingdom	95.6	4.4	88.2	11.8	63.2	36.8
United States	90.3	9.7	90.7	9.3	46.9	53.1
OECD average	82.2	17.8	92.1	7.9	79.2	20.8

Source: OECD (2003, table B4.2).

An indirect measure of the degree of homogeneity of education provision can be obtained by examining the dispersion of students' achievements in terms of literacy and numeracy. Table 5.5 reproduces the decomposition of the variation in student performance as recorded by the PISA assessment conducted in 2000 under the supervision of the OECD. Many factors contribute to the variation in average student performance within each country: subnational differences due to different jurisdictions, the size of the private sector, the presence of differentiated curricula in accordance with past performance, the socio-economic intake. The more centralised a schooling system the lower will be the overall dispersion in student tests; the less stratified and/or the lower the degree of differentiation (due to either local financing or access to private education) the lower will be the between-school variation. From this table we observe the emergence of a potential trade-off: stratified educational systems yield the highest between-school variation (Italy and Germany),[53] but this contributes less to overall dispersion whenever the country is centrally financed (Italy, but not Germany). At the other extreme, the more comprehensive the system the greater will be the performance variation within each school, whereas the overall dispersion depends on the source and the amount of funding.

Table 5.5 *Variance decomposition in literacy ability: PISA, 2000*

	Overall variation in student performance (mean = 500)	Between-school variation (%)	Within-school variation (%)	Secondary school system	Private sector in secondary schools
Germany	12.368	56.11	43.89	stratified	high
Italy	8.356	56.49	43.51	stratified	low
Japan	7.358	46.03	53.97	stratified	intermediate
Switzerland	10.408	43.40	56.60	stratified	intermediate
United Kingdom	10.098	20.57	79.43	comprehensive	intermediate
United States	10.979	44.69	55.31	comprehensive	intermediate

Source: Columns 1–3, OECD (2003, table A7.1); column 4, OECD (1996, country profiles); column 5, see table 5.4 above.

The three dimensions (namely stratification, privatisation and centralisation of the educational system) overlap with each other and are interrelated, in that they all contribute to segmentation of the 'market for education'. Standard economic theory suggests that, in a segmented market, customers are more satisfied (since each customer gets closer to his preferred bundle of consumption), but consumption inequality increases. Inequality considerations are relevant from a social point of view: if uniformity of education generates positive externalities, segmentation can be socially suboptimal. Gradstein and Justman (2002) have stressed the economic benefit of education as socialising force: instilling social norms; reducing potential conflict; favouring the assimilation of minorities.[54] They show that the public provision of uniform education financed through taxation tends to speed up the assimilation of minorities (and encourge greater productivity), since it imposes a double cost on those who wish to opt out of the public system.[55] The socialising role of schools can only be regulated centrally, since the cultural contents of education are hardly monitored when they are decided upon at local level.[56] Grossman and Kim (1998) have added the additional benefit of educating illiterate people in order to reduce the threat they pose to educated people's properties.[57] Additional social returns on the uniform public provision of schooling can be found in sustaining democratic attitudes and political participation.[58]

But there is a more substantial reason why most educational systems are centrally financed, at least at the compulsory level. Whenever educational achievement creates positive externalities there is a social interest, in that each individual in the society attains a given minimum of education (at least up to the point where private and public costs fall short of the social benefit). Since the private/local education financing stands on family resources, there is a risk to society that selfish parents do not place sufficient investment in their children (either they select low-quality schools or they go to live in communities characterised by low tax rates and low-quality schools). In such a context, the society may insure against such a risk by promulgating compulsory education laws and/or by centralising the organisation of the educational system (including its financing) in order to reduce the individual degree of choice (thus preventing the formation of local communities by parents uninterested in the quality of the education of their children).[59]

5.7 The school voucher as a solution?

Many authors have claimed that an increase in school choice opens up the ability to escape the trade-off between equality and efficiency, and some of them have advocated the introduction of school vouchers as a way to achieve this. In fact, we can deconstruct this argument into two separate propositions.

(i) Expanding school choice renders school financing dependent on enrolment, creates an incentive to expand enrolment and therefore introduces competition among schools.

(ii) Expanding the ability to access the private sector of education raises the overall level of productivity, so long as the private sector is more efficient in using the available resources.

Let us discuss these points in turn.

Transforming (partially or entirely) school financing by means of a direct payment proportional to the number of students enrolled increases school accountability, since customers can 'vote with their feet', opting for better-perceived schools and abandoning poorly performing ones. This creates a situation of *quasi-markets*, where the public sector may retain the monopoly of provision, but local agencies (the schools) have the responsibility (and the incentives) to deliver educational services to the greatest number of customers using the minimum amount of resources (so-called *X-efficiency*). However, the large-scale implementation of such a system in New Zealand during the 1990s showed that this line of reasoning encounters problems when it comes to actual implementation.[60] On the one hand, while theoretical considerations in terms of efficiency would lead to the closure of poorly performing schools, social policy concerns pull in the opposite direction. Peripheral city suburbs and rural areas would be deprived of educational structures, since all parents concerned would opt out, thus aggravating the problem instead of solving it. On the other hand, oversubscribed schools do not have an incentive to expand, because of the risk of diluting the homogeneity of social environment that made them so desirable to the parental population.[61] After some years of implementation, an increased polarisation of enrolment by ethnic groups and/or socio-economic groups was reported; the schools also differentiated, with the most popular schools attracting students concerned with academic curricula, the best teachers and better family backgrounds.

But the core of the debate over school choice is the information set of families. Since we can always think of increased school choice as a system of school vouchers covering the full cost of attendance and fully redeemable in the public sector only,[62] the problem becomes: how do families select their preferred schools? If the increased school choice creates an incentive to attract students, we would expect schools to differentiate their supply, in terms of both quality (vertical differentiation) and amenities (horizontal differentiation). However, parents are mainly concerned with labour market returns on the available alternatives, which can be assessed only with a significant time lag and have to be valued in expected terms. As a consequence, it becomes crucial to provide families with up-to-date information, but the ability to process this type of information varies with the educational attainment of the parents.[63] In addition, if parents are risk-averse, and the degree of risk aversion is inversely related to family wealth, then we expect families with poor backgrounds to prefer standardised courses to differentiated ones, since they are unable to choose between the existing alternatives.[64] Thus, it looks as if either the efficiency gains from school competition attenuate because of the reduced demand for school differentiation, or increased school choice discriminates against less educated parents.

When we associate increased school choice with the public financing of private institutions, we approach what is traditionally considered the debate over school vouchers, namely the introduction of public subsidies (partially or totally) covering school fees in the private sector (*the market choice perspective*, in Levin's (1992) terminology). While there are a great variety of experiences with school vouchers, none of them (except for the Chilean case) has been conducted on a large scale, and therefore most of the conclusions achieved in the literature have to be taken as partial equilibrium analysis.[65] This is crucial, because, if most of the expected gains in student achievement derive from student self-sorting, a large-scale experiment is destined to be ineffective, since student reshuffling does not change the average educational achievement to in the population. Suppose students' achievement are positively correlated with parental education and independent of school resources. Thanks to the positive correlation between education and incomes, the parental choices described in section 5.2 will drive the children from richer and better-educated families into private schools. If we were to measure average educational attainment, we would record an above-average performance among students in private schools; this could not, however, be attributed to better-quality education but to self-selection only. As a consequence of this potential self-selection bias, it is impossible to assess whether private schools provide better-quality education just by looking at educational attainment. The introduction of school vouchers may represent to some extent the equivalent of a natural experiment, whereby some students are randomly selected to receive a scholarship (often referred as the *treated group*), whereas some other statistically identical students do not get the same benefit (the so-called *control group*). When the random assignment property is respected, the average differences constitute a genuine effect of the residual factors, including the type of school attended.[66] Following this approach, Rouse (1998a, 1998b) has carefully analysed one of the pioneer experiments: the introduction of school vouchers in Milwaukee (Wisconsin) in 1990. These vouchers were targeted at low-income families, were redeemable only in private non-sectarian schools and were limited to 1 per cent of the student population. Thanks to the number of applications exceeding expectations, the participants in the programme were able to be randomly selected, the non-selected applicants representing an appropriate control case. Taking into account some attrition, Rouse finds that attending private schools raises the average test-scores of children from low-background families by one to two percentage points in mathematics, leaving reading and comprehending capabilities unaffected.[67]

While the Milwaukee experience suggests that there could be some positive effect for disadvantaged students in attending private schools, this conclusion does not necessarily extend to unrestricted voucher programmes.[68] The essential point is that most of the attractive features of the private sector (selectivity of the environment, attraction of better teachers) cannot be replicated on a larger scale, because they are available in limited supply.[69]

Even if we cannot expect overall gains in educational achievement or improved cost-effectiveness, vouchers could still be desirable if they were targeted at the most disadvantaged students. However, their impact is heavily dependent on how the system is designed. If schools can levy additional fees on top of the voucher and/or if transportation is not provided, poorer families may be unable to benefit from the introduction of the voucher.[70] Furthermore, if oversubscribed schools are allowed to select non-randomly among the applicants, the risk of discriminating against disadvantaged students is high. Only means-tested vouchers, perhaps made conditional on student ability, can possibly represent a useful policy instrument in increasing the equality of opportunity in accessing the higher levels of education.[71] This does not prevent the average ability of the students remaining in the public schools from declining, unless increased competition and more efficient use of teaching resources more than compensate for the decline in student inputs.

The institutional design of a voucher system also has an impact on the type of incentives it offers to school managers. Using a principal–agent approach, Gauri and Vawda (2003) describe a voucher system as a linear compensation contract (since financing is made dependent on enrolment) between a principal (the central government) and several agents (the school managers). Following the equal compensation principle, they stress the point that vouchers should be inversely correlated with student abilities.[72] Using the same principle, they notice that school vouchers do not promote innovation in pedagogical activity, because this activity is not rewarded by the compensation scheme.[73] They also show that monitoring activity is indispensable in preserving the quality of education, since otherwise schools could find it convenient to lower their standard of screening in order to attract more students and funding. Finally, following the principle of reducing the incentive effect when effort is imperfectly measured, they suggest that efficiency gains are limited when external causes (such as teacher shortages or birth-rate changes) prevent school competition.

A final point is worth mentioning with respect to political-economy considerations. As Neal (2002 p. 37) has stressed, '[T]here are good reasons to believe that families who now live in wealthy school districts or attendance zones with high-quality public schools would suffer welfare losses under most voucher plans. Because most voucher plans break the link between residential choice and the quality of publicly funded schools, families that now enjoy access to the best public schools might see their housing wealth, which is presently linked to local school quality, fall substantially under vouchers.'[74] Also, considering that, in almost all countries, the private sector of education does not concern the majority of the population, it is rather difficult to imagine the emergence of a large body of citizens supporting the generalised introduction of school vouchers.[75]

Table 5.6 *Returns on education, private and social: integral method*

	Private returns on education			Social returns on education		
	Primary	Secondary	Tertiary	Primary	Secondary	Tertiary
Sub-Saharan Africa	41.3	26.6	27.8	24.3	18.2	11.2
Asia	39.0	18.9	19.9	19.9	13.3	11.7
Europe/Middle East and North Africa	17.4	15.9	21.7	15.5	11.2	10.6
Latin America and the Caribbean	26.2	16.8	19.7	17.9	12.8	12.3
OECD countries	21.7	12.4	12.3	14.4	10.2	8.7
World	29.1	18.1	20.3	18.4	13.1	10.9

Source: Psacharopoulos (1994, table 1). Figures are percentages.

5.8 Subsidising or lending?

Some of the previous discussion is based on the implicit assumption that the demand for education exhibits sufficient elasticity with respect to its price that the lowering of net fees (through vouchers) will raise the demand for private education. However, the empirical evidence in this respect is controversial. As we have already discussed, in section 5.6, one can make a general argument for subsidising education referring to positive externalities,[76] but this argument seems more convincing with respect to compulsory education. Primary education is especially crucial in reducing transaction costs (by spreading literacy, numeracy and the adoption of a national language), facilitating the introduction of new technologies (e.g. being able to read the manual for a new appliance) and improving governance by creating an informed public. When considering developing countries, we may add improvements in child health and the reduction of family size. However, when moving to post-compulsory education, the argument supporting public subsidisation weakens, as most of the benefits of additional education accrue to the individual undertaking the investment. In addition, the over-representation of children from higher socio-economic status in tertiary education imparts a regressive trait to the public expenditure for education. Despite the fact that we have postponed a full discussion of measuring returns on education to the next chapter, from table 5.6 we get the message that the economic return on education for society is higher for the initial levels of education, due to both the lower costs of provision and the higher productivity of the educational investment.

Even if there is a general consensus towards the idea that education financing should be progressively shifted to user fees the longer one remains in education, it is unclear which the most appropriate mix of education financing is, because relatively little is known about the demand for post-compulsory education from the empirical point of view.[77]

Admission fees affect school attendance in a non-linear way, depending on family income. Using aggregate data to study the reform of student aid for college, McPherson and Shapiro (1991) find that the increase in the net cost of university attendance in the United States had a negative effect on the enrolment decision for white students from low-income families. Kane (1995) confirms these findings, providing additional non-experimental evidence for the strong impact of tuition on the college enrolment of poor and minority families.[78] However, he notices that the introduction of means-tested aid and/or subsidised loans (such as the Pell Program in the United States) in the 1970s did not modify enrolment patterns for low-income families. Nonetheless, studies based on individual data from policy experiment do suggest that enrolment decisions are strongly sensitive to financial aid.[79] Even though direct costs may not prevent investment in further education (especially for inframarginal students), they are likely to lead to a revision of students' strategies (typically including a mixture of family support, state or university grants, loans and employment) in order to finance their studies.[80]

There is much debate in the literature as to what the optimal financing strategy is for public authorities in this framework. Generally speaking, until quite recently most governments in developed countries have promoted college enrolment by keeping tuition fees low through direct university subsidisation.[81] However, rising attendance at the previous stages of schooling poses some challenge to the financial sustainability of this strategy. Some countries have partially switched to means-tested aid and/or subsidised loans, whereas some have preferred to adopt different sorts of *graduate tax* or *income-contingent loans*.[82] Both proposals are directed towards solving the problems of imperfect capital markets and the absence of insurance to cover the risks of pursuing higher education. In both systems students obtain funds from the government to cover tuition and living costs, and, having graduated, they repay a fraction of their incomes to the government in return for the funds received. With an income-contingent loan the amount of repayment has a maximum that is determined by the amount borrowed,[83] whereas with a graduate tax payments last throughout the working life. It is evident that, under a graduate tax, the amount of income insurance and the redistribution of incomes is larger because there is no ceiling on repayments; in addition, under income-contingent loans the default risk is shifted to society at large, whereas in the case of a graduate tax it is shared among graduates. The main drawback of this system is the potential reduction in university enrolment resulting from the increase in the private cost of attending universities.

In his review of the introduction in Australia of a graduate tax at the end of the 1980s (raising tuition in the meanwhile), Chapman (1997) underlines the positive impact of rendering repayment of the debt income-contingent. If the degree of risk aversion is inversely related to family wealth, families with poor socio-economic backgrounds will be prevented from applying by the greater risk they perceive to be associated with an educational investment. If the repayment is made conditional on the success of the investment, they are simultaneously receiving financial aid insurance, which should increase their willingness to enrol in universities. Women in particular seem to have taken advantage of the new system, without any sizeable reduction in enrolment from poor-background students.[84]

5.9 Summing up

In this chapter we have argued that, whenever individuals are different in terms of ability and family wealth, they face different incentives for education acquisition, which cannot easily be dealt with by market solutions. When schools differ in quality, we observe the emergence of a stratified distribution, with high-talent and/or wealthy-family children gathered in the better-quality schools.

We have then shown that the presence of externalities requires some public intervention, which does not, however, ensure the attainment of the social optimum: the democratic choice of educational investment through tax financing is very likely to lead to under- or over-investment in education, whereas the existence of a private sector providing educational services does not recreate the conditions for Pareto optimality. In addition, the presence of publicly provided education creates disincentives for investment in education for richer families, who wish to avoid the redistributive nature of public schooling, financed through general taxation. The existence of these disincentives yields macroeconomic implications, in terms of both growth and inequality persistence.

Finally, we have questioned the identical allocation of resources to all students within the private sector, showing the pros and cons of its stratification along available dimensions (the degree of curriculum stratification, the private share in education provision, local financing). The chapter closes with a discussion of the alternative strategies for providing a public subsidy to education, including school vouchers and income-contingent loans.

Appendix: Income inequality in a neoclassical model of growth

We present here a simplified version of the model devloped by Stiglitz (1969). Let us start with a standard production technology. The size of the population coincides with the size of the labour force; wage flexibility ensures full employment. Under constant returns to scale the aggregate output can be re-expressed in per capita terms as

$$\frac{Y}{L} = f\left(\frac{K}{L}, \frac{L}{L}\right) \quad \Rightarrow \quad y = \phi(k), \quad \phi' > 0, \quad \phi'' < 0 \qquad (A5.1)$$

where $y = Y/L$ is (average) per capita income and $k = K/L$ is (average) per capita capital. Whenever markets are perfectly competitive and firms are profit maximisers, each factor will earn the equivalent of its marginal contribution to production:

$$r = \phi'(k) \qquad (A5.2)$$

$$w = \phi(k) - k \cdot \phi'(k) = \phi(k) \cdot (1 - \eta) = y \cdot (1 - \eta) \qquad (A5.3)$$

where r is the user cost of capital, w is the real wage rate (the output price being normalised to one) and η is the output elasticity to capital input (depending on the curvature of the production function). Each individual i is assumed to be endowed with one unit of labour and some units of capital. His/her income will thus be defined by

$$y_i = w + r \cdot k_i \qquad (A5.4)$$

where k_i is the personal wealth of the i-th agent. In this simplified context, income and wealth distribution coincide.[85] A crucial assumption is that savings constitute a fixed proportion s of earned incomes.[86] Under such an assumption, individual capital accumulates according to personal savings, once we deduct capital depreciation δ[87]

$$\dot{k_i} = s \cdot y_i - \delta \cdot k_i = s \cdot w + (s \cdot r - \delta)k_i \qquad (A5.5)$$

Since in the aggregate the capital stock coincides with the aggregation of individual capital stocks (i.e. $k = \dfrac{K}{L} = \dfrac{1}{L} \cdot \sum_{i=1}^{L} k_i$), its dynamics can be described by the following relationship:

$$\dot{k} = \frac{1}{L} \cdot \sum_{i=1}^{L} \dot{k_i} = s \cdot w + (s \cdot r - \delta) \cdot \frac{1}{L} \cdot \sum_{i=1}^{L} k_i = s \cdot w + (s \cdot r - \delta) \cdot k$$
$$= s \cdot y - \delta \cdot k \qquad (A5.6)$$

It is interesting to note that the aggregate accumulation of capital is independent of income or wealth distribution, and, crucially, impinges on the assumption that each individual is at the same time worker and capitalist (even allowing for different degrees of wealth possession). Equation (A5.6) is characterised by steady-state capital stock, $k^* = \frac{s \cdot y(k^*)}{\delta}$, such that, when the economic system hits it, the growth process comes to a halt.[88] When the steady state corresponds to a stable equilibrium,[89] the economic system will converge to that level of productive capacity. When looking at individual accumulation plans, we make use of equation (A5.6) to re-express equation (A5.5) in the following way:

$$\dot{k_i} = s \cdot w + (s \cdot r - \delta) \cdot k - (s \cdot r - \delta) \cdot k + (s \cdot r - \delta) \cdot k_i$$
$$\qquad (A5.7)$$

$$= [s \cdot y - \delta \cdot k] + (\delta - s \cdot r) \cdot (k - k_i) = \dot{k} + (\delta - s \cdot r) \cdot (k - k_i)$$

From equation (A5.7) we may infer that, during the transition to the steady state, the capital stock of individuals endowed with wealth below the mean (i.e. $(k - k_i) > 0$) will grow more quickly, whereas the opposite situation will occur with richer than average individuals. Given the fact that stability conditions are identical at both aggregate and individual levels, the steady-state capital stock will be identical for all agents and will correspond to k^* independently of the initial level of wealth. In the long run wealth (and income) inequality spontaneously disappears, without any redistributive intervention by the public sector.

Notes

1. 'A stable and democratic society is impossible without a minimum degree of literacy and knowledge on the part of most citizens and without widespread acceptance of some common set of values' (Friedman, 1962, p. 86).
2. 'Government could require a minimum level of schooling financed by giving parents vouchers redeemable for a specified sum per child per year if spent on "approved" educational services' (Friedman, 1962, p. 89).
3. An account of this approach can be found in the appendix to this chapter, where the long-run convergence properties of the neoclassical models are shown along the lines of the model expounded in Stiglitz (1969).
4. We follow the base model proposed by De Fraja (2001).
5. This corresponds to proposition 3 in De Fraja (2002).
6. The first-order conditions are $\frac{\partial U}{\partial E} = -p_E U'_C + U'_Y W_E = 0$ and $\frac{\partial U}{\partial X} = -U'_C + r U'_Y = 0$. By making use of the latter into the former we get equation (5.5) in the text. In the absence of monetary transfer, equation (5.5) would be replaced by the condition $\frac{U'_C}{U'_Y} = \frac{W_E}{p_E}$: the marginal rate of substitution of the parental choice must be equal to the market rate of return of the educational investment.
7. It is sufficient to observe that $\frac{dE^*}{dA} = \frac{W''_{EA}}{W''_{EE}} > 0$.
8. Piketty (1997) includes a lengthy discussion on the reasons why potential lenders will deny credit to parents wishing to finance the education of their children using their future income to guarantee debt repayment. His main point is based on the idea that children's effort in the labour market might be unobservable, thus providing an opportunity for problems of moral hazard.
9. The first-order condition is now given by $\frac{\partial U}{\partial E} = -p_E U'_C + U'_Y W_E - \mu p_E = 0$, where μ is the Kuhn–Tucker multiplier associated with the inequality constraint $p_E E^*_{i_{t+1}} \leq Y_{it}$.
10. De Fraja (2002) presents a model in which ability and education are complements in generating labour income for the children, and parents' willingness to pay is exploited by the government, which does not observe the true ability endowment of children: 'Those who get the most out of the education system are the bright children of sufficiently well-off parents . . . Because of these features, the optimal education policies operate in a direction opposite to a redistributive policy: brighter children are subsidised by the taxpayer and by the average children' (p. 458).

In a similar context, De Fraja (2001) shows that admission tests based on student ability induce a flatter relationship than the one depicted in figure 5.1: fewer students gain access to the higher level of education (university, in his paper), but their average ability is increased.

11. Private schools are typically assumed to be of better quality, on the argument that rational agents would not pay a price for a service of similar quality that is freely provided by the public sector. However, private schools could be chosen for additional features: some parents elect to send their children to private schools because they explicitly support certain values, such as religion (Sander, 2001); others because private schools have better facilities, such as libraries and laboratories, or lower transportation costs. Sometimes the quality of education or the facilities is not even the main issue. Some people consider private education a status symbol (Fershtman, Murphy and Weiss, 1996), a way of improving their own and their children's social networks, of shielding their children from social problems, avoiding contact with immigrants and children with disabilities, or simply because they do not approve of the open and more heterogeneous public school environment (Gradstein and Justman, 2001). Empirical evidence on the returns to private schooling is mixed: see Wright (1999) for the British evidence, and Brown and Belfield (2001) for a survey of the existing literature on the overall effect of private school attendance (in terms of achievement, attainment, social outcomes and earnings). The crucial issue is how to control for sample self-selection: see the discussion in Mocan, Scafidi and Tekin (2002).

12. Epple and Romano (2002) (building on Epple and Romano, 1998) propose a model based on this type of self-sorting: the peer effect makes school quality dependent on the ability composition of a school students' body; this creates an incentive for schools to resort to cream-skimming (i.e. attracting the best students). An unconditional voucher possibly exacerbates the problem, promoting a quality hierarchy of schools, whereas 'a simple tuition restriction combined with ability linked vouchers induces equal quality, competing and technically efficient schools' (p. 3). Otherwise, the market equilibrium results in better private schools charging higher prices, and state-run schools retaining the worst students.

13. Indirect evidence for this effect in the case of university attendance in Italy can be obtained by specific surveys of labour market transitions after graduation. In a survey of students from the State University of Milan who graduated in 1997 and were interviewed in 2001, the median (net) income was €1,394 and the median wait for the first job after graduation was twenty-one months. In a similar survey conducted with students from the Bocconi University, a private university in the same

city for the same year, the median income was €1,549 and the median wait was less than three months. Both elements suggest the existence of a positive premium in expected earnings from attending a private university in Italy. Similarly, Naylor, Smith and McKnight (2002) find a positive premium for attending a private secondary school in England in the order of 3 per cent six months after leaving, and explain the premium as being related to social networks associated with private schools.

14. Data come from the administrative archives of the State University of Milan, Faculty of Economics, and of the Bocconi University, a private institution mainly offering courses in economics. In the city of Milan there is a second private university, the Catholic University (Università Cattolica del Sacro Cuore), which did not make its information available to us. We suspect that Catholic University attendance includes an ideological bias towards religious education (students are required to take an extra course in theology each year) that we cannot account for. These data were collected in a joint research project with Andrea Ichino and Francesco Franzoni.

15. Income data for the entire population are obtained from the Bank of Italy's 1995 survey on household income and wealth, with the sample restricted to families with children aged between nineteen and twenty-six. Data on secondary school marks are obtained from a different source (Gasperoni, 1997, table 4) and refer to the academic year 1994/95, whereas students' marks incorporate data from the period between 1990/91 and 1996/97.

16. Ganderton (1992) presents similar results with respect to college application and quality selection in the US case: 'Wealth as proxied by the socio-economic status measure, high school grades and test scores all have a positive effect on the probability of applying to college. [. . .] Wealth, as proxied by the socio-economic status, and ability, as measured by test scores, both have a negative effect on the probability of choosing a public college' (p. 283).

17. It is worth noting that a child from a poor family should in principle apply for private university attendance, spending even less than attending a public one. However, entry tests based on both logic/numeracy/literacy task assessments and marks from previous schooling should ensure that only the most brilliant of them would gain admission. In this way, the private institution can attract the best students from the poorest backgrounds.

18. The correlation between our proxy for talent and (log) family income is -0.086 (2.99) among the students at public university and -0.12 (10.4) among the students at private university.

19. The sample is self-sorted twice, both for university attendance and the choice of a faculty of economics. The first choice is typically related to parental education and the type of secondary school attended (see Checchi, 2000). The second choice is more difficult to assess, in the absence of specific studies. The common perception of a course in economics in Italy is that it is a quantitatively oriented course, thus discouraging students with some interest in humanities.

20. Checchi (2003a) studies how the Italian educational system sorts students according to their family background, showing that early tracking during lower secondary school is highly correlated with parental education.

21. On the notion of social networking, see the paper by Montgomery (1991), where he presents a model incorporating the unobservable ability of the applicants. If a firm observes that social relations are more likely between individuals of identical ability, then it will base its hiring policy on recommendations of peers as a way of acquiring information.

22. This is particularly true if the dominant channel for obtaining employment is represented by personal connections. At the beginning of the 1990s 47 per cent of interviewees in Italy declared that they had found their current job through informal connections, whereas the comparable figures were 32 per cent for the United Kingdom and 35 per cent for the United States. See Pistaferri (1999).

23. Banerjee (2004) shows that inequality persistence can either be the consequence of the absence of financial markets (as in Galor and Zeira (1993), where the family acts as an imperfect substitute for the missing market) or be attributed to the *symbolic consumption* of education, defined as the presence of children's education in the utility function of the parent in an intergenerational model of educational choice: 'Symbolic consumption covers things like the "warm glove" of giving to one's children . . . , pride in having children who are well educated or rich and the pleasure of being able to say that one's children go to an expensive school' (p. 7).

24. A pure collective good is defined as such if the cost of excluding an additional consumer is infinite (non-excludability) while the cost of an additional consumer is nil (non-rivalry). See Johansson (1991, pp. 63–4).

25. This is the definition adopted by Stiglitz (1974, p. 356).

26. Should we abandon the assumption of perfect financial markets, the optimal investment of education could be upper-bounded by the available inheritance, and equation (5.15) has to be replaced by $E_{it}^{priv} = \min\left\{\left[\frac{\beta A_{it}^{\gamma}}{R}\right]^{\frac{1}{1-\beta}}, X_{it}\right\}$. This implies an inefficient outcome, because all

individuals who are rationed according to family wealth have marginal returns exceeding the marginal cost of their education.

27. Rather implausibly, we are assuming that the optimal tax rate is chosen by the young generation before entering the labour market. An alternative framework would require that parents choose both the educational investment and the optimal tax rate: see Stiglitz (1974).

28. Individual preferences are characterised by a unique global maximum with respect to the desired tax rate, and therefore the median voter theorem applies: see Grandmont (1978).

29. Bertola and Checchi (2001) show that when the secondary school system is stratified this presumption may prove false, because the brightest students tend to choose high schools rather than vocational ones. In this way private schools retain a role as remedial schools for less talented children from rich families.

30. Using a representative sample of Italian families interviewed in 1993, Checchi and Jappelli (2004) show that the probability of attending a private school is negatively affected both by subjective judgements on the quality of the local public school and by objective measures of available resources in the public sector (such as pupil/teacher ratios).

31. The property of single-peakedness gets lost because people enrolling in private schools will vote for zero taxation (since they do not want to subsidise other people remaining in the public sector). Conversely, the outflow of the ablest students lowers the talent endowment of the median voter, who now has the incentive to raise his/her optimal tax rate in order to obtain subsidisation from people attending private schools. See Stiglitz (1974, sect. 5.4).

32. Checchi (2004) studies the relationship between educational inequality and income inequality, finding some evidence of an inverted U-shaped relationship between the two (when measured by Gini concentration indices). Teulings and vanRens (2002) analyse the crucial role played by the constant return rate assumption when studying this relationship.

33. We base our exposition on the model proposed by Glomm and Ravikumar (1992).

34. The identity $W_t = H_t$ can be thought of as the result of a simplified production technology exhibiting constant returns to scale where the sole production factor is given by human capital.

35. Notice that these resources are earmarked for education financing, since the individual does not have the ability to divert them to alternative uses, such as consumption.

36. Again, for simplicity, there is no intertemporal discounting.

37. These solutions can easily be obtained by a two-step procedure: initially suppose a given W_{t+1} and find the optimal choices for C_{t+1} and X_{t+1};

then substitute these optimal choices into equation (5.31), make use of equation (5.30) and solve for S_t.

38. When a variable $h = \log(H)$ is normally distributed, its density function is given by $f(h; \mu, \sigma^2) = \frac{1}{\sqrt{2\pi}\sigma} \exp\left[-\frac{(h-\mu)^2}{2\sigma^2}\right]$, where μ and σ^2 are, respectively, the mean and variance of h. Then $H = \exp(h)$ will be lognormally distributed, with a density function $f(H; \mu, \sigma^2) = \frac{1}{H\sqrt{2\pi}\sigma} \exp\left[-\frac{(\log H - \mu)^2}{2\sigma^2}\right]$. In such a case the mean and variance are given by $E(H) = \exp\left[\mu + \frac{1}{2}\sigma^2\right]$ and $\text{Var}(H) = \exp(2\mu + 2\sigma^2) - \exp(2\mu + \sigma^2)$. In addition, if $H \sim \log N(\mu, \sigma^2)$ then $\alpha H^\beta \sim \log N(\log \alpha + \beta\mu, \beta^2\sigma^2)$.

39. If $(\gamma + \beta) = 1$ there is a unique equilibrium if $\Theta = 1$; in such a case $H_{t+1} = H_t$ and there are a multiplicity of equilibria (like the hysteresis in the unemployment literature). If $(\gamma + \beta) > 1$ the equilibrium is unstable, and incomes diverge towards $\pm\infty$, according to the initial conditions.

40. Obviously, things are reversed if $(\gamma + \beta) > 1$, but this corresponds to an unstable equilibrium.

41. Since H_{t+1} is a concave function of H_t in equation (5.47): see the demonstration of proposition 6 in Glomm and Ravikumar (1992).

42. Rothschild and White (1995) have shown that such allocation can also be achieved in a private system through appropriate tuition fees. By taking into account the fact that students are at the same time inputs and customers in the educational production sector, it is possible to devise a pricing policy based on the added value received by each student. However, this policy has the unwelcome feature of charging lower fees (per unit of human capital) to the brightest students, since their attendance creates a positive externality for all remaining students: 'If the desirable students enhance the educational experience of other students, the university should be able to charge higher tuitions to the latter' (Rothschild and White, 1995, fn. 15). Similar conclusions are reached in De Fraja (2002); see note 10 above.

43. 'Generally the decision about school track is taken by both parents and the local educational authorities, but children's measured ability remains the most important factor determining the selection process' (Schnepf, 2002, p. 7).

44. 'The high level of credentialism, i.e. matching qualifications to labour market positions, and the occupational segmentation of the German labour market, tends to limit the likelihood of post-school correction' (Schnepf, 2002, p. 13).

45. Most studies compare students from different ability groups to heterogeneously grouped students, finding evidence that the most able students are helped by ability grouping, whereas the least able students are

harmed, resulting in a net effect that can be positive or negative, but which is usually close to zero. See Betts and Shkolnik (2000). Similarly, Figlio and Page (2002) have shown that the academic performance of low achievers is not hampered by ability tracking in US schools.

46. The preference revelation property is the core of Tiebout's (1956) argument: since a public good provision creates incentives for free-riding, people would not reveal their true preferences and so avoid sustaining the cost of provision. Local financing and residential sorting would solve the problem of preference revealing.

47. Hoxby (1996b) asserts that local financing achieves both *allocative efficiency* (supplying to each agent what they prefer) and *productive efficiency* (supplying at a minimum cost, since it exerts a more direct control on resource utilisation). In addition, it embeds a self-reinforcing mechanism: financing education with property taxation gives more resources to schools located in richer areas; if additional resources translate into better quality, the presence of better-endowed schools makes these areas more attractive, raising property prices and thus increasing the asset values of the schools themselves.

48. The overall effect on human capital accumulation is ambiguous, since the uniform provision of education raises educational attendance, whereas it nullifies the extra investment that some families would undertake in a private/locally financed system. Using a theoretical model calibrated on the US economy, Fernandez and Rogerson (1998) estimate an overall gain equivalent to 3.3 per cent of GDP (measured in terms of *compensative variation*) when passing from local financing to central financing, owing to the dominance of the former effect over the latter.

49. See the account of passing the *Serrano proposition* (from the name of the judge raising the issue) in Fernandez and Rogerson (1999), see also Fernandez and Rogerson (2003).

50. 'We believe the data are consistent with the existence of a modest effect of school finance reforms on the gap in test scores between children from different background groups, but the evidence is mixed' (Card and Payne, 2002, p. 3).

51. Nechyba (1996) makes use of a general equilibrium model with endogenous residential choice and a contemporaneous presence of public and private schools, showing that local financing may reduce territorial segregation, because rich families have an incentive to relocate in poor areas (in order to pay lower taxes) and send their children to local private schools. See also Nechyba (2000) and Neal (2002).

52. It is difficult to find similar information along the central/local dimension of financing. In 1993 74.3 per cent of educational expenditure was locally financed in the United States, while the corresponding figure was

16.0 per cent in Italy (OECD, 1996, table F12.1). On the comparison of different educational systems, see Checchi, Ichino and Rustichini (1999).

53. 'In school systems with differentiated school types, the clustering of students with particular socio-economic characteristics in certain schools is greater than in systems where the curriculum does not vary significantly between schools. In Austria, Belgium, the Czech Republic, Germany, Italy and the Netherlands, for example, the between-school variation associated with the fact that students attend different types of school is considerably compounded by differences in social and family backgrounds' (OECD, 2003, p. 82).

54. 'The economic benefits of education as a socializing force are realized in various ways. Instilling civic virtues from an early age, through education, can reduce the cost of enforcing desirable social norms. Relatedly, when society is divided along ethnic or religious lines, uniform schooling in a common culture can lessen the potential for redistributional conflict among distinct social groups. The present paper focuses on a third benefit of common socialization: the role of state schooling in reducing transaction costs by shrinking the "social distance" between individuals in the economy' (Gradstein and Justman, 2002, p. 1192). Gradstein and Justman (2000) argue that uniform/public education reduces the potential for conflict over rent-seeking activities between competing ethnic groups.

55. Parents in the minority group face a dilemma: raising children more in line with the mainstream increases their productivity (because they reduce their distance in social transactions), but incurs the psychological cost of dissonance with their own offspring. See also Gradstein and Justman (2001), who show that majority parents have an incentive to subsidise minority parents in order to reap the externality implied by the reduction of social distances.

56. See their main result: 'Proposition 3: When the government has coercive powers to impose school curricula, centralization leads to more uniform schooling and faster income growth than decentralization, but only by imposing a greater psychic [sic] cost for parents, which may or may not outweigh its benefits. In any case, coercive centralization induces overly rapid convergence to complete uniformity, which parents find strictly inferior to the unconstrained Pareto optimum. Noncoercive centralization is a Pareto improvement over decentralized education' (Gradstein and Justman, 2002, p. 1192).

57. 'An egalitarian educational policy makes production more lucrative for all the poorly endowed people, and thereby decreases the amount of guarding against predators that is necessary to deter poorly endowed

people from choosing to be predators' (Grossman and Kim, 1998, p. 4).

58. Dee (2003) finds that educational attainment has large and statistically significant effects on subsequent voting participation and support for free speech. He also shows that additional schooling appears to increase the quality of civic knowledge, as measured by the frequency of newspaper readership. Yet critics of the public financing of schooling object that totalitarian governments spend more on education as a way to achieve the support of public opinion for their actions: 'Like public ownership of the news media, government-provided schooling decreases the cost of wealth transfers by changing the relative cost of acquiring different information and predisposing students to support certain transfers' (Lott, 1999, p. S129).

59. Eckstein and Zilcha (1994) present an overlapping generation model in which agents are differentiated in terms of altruism and ignore the positive spillover of education onto the growth potential of the society. In such a context, a benevolent dictator can achieve higher levels of productivity by imposing a compulsory education level, and this second-best solution is superior to decentralised optimisation. A further argument in favour of compulsory education and reduced variation in schooling standards is offered by the sequential nature of the educational process: by forcing families to achieve a given threshold of education, a government raises the probability of the transition to further levels of education. See Appleton, Hoddinott and Knight (1996).

60. See the interesting account of this policy experiment reported by Fiske and Ladd (2000).

61. In the New Zealand experience, oversubscribed schools were entitled to choose among students, thus shifting the system from 'parental choice' to 'school choice'.

62. Equivalent to the *public choice perspective* defined by Levin (1992) in his survey on school vouchers.

63. However, 'parents might use the socio-economic level of the parents of other children in the school as a proxy for school quality, based on the well-documented observation that the average achievement of students within a school is highly correlated with the socio-economic and racial composition of the student body. The positive correlation between the socio-economic composition of a school and the performance of its students largely reflects what happens at home rather than at school' (Ladd, 2002, p. 7).

64. This point is stressed by Manski (1992). It is worth noting that, whenever school quality is proportional to the average ability of the students enrolled, it is necessary to impose some consistency requirement

on expectation formation, in order to be able to characterise an equilibrium distribution of students; for this reason, both Manski (1992) and Nechyba (1996) assume perfect information on school quality when performing policy simulations in their models.

65. Surveys of existing experiences of school vouchers are reported by Neal (2002), Ladd (2002) and Gauri and Vawda (2003).

66. 'In order to estimate the true effect of choice schools, one must control for family background (such as family income and parental education) and student ability. The goal is to control for all individual characteristics that are correlated with attending the choice school and explain higher test scores such that the only difference between the two groups of students is whether or not they have enrolled in a choice school. In general, the more similar the two groups of students are to begin with, the more credible the evaluation of the program' (Rouse, 1998b, p. 65). One method used to check the random assignment property is matching scores: see, for example, Becker and Ichino (2002).

67. Rouse (1998a) is very careful in interpreting her results in terms of the *intention-to-treat* effect: 'Thus, the reduced-form estimates reflect the overall potential gains from offering the vouchers. Second, as in many experimental settings, the randomisation only occurred in the intention-to-treat and as such, the reduced-form estimate is the only unambiguously unbiased estimate that one can obtain from an ordinary least squares (OLS) regression, assuming the initial selection was truly random' (p. 562). A similar approach is adopted by Krueger and Zhou (2002).

68. Also, in the case of the New York experiment, involving 1,300 students per year, Krueger and Zhou (2002) raise doubts as to the previous finding of significant gains in test scores for voucher recipients relative to non-recipients for African-American students only.

69. 'Thus, one should expect neither higher overall achievement nor lower resource costs as a result of a shift of students from public to private schools. At most, there are likely to be small achievement gains for a selected group of African-American students. Furthermore, a universal voucher program could possibly require the government to spend more public funds on education, because some of the voucher funds would undoubtedly go to families who would otherwise have paid all of the cost of putting their children in private schools' (Ladd, 2002, p. 13).

70. In the case of the New York experiment, up to a quarter of the selected applicants did not use the offered voucher, whereas in the Milwaukee case the percentage was even higher.

71. The simulations of Manski (1992), Nechyba (1996) and Epple and Romano (1998, 2002) are unequivocal in predicting that unconditional vouchers yield an over-representation of students from richer families among school voucher recipients.

72. 'Some European countries with voucher systems, recognizing the incentive that flat per-pupil payments create for schools to select relatively advantaged students and for parents to choose those "successful" schools, transfer additional resources to schools based on the composition of the student body enrolled. Holland pays 1.9 times the standard voucher value for each minority student and 1.25 times that value for an economically disadvantaged student. Sweden also transfers additional resources based on numbers of minority students and students with learning disabilities' (Gauri and Vawda, 2003, p. 13).

73. 'Voucher programs in Chile, New Zealand, England and Wales, Bangladesh, and Côte d'Ivoire did not promote pedagogical innovation; in fact, case studies suggest that pedagogy might have become more uniform in those countries. In voucher programs, governments will need to continue to finance and support teacher training and professional development in private schools' (Gauri and Vawda, 2003, p. 19).

74. Gibbons and Machin (2003) discuss an empirical relationship between housing prices and primary school performance, as measured by the proportion reaching target grades in age-11 standard assessment tests, with respect to the UK case. For evidence on the US case, see Clapp and Ross (2002).

75. However, Bearse, Glomm and Ravikumar (2000) have considered a political-economy model contrasting the introduction of means-tested vouchers against uniform vouchers. By calibrating their model on the US economy, they find that the poorest 45 per cent and the richest 18 per cent of families prefer means-tested vouchers, obviously for different reasons: the poorest favour means-testing because they receive more, the richest because means-tested vouchers are associated with lower educational expenditure.

76. Appleton (2001) offers a lengthy discussion of these externalities, ranging from inequality reduction, the absence of perfect capital markets and/or insurance markets, and the imperfect altruism of parents, up to the merit-good argument (since education may be undervalued by those who have never experienced it). Barr (1993) adds the point of the 'tax dividend': by subsidising investment in human capital, a government will collect additional tax revenues in the future.

77. Some degree of public subsidisation of higher education can be justifiable on efficiency grounds whenever there exists complementarity in production between skilled/educated workers and unskilled/uneducated workers; see Johnson (1985).

78. He estimates that a between-state difference of $1,000 in tuition is associated with a gap in two-year college enrolment of somewhere between 11 per cent and 29 per cent (depending on the data set). This is also consistent with the impact of minimum wage legislation, taken as a proxy for forgone incomes, which represent the bulk of the cost of college attendance. Canton and deJong (2002) reach similar conclusions studying aggregate time-series data on university attendance in the Netherlands in the post-war period.

79. Dearden et al. (2003) analyse individual British data from a pivotal experiment conducted in 1999 in ten areas, where a means-tested allowance was granted to students proceeding with post-compulsory education. They find that an allowance replacing between a quarter and a third of forgone income has a substantial and persistent impact on school access, raising enrolment in 'treatment' areas by 3.7 additional percentage points. Surprisingly, very similar conclusions are obtained in a developing country context: Ravallion and Wodon (2000) report that the programme 'Food for education', granting an in-kind subsidy (rice) equivalent to between 13 and 20 per cent of the monthly wage of working children in exchange for school attendance, was able to reduce child labour and increase school attendance (with the latter effect dominating the former one).

80. Christou and Haliassos (1994) estimate a model in which different sources of financing are combined into a production function generating educational expenditure, and individuals optimally select their preferred financial strategy.

81. Ganderton (1992) raises the issue that in-kind subsidies (such as subsidised tuition in public colleges) in a context characterised by quality differences can induce suboptimal matching between student ability and college quality (as measured by the average ability of applicants).

82. See the discussion of the original proposal by Friedman and Kuznets reported by Nerlove (1975), and the reappraisal by Barr (1993) and Jacobs (2002).

83. The repayment is quicker for more successful graduates, however; this distinguishes an income-contingent loan from a mortgage-type loan, with repayments in fixed instalments over a fixed period (like the one introduced and found immediately to be unsuccessful in the United Kingdom in 1988; see the discussion in Barr, 1993).

84. An analogous system exists in Sweden (see Morris, 1989). For a proposal of introduction and related cost simulations in the Netherlands, see Jacobs (2002). See also the general review contained in chapter 7 of Jones (1993).

85. In the original model of Stiglitz (1969), the population is composed of groups of equal size, and all groups grow at the same growth rate, leaving

the population distribution across groups unaffected. He also excludes inheritance strategies favouring primogenitures, and cross-group marriages. In the text we assume that each group is composed of one individual, abstracting from population growth.

86. This result can easily be obtained under specific utility functions, and it plays the role of separating the problem of growth from the problem of distribution. Were savings a concave function of income (the marginal propensity to save would decline with individual income), the results would be unaltered. In contrast, when savings are a convex function of income (rich people exhibit a higher propensity to save than poor individuals) then wealth distribution converges towards a non-egalitarian distribution. The last situation has been analysed by Bourguignon (1981), who shows the Pareto superiority of this latter case.

87. In the original model, capital depreciation is neglected, but the same result obtains in per capita terms because of the population growth.

88. There are, in fact, two steady states associated with the differential equation (A5.6): the case of $k = 0$ and the case discussed in the text. The former is dynamically unstable, while the latter is stable.

89. This applies whenever $sr < \delta$; that is, when the capital stock is sufficiently high to keep its productivity sufficiently low.

6 | *The return on education*

6.1 Introduction

The discussion of educational investment presented in chapter 2 was based on the assumption that an increase in education was associated with an increase in potential (permanent) income. While this remains true from an individual perspective (that is, families take this to be a stylised fact, as in any partial equilibrium model), in this chapter we look into why this may be true in the aggregate. We face competing explanations here, and will review them in turn, starting from the aggregate evidence supporting the view that human capital raises firms' productivity (in line with the human capital approach). We then proceed with a more recent view, according to which education is associated with non-cognitive abilities. Next we present the credentialist approach, where education is just a signal of unobservable ability. The remaining part of the chapter is devoted to the problem of measuring the return on education, from both theoretical and econometric perspectives.

6.2 The productivity of human capital

While the positive correlation between education and earnings at the individual level is one of the most established facts in economic literature, the existence of a causal relation between the two is not yet widely accepted. The strongest doubts arise from the consideration that earnings and schooling could both depend on additional factors not observed by the researcher, thus constituting a patent case of spurious correlation. An incomplete list of unobserved factors that could affect both variables includes parental education (children's education is favoured by educated parents, offering wider cultural stimuli, helping with homework, selecting better schools, and so on; moreover, better-educated parents are located in higher-ranking social networks, thus offering better job opportunities to their children), behavioural traits (self-consciousness and self-esteem are rewarded both during the educational progression and in the labour market), school quality based on peer effects (attending a school with brighter classmates raises educational attainment, at the same time creating social networks that may be helpful when entering the labour market) and discrimination (ethnic or gender discrimination can prevent access to the best positions in highly ranked colleges and in top-paid jobs, sometimes leading to self-fulfilling expectations).[1]

However, we now possess a large body of evidence that, despite all the unobservable differences, education still plays a causal role in earnings determination, even if standard Mincerian regressions (whereby earnings are regressed onto education) do not account for more than one-third of the observed variance. One of the most convincing pieces of evidence comes from studies on identical twins.[2] Twins are, in general, identical in terms of family background; in addition, fraternal (monozygotic) twins are biologically identical. Under the debatable (and debated) assumption that intelligence is genetic, and that intelligence represents the bulk of unobservable ability, one can take the difference in educational attainment between twins and use it as a regressor measuring its effect on earnings differences. By analysing a sample of Australian twins, 60 per cent of whom were monozygotic, Mulvey, Miller and Martin (1997) compare the estimated return obtained from monozygotic twins with analogous estimates from dizygotic ones. Suppose that earnings are determined in their general form as follows:

$$w_{ij} = \alpha_0 + \alpha_1 A_{ij} + \alpha_2 H_{ij} + \alpha_3 X_{ij} + \beta S_{ij} + v_{ij} \qquad (6.1)$$

where w_{ij} are earnings of twin j, $j = 1, 2$ in family i, A_{ij} is his/her (unobservable) ability, H_{ij} measures the family background (education, income, socio-economic status), S_{ij} is his/her schooling and X_{ij} represents additional information (such as gender, age, experience). v_{ij} indicates the error term. By taking the difference between twins,

$$w_{i1} - w_{i2} = \alpha_1(A_{i1} - A_{i2}) + \alpha_2(H_{i1} - H_{i2}) + \alpha_3(X_{i1} - X_{i2})$$
$$+ \beta(S_{i1} - S_{i2}) + (v_{i1} - v_{i2})$$

$$(6.2)$$

If the twins are monozygotic then $(A_{i1} - A_{i2}) = 0$, and plausibly also $(X_{i1} - X_{i2}) = 0$. In addition, if they are reared together, $(H_{i1} - H_{i2}) = 0$, and then a least square projection of $(w_{i1} - w_{i2})$ onto $(S_{i1} - S_{i2})$ yields an unbiased estimate of the true impact of education on earnings β. When the same procedure is applied to dizygotic twins, the estimates of β will be biased by the omission of the unobservable difference in ability, the extent of which can be assessed by comparing with the estimate obtained for monozygotic twins.[3] When we take into account the presence of unobservable family characteristics, as in the case of Ashenfelter and Rouse (1998),[4] and we introduce the additional assumption of a potential correlation between the family's ability and children's schooling, the return on education can be estimated from

$$\begin{cases} w_{i1} = \alpha_0 + \alpha_2 H_{i1} + \alpha_3 X_{i1} + \beta S_{i1} + \gamma \dfrac{S_{i1} + S_{i2}}{2} + v_{i1} \\ w_{i2} = \alpha_0 + \alpha_2 H_{i2} + \alpha_3 X_{i2} + \beta S_{i2} + \gamma \dfrac{S_{i1} + S_{i2}}{2} + v_{i2} \end{cases} \tag{6.3}$$

where this reduced form is characterised by correlated random effects.[5] The additional advantage of using twins' data is that in most cases they allow the assessment of the measurement error for schooling, by comparing one twin's recall of his/her schooling experience with the other twin's recall of the same experience.[6]

The main objection raised against the analysis of twins is the small sample size; in addition, some of these samples were collected for other purposes (typically medical) and could, in principle, contain systematic biases. However, two other pieces of evidence can be invoked in order to sustain the proposition that education has a causal impact on earnings independent of unobservable ability. The first one comes from instrumental variable estimates, while the second is from the more recent literature on natural experiments. Ideally, in order to assess the existence of a causal role for education one would be able to allocate individuals randomly to acquire additional education, and then measure income differences subsequently. However, ethical and political considerations stand in the way of preventing some children from acquiring education for scientific research purposes, and therefore researchers have to resort either to relative comparisons or to exogenous variations attributable to events that go beyond the control of individual subjects.

The approach based on instrumental variables hinges crucially on the ability of the researcher to identify a variable (or a group of variables) correlated with the educational choice (which is likely to be correlated with unobservable ability) but not with earnings. If this variable exists, it is possible to obtain unbiased estimates of the return on education. In symbols, we replace the previous equation (6.1) with a system of two equations:

$$w_i = \alpha_0 + \alpha_1 X_i + \beta S_i + v_i \qquad (6.1')$$

$$S_i = \gamma_0 + \gamma_1 X_i + \gamma_2 Z_i + \varepsilon_i \qquad (6.4)$$

where Z_i represents the potential instrument affecting education but not earnings.[7] The return on education can then be estimated by replacing the observed education S_i with the predicted value $\hat{S}_i$ obtained from equation (6.4), since there is no reason to expect this variable to be correlated with the error term in equation (6.1').

Several instruments have been proposed in the literature, and we will recall here only the most important ones.[8] The first possible candidate for the Z_i instrument is parental education: it has a close correlation with the educational attainment of children, and in principle should be uncorrelated with their future earnings. However, where social networks are an important channel of access to the labour market, better-educated parents may prove crucial in favouring the entrance to better jobs (which are obviously better paid as well). A second candidate that has been used is school (college) proximity, since students living nearby face lower costs of attendance (in terms of transportation and/or living away from home). This represents a better alternative, although one could always devise a potential correlation with earnings (cities with colleges experience an extra supply of graduates, which may depress the local rate of return on the college). A third alternative concerns the time of year in which the individual was born, the argument being that people born at the beginning of the year reach compulsory leaving age earlier, and therefore have fewer incentives to proceed further in education. While this in principle represents purely exogenous variation, it has been challenged on the grounds that the season of birth may be correlated with family background.[9]

The last instrument points to compulsory education legislation as a source of exogenous variation. Effectively, several papers have utilised educational reforms as an instrument to estimate the return on education, finding a consistent pattern of higher estimated returns (in the order of a 20 per cent greater return than ordinary least squares).[10] Even if in this case too doubts can be raised about the selection of this instrument,[11] a more relevant problem arises when we question the assumption of a constant return in the population. So far we have taken for granted the existence of a single measure of return, identical for all the population. When we take into account potential heterogeneity in the return on education, least square estimates (whether biased or unbiased) provide a measure of the average return on education in the population. In such a framework, the instrumental variable estimations are to be reinterpreted as a measure of the causal effect of education on the sub-group of the population that was actually affected by the educational reform.[12]

In all attempts to provide an unbiased estimate of the return on education (either using twins or using an exogenous source of variation) we find a consistent result: *differences in education explain differences in earnings, even accounting for unobserved difference in abilities, and these outcomes can be taken as evidence for a productivity-enhancing effect of schooling.*[13] Nevertheless, even leaving aside the problem of measuring the relative contribution of unobservable ability, the estimated return provides a measure of the private return on education – i.e. the increase in productivity converted into earnings for the recipient of the additional education. Yet we should not forget that, when we consider the optimal investment in education (as in chapter 2), we take the return on education as a given, as in any partial equilibrium analysis. But, when we aggregate individual choices, we should not forget that in a Walrasian perspective aggregate prices (and returns) reflect relative scarcity, and could be partially unrelated to real productivity.[14] Cyclical fluctuations of returns on education can be observed independently from technological shocks, and can be attributed to both supply and demand shifts that are unrelated to changes in individual productivity.[15] Acemoglu (1999, 2003) provides an elegant model to account for the different dynamics observed in wage inequality in the United States and Europe: a skill-biased technology (such as the introduction of computers in production) should raise the relative return on education, under the assumption that new technologies are complementary to education (since educated workers are more able in managing software-driven activities). This represents a genuine increase in productivity that converts into earnings, and is actually observed in the United States. However, if labour market institutions compress wage distribution, as in Europe, firms will have an incentive to adopt technologies that raise the relative wage of the unskilled, thus reducing the return on education.[16] Alternatively, if the supply response is sufficiently quick, the greater availability of skilled labour may offset the effect of technological change, leaving the return on education unaffected.[17]

The fact that private returns on education incorporate market equilibrium effects that are independent of individual productivity works against the claim that human capital is productive per se. Nevertheless, further supportive elements can be found in the literature on education and growth.[18] While a consolidated practice among growth theorists consists of controlling for initial conditions with various measures of educational attainment in the population (see Barro, 1997), more recently greater attention has been paid to the implications of what Krueger and Lindahl (2001) call the 'macro-Mincer' model.[19] By replicating equation (6.1) in a different context, let us express the determinants of earnings of individual i working in country j at time t:

$$w_{ijt} = \alpha_0 + \alpha_1 A_{ij} + \alpha_2 H_{ijt} + \alpha_3 X_{ij} + \beta S_{ijt} + v_{ijt},$$
$$i = 1, .., n; \, j = 1, \ldots, m; \, t = 0, \ldots, T \quad (6.5)$$

By aggregating across individuals within a country we obtain

$$\overline{w}_{jt} = \sum_{i=1}^{n} w_{ijt} = \alpha_0 + (\alpha_1 \overline{A}_j + \alpha_3 \overline{X}_j) + \alpha_2 \overline{H}_{jt} + \beta \overline{S}_{jt} + v_{jt}$$
$$= \eta_{0j} + \eta_1 \overline{H}_{jt} + \beta \overline{S}_{jt} + v_{jt},$$
$$j = 1, \ldots, m; \, t = 0, \ldots, T \quad (6.6)$$

Equation (6.6) suggests an additional implication of the productive role of human capital at the macro-level: average[20] labour earnings must correlate with average educational attainment; this proposition can be estimated using cross-sectional data at country level, including a country fixed effect (η_{0j}) and other covariates to capture the country wealth or income ($\overline{H}_{jt}$). With additional assumptions regarding the features of the aggregate production function (and specifically the presence of constant labour share), equation (6.6) can easily be converted into a growth equation, in which the current level of output is taken as a function of the current stock of human capital, its dynamic equivalent being that the output growth rate is a function of the change in average educational attainment.[21] The empirical analysis has found that the initial stock of human capital shapes future growth paths, and that secondary education is more important than primary.[22] Krueger and

Lindahl (2001) analyse several problems connected with the absence of any significance of changes in human capital on output growth, including measurement errors for human capital (reliability ratios[23] are obtained using information from different sources), the length of the time horizon, the heterogeneity of impact across countries, the potential endogeneity bias and the linearity assumption. Under some specifications the estimated impact of human capital on growth (coefficient β) is much higher than the private return on education, ranging from 18 per cent to 30 per cent.[24] If the return on education estimated at the aggregate level exceeds the corresponding estimate based on individual information, this provides a clue to the potential existence of externalities – i.e. beneficial spillover effects deriving from individual choices.[25] However, the aggregate return does not necessarily measure the social rate of return, since this latter concept includes other externalities that may not necessarily affect output growth, despite being important from a policy point of view: think of greater educational attainment being positively correlated with lower crime rates, reduced welfare dependence, better public health, better parenting, wider political participation and greater social cohesion (Blöndal, Field and Girouard, 2002).

Overall, this section has put forward several pieces of evidence supporting the view that human capital raises individual productivity, possibly introducing positive externalities into aggregate output. In both micro- and macro-analyses human capital has been measured by years of education, thus implying that school attendance has a beneficial effect per se. However, the true reason why staying at school should increase productivity has not yet been well understood, and this subject will be discussed in the next section.

6.3 Effort-enhancing preferences

If education has a productivity-enhancing effect, this can occur either because it provide students with know-how that will prove important once inserted into a productive process or because it reveals information about the students' abilities. In principle we can partially control for both these channels, inserting into an earnings function such as (6.1) proxy measures of specific skills learned at school (such as specific subjects taken during high school or when at college) or test measures of general intelligence (such as IQ test, AFQT (Armed Forces

Qualification Test) scores, and the like).[26] Nevertheless, Bowles, Gintis and Osborne (2001a) report a meta-analysis on empirical estimates of returns on education in which some measure of cognitive ability was included among the regressors. If the effect of schooling on earnings is due to acquired abilities, explicitly accounting for them should lead the coefficient on education to statistical non-significance and/or it should raise the variance explained by the regression (which typically does not exceed 30 per cent in Mincerian regressions such as equation (6.1)). Surveying twenty-five studies reporting empirical estimates of the determinants of earnings in the United States from the late 1950s to the early 1990s, Bowles, Gintis and Osborne find that the introduction of a measure of cognitive performance into an equation using educational attainment to predict earnings reduces the coefficient of years of education by an average of 18 per cent, without exhibiting any specific time trend.[27] By implication, they conclude: 'This suggests that a substantial portion of the returns to schooling are generated by effects or correlates of schooling substantially unrelated to the cognitive capacities measured on the available tests' (Bowles, Gintis and Osborne, 2001a, p. 1149).

Finding limited explanatory power for cognitive skills in accounting for earnings does not answer the underlying question of why firms are disposed to pay higher wages to individuals who have spent more time at school. In addition to enhancing productivity on the job, firms may prefer educated individuals because they are self-selected according to their ability to identify with authority, or, even more simply, because they believe that achieving educational degrees is a signal of non-cognitive ability. The first perspective does not necessarily require acquired knowledge to induce its owner to introduce better techniques of production, to discover new products, and so on. The 'human capital' concept is wide enough to include the lifestyle of its owner.[28] If additional education is correlated with a healthier lifestyle and improved family planning, education is valuable to a firm, since it is associated with a more reliable job performance.[29] Human capital can, therefore, alternatively be described as the *quality of job performance* yielded by a person that can be modified through increased education.

This view has to be inserted into the capitalist framework of labour exchange. From this point of view the use of the term 'capital' is ambiguous, since it suggests the idea that every person owns some sort of capital, whether in monetary form or in intangible form through education. Nevertheless, except for the case of self-employment, human capital does not represent a true productive input, since its owner is forced to sell his/her labour in the market in order to get the return on his/her human capital.[30] But any seller of human capital in the capitalist labour market does not have any incentive to achieve his/her best performance, since the residual claimant of any increase of productivity is typically the firm. The non-observability of the work effort pushes firms to adopt higher wages (known in the literature as *efficiency wages*) and/or random monitoring accompanied by the threat to fire in the case of non-compliance (known in the literature as *contingent renewal*).[31] Whenever acquiring education modifies individual preferences, such that the agent's (i.e. the worker's) objective function becomes more in line with the principal's (i.e. the firm's), then the firm can reduce its surveillance costs and share with the worker these potential extra revenues. In such a case we will observe a positive relationship between education and wages, due to the inefficiency reduction associated with the imperfect observability of effort.

From an empirical point of view, this perspective is observationally equivalent to alternative ones, based on the productive role of knowledge or ability signalling. And it is not easy to provide an empirical test of this claim. We have already mentioned the fact that education retains significant explanatory power despite controlling for cognitive abilities in earnings regressions, and this could be taken as indirect evidence of the potential existence of behavioural traits that are imparted in schools and are valuable for firms.[32] Bowles and Gintis (1976) claim that schools in capitalist economies are designed to transmit skills that are appropriate to the hierarchical role to be followed in the labour market: thus, vocational schools reward adherence to rules and the carrying out of assigned duties, whereas university and higher stages of education, destined for the offspring of the elite, enhance creativity and problem-solving abilities.[33]

Let us now offer a formal representation of these ideas. We take as our starting point the model of contingent renewal proposed by Bowles (1985), in which effort is unobservable and the firm can use either wage incentive and/or surveillance to extract effort from workers.[34] In this framework we study the impact of changes in workers' preferences, which can be seen as behavioural traits imparted at school. Under a given set of parameters, the model predicts a positive correlation between education and wages. Let us define the production technology by

$$Y = f(L, K) = L^\beta K^{1-\beta}, \quad \beta < 1 \tag{6.7}$$

where Y is output and K are all intermediate inputs, taken as given in the short run. While in standard neoclassical models L, the labour input, is a homogeneous contractible commodity, in the present context we assume that the labour contract fixes the amount of hours L_p during which a worker becomes subordinate to firm managers' authority, but that the effective productivity of these hours depends on the worker's choice. If we consider that only two alternatives are available in each instant, either producing or shirking, then we indicate with λ the fraction of time devoted to production, and the labour input is defined accordingly as

$$L = L_p \cdot \lambda \tag{6.8}$$

While L_p can be taken as given from the institutional context and cannot be modified in the short run, the labour input varies according to the worker's behaviour. We assume that λ cannot be observed continuously by the firm (unless at very high costs), but monitoring techniques can be introduced at some cost, rendering shirking detection feasible in probabilistic terms.[35] When a worker is caught not producing he/she is fired, goes back into the pool of unemployed and looks for another job, which is found with a probability that depends on labour market conditions.

The worker chooses λ according to two considerations: the unpleasantness of the effort exerted in production, and the cost associated with the risk of being fired in case of being caught shirking. A rational worker equates the marginal utility of expected income to the marginal (disutility) cost of effort.[36] The expected income R is given by the contractual wage W times the probability of not being caught shirking (which has an upper limit of one for a worker who never shirks). In the case of dismissal for not being productive, a worker enters the unemployment pool, where he/she faces two alternative events: either finding a new job (which in equilibrium offers the same contract and the very same wage) or remaining unemployed and living on the dole. We summarise all these events in the following definition:

$$R = W \cdot (\lambda + (1 - \lambda) \cdot (1 - p)) + p \cdot (1 - \lambda) \cdot [(1 - u) \cdot W + u \cdot b]$$
$$= W - (W - b) \cdot u \cdot p \cdot (1 - \lambda) \tag{6.9}$$

where $p = p(m)$ is the probability of detection, which is a function of the amount of surveillance m introduced by the firm, u is the unemployment rate (which for simplicity we assume to be equal to the unemployment probability)[37] and b is the unemployment subsidy. In order to get an analytic solution for the model, we introduce a specific functional form for the detection probability function P:

$$p = \frac{m}{m+1}, \quad p' > 0, \; p(0) = 0, \; p(\infty) = 1 \tag{6.10}$$

The worker's preferences are defined over income and effort. We parameterise individual preferences by the parameter α_i, $i = 1, \ldots, n$, intended to capture the relative disutility of effort (or the relative appreciation of income) for worker i. This parameter is taken as given by each worker when optimally selecting his/her level of effort, but can capture the impact of schooling experiences: we assume that more education lowers α_i, due to the lower cost of effort and/or to the higher utility associated with income.[38] Once again, we make use of an explicit Cobb–Douglas functional form for preferences:

$$U(Y, \lambda) = (1 - \alpha_i) \cdot \log(R) + \alpha_i \cdot \log(1 - \lambda_i) \tag{6.11}$$

The worker chooses the optimal level of effort by maximising equation (6.11) after substituting the definition of R given in equation (6.9):

$$\lambda_i^* = 1 - \frac{\alpha_i \, W}{(W - b) \cdot u \cdot p} = 1 - \frac{\alpha_i \, W \cdot (1 + m)}{(W - b) \cdot u \cdot m}$$

$$= \lambda \left(\underset{+}{W}, \underset{-}{b}, \underset{+}{m}, \underset{+}{u}, \underset{-}{\alpha_i} \right) \tag{6.12}$$

The worker is more likely to produce the higher the wage paid by the firm and/or the lower the unemployment benefit – i.e. the higher the cost of job loss. A similar impact is produced by the unemployment rate: a higher unemployment rate, soliciting a greater effort as a consequence of the increased risk of permanence in unemployment, allows the firm to reduce either wages or monitoring. Bowles (1985) labels equation (6.12) as the *labour extraction function,* because it displays alternative combinations of tools available to the firm: the 'carrot', accounted for by the wage, and the 'stick', provided by surveillance.[39] We can therefore define isoquants associated with the effort production function (6.12) in the (W, m) space (let us call them *iso-effort schedules*), and the firm will select its optimal combination of stick and carrot, according to their relative costs. What are the consequences of different values

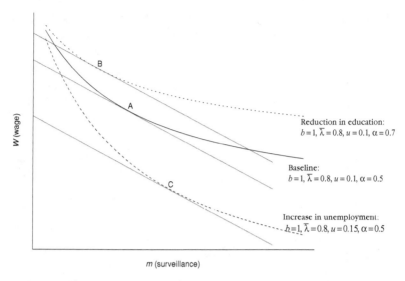

Figure 6.1 Alternative isoquants from the optimal effort function

of the α parameter – for example, associated with differences in educational backgrounds? A lower α implies a lower disutility of effort, allowing the firm to reduce monitoring m and/or wage W while eliciting the same level of effort.[40] Figure 6.1 shows alternative configurations of iso-effort schedules derived from equation (6.12).

The firm anticipates the worker's best response and will select the optimal combination of wage W_i and surveillance m_i for worker i that achieves the maximum profit in the short run:

$$\max_{L_p, W_i, m_i} \quad Y - (W_i + p_m \cdot m_i) \cdot L_p - p_k \cdot \overline{K} \tag{6.13}$$

under the constraint represented by equation (6.12) and the definition of Y given in equation (6.7). p_m is the unitary cost of per capita surveillance. First-order conditions for profit maximisation require that

$$\frac{\partial \Pi}{\partial L_p} = \lambda \beta (L_p \lambda)^{\beta-1} \overline{K}^{1-\beta} = W + p_m m$$

$$\frac{\partial \Pi}{\partial W} = L_p \beta (L_p \lambda)^{\beta-1} \overline{K}^{1-\beta} \frac{\partial \lambda}{\partial W} = L_p \tag{6.14}$$

$$\frac{\partial \Pi}{\partial m} = L_p \beta (L_p \lambda)^{\beta-1} \overline{K}^{1-\beta} \frac{\partial \lambda}{\partial m} = p_m L_p$$

where, for notational simplicity, the subscript i has been ignored. The first condition is the standard equality between the marginal productivity of labour (measured in efficiency units) and its marginal cost (including monitoring). Dividing the second condition by the first one we get

$$\frac{\partial \lambda}{\partial W} \cdot \frac{W + p_m m}{\lambda} = 1 \qquad (6.15)$$

which is the standard Solow's condition, stating that any efficiency wage must equate at the margin the rate of change of effort with the rate of change of the wage. By contrast, if we divide the third condition in (6.14) by the second we get

$$\frac{\frac{\partial \lambda}{\partial m}}{\frac{\partial \lambda}{\partial W}} = p_m \qquad (6.16)$$

Condition (6.16) suggests that the firm will select the lowest iso-cost schedule that is tangent to the iso-effort curve, since the left-hand side of (6.16) is the (inverse of the) slope of the schedule implied by equation (6.12) and the right-hand side is (the inverse of the) slope of a per capita cost function such as $C = W + p_m m$. It tells us that the cost of monitoring has to equate the marginal rate of substitution in the effort extraction function between the cost of job loss and the probability of being detected. This corresponds to point **A** in figure 6.1. If we now wonder about the consequences of a better-educated labour force in this context, we have to recall that less education implies a higher cost of effort, thus raising the iso-effort locus: in order to extract the same amount of effort for a less educated worker it is necessary to offer a higher wage and/or to introduce greater surveillance (point **B** in figure 6.1). Thus, in general equilibrium, better-educated workers will be in greater demand, since they are characterised by a lower cost of incentives, while less educated workers will suffer greater unemployment. Higher unemployment creates the opposite situation to an increase in α, since it lowers the need of incentives to elicit the same amount of effort (see point **C** in figure 6.1). The overall effect is ambiguous, depending on labour market equilibrium, which has to be stratified for educational attainment, since the supply is inelastic in the short run. If unemployment effects are stronger than the relative demand for better-educated workers, we will obtain a positive correlation between education and wages, which does not depend on the productivity of human capital but relies on behavioural traits supposedly induced by education (which can be referred to as *affective capital*).[41]

6.4 Education as a signal or as a screening device

A complementary explanation for the returns on education considers the role of *information revealing* associated with schooling experience. This is consistent with the empirical observation that a large share of class activity in schools is devoted to testing students and marking their performance, and with the fact that student's previous academic record is revealed to be a strong predictor of their current record. The easiest way to frame this argument is to think of personal abilities (which might include affective capital, as in the previous section, or simply talent, discussed in chapter 2); the ability endowment is regarded as students' private information. Ability is valuable for firms, since productivity rises with ability. We know from the literature (see Riley, 2001 for a survey) that imperfect information can lead to adverse selection phenomena, up to the complete disappearance of the market. However, agents may devise alternative strategies to overcome these imperfections. One of these strategies is the giving of signals that are (imperfectly) correlated with the hidden information. Another is to adopt wage policies that induce individuals to undertake costly screening procedures, eventually revealing the hidden information. The common trait of this approach is that education and wages are positively correlated, but it is a classical case of spurious correlation, since both correlate with unobservable ability. The other common trait is the absence of any direct impact of education on productivity, which portrays expenditure on education as a waste of resources.

Let us review these approaches more formally. We assume that individual talent A_i constitutes a productive factor for firms (i.e. it enters positively the output production function), but it is not directly observable. If it could be observed then, in equilibrium, each profit-maximising firm would pay each unit of talent its marginal product; as a consequence, better-endowed individuals would earn higher wages. Otherwise, each firm (supposed to be risk-neutral, for simplicity) will offer the same wage to all workers, based on the productivity of a worker endowed with the expected level of talent in the population.

The absence of perfect information regarding individual ability introduces potential conflicts of interest among the agents, thus rendering self-declarations non-trustable. On the one hand, there is an inherent conflict between firm and worker, since the latter has an incentive to self-declare the highest endowment of talent, given the impossibility of checking it; conversely, the former (the firm) has an incentive to deny the presence of talent, since its declaration cannot be disproved. On the other hand there is a conflict between workers with different endowments of talent. Let us suppose the existence of only two types of workers: the 'talented', with talent endowment equal to A_2, and the 'not talented', with talent endowment equal to A_1, $A_1 < A_2$.[42] The first group represents the fraction n of the labour force, while the second reaches the complementary fraction $(1 - n)$. From past experience, we presume that firms know the talent distribution in the population – that is, the parameters A_1, A_2 and n. In the absence of any further information, the best strategy for the firm is to assume that each worker is randomly extracted from the pool of job seekers and that his/her talent endowment corresponds to the expected value in the population (equal to sample mean $\overline{A} = nA_2 + (1 - n)A_1$). As a consequence, the firm will offer an identical wage to all job seekers; if φ represents the marginal revenue of talent, competition between firms will push the unique wage rate to the point indicated by the following condition:

$$\overline{W} = \varphi\overline{A} = \varphi[nA_2 + (1 - n)A_1] \tag{6.17}$$

According to equation (6.17), talented workers receive less than their actual productivity; if talent were freely observable, they would get $W_2 = \varphi A_2 > \overline{W}$. Conversely, less talented workers take advantage of the absence of information, since under perfect information they would get $W_1 = \varphi A_1 < \overline{W}$. Thus, the absence (or the high cost) of the observability of talent leads to a compression of the wage distribution (in the limiting case resulting in the disappearance of wage differentials), with implicit subsidisation from talented workers towards non-talented ones. If the former group of workers could obtain the recognition of their true endowment from the firm, they would not hesitate in pursuing it, thus raising their own wages and implicitly lowering the wages of the latter group.

In such a context, two alternative interpretations of educational attainment have been proposed, as responses to asymmetrical information. The first interpretation regards the achievement of education as a signal that workers give to firms, in order to reveal their true endowment of talent.[43] Suppose that a firm offers a wage schedule such that the offered wage rises more than proportionally with the amount of obtained education:

$$W_i = \beta(S_i) \cdot S_i, \beta' > 0, i = 1, 2 \qquad (6.18)$$

where β can be thought of as the marginal return on education, with the counter-intuitive property that $\beta(S_2) > \beta(S_1)$ for any $S_2 > S_1$.[44] If the firm's conjecture is confirmed by individuals choosing different amounts of education for different talent endowments (thus conforming to their future employer expectations) then acquiring education constitutes an effective signal, able to overcome the inefficiencies introduced by imperfect information.

However, the necessary (but not sufficient) condition for a potential signal to become an actual one is that signalling costs are negatively correlated with an individual's unknown talent.[45] In other words, we are requiring the unitary cost of education for talented individuals to be lower than the corresponding cost for less talented ones. In addition, we require the offered wage schedule to encourage talented individuals to acquire education (yielding a net gain for them), in the meanwhile discouraging less talented people from imitating talented ones in acquiring education (thus associating a net loss with this choice). More formally, a separating equilibrium requires the amount of signalling emitted by each type of individual to be a dominant strategy against all the other strategies available. Let us assume that individual preferences are simply described by

$$V_i = W_i(S_i) - \gamma(S_i, A_i), \gamma_S > 0, \gamma_A < 0, i = 1, 2 \qquad (6.19)$$

where $\gamma(S_i, A_i)$ represents the direct and indirect costs of achieving the S_i amount of schooling for an individual with talent A_i. The cost of attendance clearly increases with more schooling and decreases with more talent. This assumption implies that, for any amount of education, talented individuals face a lower cost than less talented ones.[46]

Given the wage offer described by equation (6.18), less talented people do not find it profitable to imitate the behaviour of talented people whenever $W_2 - \gamma(S_2, A_1) \leq W_1 - \gamma(S_1, A_1)$, where the first term indicates the utility of emitting the highest signal S_2 for a less talented individual (denoted by his/her talent endowment A_1), while the second term corresponds to the utility associated to emitting the signal S_1. In order to obtain a separating equilibrium, we also need a participation constraint for talented individuals, who have to find it convenient to give off the signal under the wage offer (6.18). This corresponds to the condition $W_2 - \gamma(S_2, A_2) > W_1 - \gamma(S_1, A_2)$. By combining the two previous inequalities, we get

$$\gamma(S_2, A_1) - \gamma(S_1, A_1) \geq W_2 - W_1 > \gamma(S_2, A_2) - \gamma(S_1, A_2) \qquad (6.20)$$

Condition (6.20) shows that the wage differential proposed by the firm must lie in an intermediate position, between the cost differentials faced by a less talented individual when considering the possibility of emitting the signal S_2 and the corresponding cost differential faced by a talented individual. When the left-hand side of inequality (6.20) is violated, less talented individuals will find it convenient to imitate talented individuals in achieving the amount S_2 of education; in contrast, when the right-hand side is violated, talented individuals will not find it convenient to emit the signal, and they will become indistinguishable from the less talented ones.

This situation can be visualised with the help of figure 6.2, where we have drawn two indifference curves corresponding to the two types of individuals, with flatter indifference curves being associated with more talented people. The two straight lines exiting from the origin describe the wage offer by the firm; the first line applies to individuals choosing the amount S_1 of education, while the second schedule refers to those choosing S_2 of education. Conditional on the firm's wage offer, less talented individuals will maximise their utility by selecting the amount S_1 of education (point **A**), while talented individuals will achieve their maximum choosing S_2 of education (point **B**).[47] This corresponds to a separating equilibrium, where no agent has an incentive to deviate: if talented individuals were to select education S_1^*, they would end up on a lower indifference curve; similarly, if less talented individuals were to choose S_2^* they would not improve their welfare. Finally, a firm offering a wage exceeding $W_i = \beta(S_i) \cdot S_i$ would make losses, despite being able to attract only talented individuals.[48] We have, therefore, shown that an appropriate wage announcement by firms is able to induce individuals to self-sort according to their unobservable characteristics,

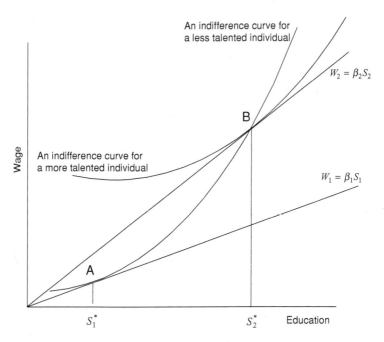

Figure 6.2 The signalling equilibrium

thus revealing their hidden information. The workers' choices confirm firms' conjectures, thus satisfying the equilibrium requirements.

It is important to remember that, in this framework, acquiring education does not increase a worker's productivity per se; nevertheless, education is positively correlated with productivity thanks to its information-revealing property. Signalling models are characterised by the informed side of the market (the workers in the present case) acting as first mover, with the uninformed side, the firms, forming (and/or updating) their expectations on the relationship between education and productivity, and consequently offering wage contracts analogous to those reported in equation (6.18).[49] Despite the revelation of hidden information through educational choice, this equilibrium is a constrained Pareto-efficient equilibrium, since resources are wasted in emitting the signal.

A different situation emerges when we abandon the assumption of talent-based differences in the cost of educational achievement; what types of equilibria emerge in this framework? Let us assume the existence of a screening device, able to reveal the unobservable information.

Accessing the screening has a fixed cost equal to γ for any type of agent; afterwards, information concerning the examined agent becomes freely available to anyone. Some aspects of the schooling experience, and in particular some crucial turning points (such as completing compulsory education, graduating from high school, taking tests for college admission), may conform to this view.[50] As in the previous case we assume the existence of only two types of agents, talented (type A_2) and non-talented (type A_1). Their existence and their distribution in the population is common knowledge.

Given the availability of an information-revealing tool, firms announce a different wage policy: they will pay a wage $W_2 = \varphi A_2$ to any worker accepting the screening and shown to be talented, and a wage $W_1 = \varphi A_1$, $W_1 < W_2$, otherwise. If no worker agrees to be screened, firms operate effectively under perfect ignorance about the talent attributes of job applicants, and therefore will pay an identical wage to everyone, based on the mean ability in the population (as described by equation (6.17)). If firms are paying an identical wage to all workers, more talented people have an incentive to stand out from the others, in order to appropriate the implicit rents associated with their endowment. However, they will not find it convenient to undertake the screening if

$$\gamma > W_2 - W_1 = \varphi(A_2 - A_1) \tag{6.21}$$

If the cost of screening rises above a certain level, there is no incentive to use it because the net income for a talented worker ($W_2 - \gamma$) exceeds the income that he/she would be granted even under the worst situation (such as being misclassified as less talented). When inequality (6.21) is satisfied, we observe a single wage paid to all workers, despite their different (but unobservable) quality. This situation is classified as a *pooling equilibrium.*

We now consider an opposite situation, where the screening cost is sufficiently low to satisfy

$$\gamma < W_2 - \overline{W} = \varphi A_2 - \varphi[n A_2 + (1 - n) A_1]$$
$$= \varphi(1 - n)(A_2 - A_1) \tag{6.22}$$

In such a case talented people find it convenient to afford the cost of screening in order to signal their ability endowment to the firm. Whenever some workers undertake the screening, the firm reduces the wage paid to the remaining workers to W_1, under the presumption that they are less talented. This will convince some reluctant and talented workers to undertake the screening. For a sufficiently low cost of screening, the information is revealed and a separating equilibrium emerges.

Next we need to know what happens in the intermediate case, when the screening cost lies in the interval

$$W_2 - \overline{W} < \gamma < W_2 - W_1 \qquad (6.23)$$

or, alternatively,

$$\overline{W} > W_2 - \gamma > W_1 \qquad (6.24)$$

In this case talented workers do not have an incentive to submit themselves to the screening, for their net income is reduced. Nevertheless, firms can force them to do so by threatening to consider all workers less talented, therefore reducing the general wage from $\overline{W}$ to W_1. Once again we obtain a separating equilibrium, which is, however, Pareto inferior to the pre-existing pooling equilibrium. In fact, all workers experience a wage reduction, because talented workers obtain $W_2 - \gamma < \overline{W}$ and less talented workers receive $W_1 < \overline{W}$.[51] This is due to the specific assumption we made at the beginning of the section, where we considered the resources spent to acquire education as wasted.

We can sum up the different cases by stating that, under asymmetric information, the ability to screen (to be interpreted as either a cost of schooling or a cost of on-the-job training and selection) is associated with multiple equilibria, parameterised over the cost of screening γ. However, unlike previous results, the demand for education does not vary continuously with its price. This is due to the fact that the ability to screen improves the quality of matching (unobservable) talents to job opportunities, at the cost of greater earnings inequality. Indeed, there is an underlying conflict about the value of information. Talented individuals (type-2 agents) have an interest in seeing the recognition of their endowment, in order to raise their market value. For different reasons, a single firm also has the same interest, conditional on being able to conceal the information: if better workers can be identified without public recognition of the sighting, they can be allocated to more appropriate jobs, securing the extra profit associated with the productivity difference ($W_2 - \overline{W}$). However, as soon as the information is disclosed to the public, competition among firms drives the extra profit to zero, and talented workers obtain a fair reward for their talent endowment.

Things are slightly different under the case of imperfect symmetric information – namely when both workers and firms cannot freely observe the talent endowment. If workers are risk-averse they will never accept being screened, since they do not want to incur the risk of wage reduction once identified as 'less endowed'. In fact, indicating with $U(W), U' > 0, U'' < 0$ the risk-averse worker preferences, we know that

$$U(\overline{W}) = U(nW_2 + (1-n)W_1) > nU(W_2 - \gamma)$$
$$+(1-n)U(W_1 - \gamma) \tag{6.25}$$

Inequality (6.25) tells us that individuals always refuse to be screened even in the case of a zero cost of screening. It may be that they are induced to afford the screening only if they are subsidised to do so (as in the case of $\gamma < 0$). If firms have to meet the expense of screening, the assumptions we introduce over the shape of their objective function become crucial.[52]

There are several objections that can be made to this approach. The most immediate one is that we do not observe an empirical equivalent of what we have termed 'screening'. If the term has to be taken as equivalent to 'educational progression' then, typically, it provides an imprecise assessment of individual abilities. No employer will base his/her offered wage on the grades obtained in a specific subject! In addition, ability is a multidimensional concept, and different school subjects typically call into play different types of abilities (creativity, logic, expressivity, and so on). If screening has to be taken as an 'admission test' for job applicants, it seems implausible that firms should base their entire wage policy on these results, when they may hire a worker on a temporary basis and test him/her directly on the job. The same type of objection applies to regarding screening as being equivalent to 'possessing a school diploma': why should a firm rely on an educational certificate released by a college that is often unknown once it has the opportunity to test the worker directly?

With respect to the empirical validity of the signalling hypothesis, and particularly to the relative importance of the signalling versus human capital explanations, we find in the literature several attempts to discriminate between the two. Starting from the idea that, in a signalling perspective, education is worthless whenever no screening is required, earlier attempts focused on sectoral differences in the return on education (Layard and Psacharopoulos, 1974). Similarly, significant differences in returns on education between employees and the self-employed are compatible with the idea that self-employment does not require any screening at the entrance to the job.[53] However, as clearly recognised by Riley (2001), in cross-sectional analysis the human capital and the signalling/screening approaches are observationally identical, since both are based on the assumption that individuals optimally select the amount of education that will maximise their expected utility, and that firms reward education because it is associated with greater productivity. In addition, empirical tests based on sample splitting are not robust against sample selection bias.

A different approach has been followed by Riley (1979) and Groot and Oosterbeek (1994), among others. The first author considers the fact that, within a sorting framework, extra information about worker productivity (through admission tests or job tenure) reduces the importance of education as a signal. His results are consistent with a sorting model based on unobservable ability, but also with self-sorting based on different degrees of risk aversion. In addition, he finds few differences between acquiring and not acquiring qualifications (an absence of sheepskin effects), providing additional support to the human capital hypothesis. The second paper focuses on the different information content possessed by years of education when distinguishing repeated, skipped or drop-out years. They exploit the idea that repeating one year should have a non-negative effect on wages in the human capital approach, and a negative effect according to the screening model. The opposite situation applies to skipping years. Using Dutch data, they find an absence of impact from repeated years and a negative impact from skipping years, both results pointing towards the human capital approach.

A more ingenious approach has been to follow a route similar to the natural experiment approach. Lang and Kropp (1986) start from the assumption that ability differentials give rise to a separating equilibrium based on a continuum of ability classes, and make the following observation (p. 613): 'In any sorting model the wage associated with a given level of education depends on the innate ability of the individuals who obtain that level of education ... Suppose then that for some reason a group of (lower-ability) workers who previously would have left school after education $(s - 1)$ remain in school through s. Since the average ability among workers with schooling s declines, the wage associated with s declines. Consequently the benefit of obtaining $s + 1$ increases.' Building on this consideration, they propose a discriminatory test between the human capital and the screening approaches based on relative enrolment rates: according to the former approach, educational reforms affecting the school leaving age should affect only students who were previously prevented from attending, leaving all the others unaffected; vice versa, according to the latter approach, the entire distribution of enrolment is modified, because the informational content of different achievements is modified.[54] On similar lines, Bedard (2001) presents a model of sorting in which some of the agents are constrained from achieving education by reasons that are uncorrelated with ability (think of family income). In a threefold partition (dropping out, graduating from college and reaching university), college proximity corresponds to an exogenous variation that reduces the mean ability of the intermediate group, since it eases the access to college. Because of the reduction of the signalling value of the credentials of the intermediate group (graduates from high schools), an increase in dropping-out rates is expected (i.e. members of the first group), which cannot be accounted for by the standard human capital theory. She finds significant evidence for the sensitivity of ordered probit thresholds to college proximity in National Longitudinal Survey (NLS) data for individuals who completed their schooling experience in the late 1960s and early 1970s.

Overall, we may conclude this section by stating that education may have a return in the labour market as a signal for unobservable components. However, the empirical evidence in support of this view is not entirely convincing, and we should limit ourselves to saying that educational credentials convey information to potential employers who do not have the time or ability to assess all self-declared competences. But the information concerns much more the amount of knowledge incorporated by the job applicants than their unobservable skills.

6.5 On-the-job training

The return on education has to be assessed not only with respect to differences in average earnings but also in terms of lifelong earnings. Figure 1.3 in chapter 1 showed a typical age–earnings profile, which

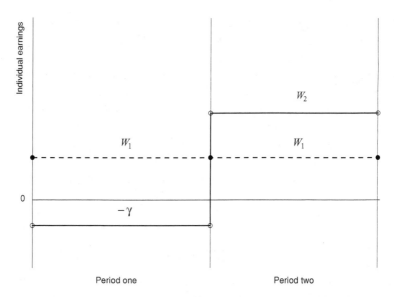

Figure 6.3 Alternative earnings profiles

is characterised by a hump-shaped contour, with the profiles differing according to the educational attainment obtained.[55] The rising portion comes to a standstill during the first half of the forties and then begins to decline subsequently, but the turning point is postponed for higher educational attainment, and in the case of tertiary education it is estimated to occur after the retirement age. As a consequence, the returns on education are not restricted to entry into the labour market, but appear along the entire working life of individuals.

From a theoretical viewpoint, it is challenging to provide an explanation of this dynamics. In the appendix to chapter 2 we have advanced an explanation based on the human capital investment theory. If we accept the idea that human capital can be acquired at any point in life (although the incentives decline with the shortening of the expected duration of life), and that it decays at a constant rate along the entire lifespan, we obtain the hump shape seen in figure 1.3: during the initial portion of life individuals devote all their available time to human capital investment (conditional on talent endowment and family background); when entering the labour market the amount of time devoted to human capital formation shrinks but does not disappear, thus helping to explain the upward-sloping portion of the line; but then the obsolescence of acquired knowledge sooner or later becomes dominant, and the downward sloping part of the profile appears.

Alternative explanations have been put forward for the upward trend in the earnings profile. The initial one invokes the existence of *learning by doing* (Arrow, 1962). If individual productivity is positively correlated with tenure because each worker improves his/her performance through practice in a job, competitive markets predict a positive correlation between age and earnings. A second explanation concerns the screening approach to the return on education: if the unobserved talent is gradually revealed by the observed on-the-job performance of the worker, firms may be willing to pay higher wages for more able workers, in order to retain them.[56] A third explanation combines the problem of revealing the hidden characteristics of the worker (the *talent allocation*) with the need to provide the right incentive to put effort in a context of imperfectly observable action (*objective alignment*). Promotions are, typically, a low-frequency, high-impact wage change that may be used by management to motivate and retain their personnel.[57] However, all these explanations have problems in explaining the declining segment, unless demotions and lay-offs are introduced as possibilities.

A fourth explanation, which we will discuss at some length in this section, extends the paradigm of human capital to the entire working life. If we consider that human capital can also be accumulated through job training (which is a mixture of formal schooling, work experience and interaction with senior colleagues), and we allow for positive correlation between human capital, productivity and wages, we obtain the upward portion of the age-earnings profile. When we then consider the decreasing marginal productivity of job training, sooner or later the accumulation of human capital ceases and the profile becomes flat. Eventually, obsolescence is responsible for the decline in earnings in the final stages of the working life.

Unlike schooling decisions, the job training decision involves two agents, the worker and the firm. It is not just that the cost of the training can be borne by one or the other, or shared between them, but also that the content of the training can be jointly determined. In sectors characterised by rapid technological change, competitiveness requires a rapid adaptation to new technologies, and the employed labour force is required to learn quickly how to operate with improved equipment. Both firm and worker have a common interest in this state of affairs, the former to enhance its competitiveness, the latter to lengthen the expected duration of employment through being indispensable to the production process. This attitude requires on both sides the expectation of a long-lasting labour relationship: if either one or the other side expects the labour contract to terminate soon (because of low wages, bad jobs, absence of firing costs, etc.), it is difficult for the human capital investment associated with on-the-job training to materialise.

Table 6.1 reports some measures of the diffusion of training in European firms. Apart from the wide variation across countries, which is correlated with the countries' technological level (and therefore with the level of GDP per capita[58]), it can be noted that the countries offering more opportunities for training are also the countries where the percentage of participating workers is higher: the (unweighted) sample correlation between 'offer' and 'participation' is 0.64. At the same time, most of the country differences are related to the structure of the vocational system: countries where vocational schooling is less pervasive[59] are countries where the participation and the intensity of job training are also low.

This aggregate evidence could, however, mix different sources of variation, including the gender composition of the labour force, the sectoral composition of employment, educational attainment, and so on. Table 6.2 reports information extracted from the 1996 wave of the European Community Household Panel, concerning male employees aged between thirty and sixty, working full-time in the non-agricultural private sector. From this table one may easily appreciate that training opportunities are not evenly distributed among workers: previous schooling seems complementary to subsequent training, which is also more frequent among high-rank occupations.

From a theoretical point of view, whenever we observe occurrences of training a crucial question can be asked about who is paying the cost. The cost of training incidence reported in table 6.1 includes direct costs (teachers, enrolment, materials) and personnel absence costs, with relative shares ranging from 78 per cent in direct costs for the United Kingdom to 62 per cent in absence costs for Spain. Direct costs can be paid either by the firm or by the worker, whereas when the training is imparted during working hours the opportunity cost is paid entirely by the firm. A useful distinction introduced by Becker is that between *perfectly general training* (general skills that are useful with other employers and that increase labour productivity by the same amount with all employers) and *perfectly specific training* (skills that

Table 6.1 *Selected indicators of training: Europe, 1999*

	Offer[a]	Participation[b]	Intensity[c]	Cost[d]	GDP per capita[e]
Austria	72	35	29	1.3	111.3
Belgium	70	54	31	1.6	106.5
Bulgaria	28	28	35	1.0	28.3
Czech Republic	69	49	25	1.9	59.1
Denmark	96	55	41	3.0	118.8
Estonia	63	28	31	1.8	38.7
Finland	82	54	36	2.4	100.7
France	76	51	36	2.4	99.7
Germany	75	36	27	1.5	106.4
Greece	18	34	39	0.9	66.1
Hungary	37	26	38	1.2	49.0
Ireland	79	52	40	2.4	112.3
Italy	24	47	32	1.7	103.4
Latvia	53	25	34	1.1	28.6
Lithuania	43	20	41	0.8	34.5
Luxembourg	71	48	39	1.9	188.8
Netherlands	88	44	37	2.8	114.6
Norway	86	53	33	2.3	129.0
Poland	39	33	28	0.8	39.0
Portugal	22	45	38	1.2	72.3
Romania	11	20	42	0.5	23.8
Slovenia	48	46	24	1.3	68.5
Spain	36	44	42	1.5	82.2
Sweden	91	63	31	2.8	105.2
United Kingdom	87	51	26	3.6	100.6

[a] Enterprises offering continuing training as a proportion of all enterprises (per cent).
[b] Participation rate in enterprises offering training courses (per cent)
[c] Participation hours per participant.
[d] Costs of training courses as a proportion of the total labour costs of all enterprises (per cent).
[e] per capita in Purchasing Power Standard (Europe15 = 100).
Source: Eurostat (2000).

Table 6.2 *The incidence of training: selected European countries, 1996*

	Percentage of individuals receiving on-the-job training
Country	
Austria	21.1
Belgium	19.9
France	15.5
Germany	19.9
Italy	6.7
Spain	11.8
United Kingdom	39.1
Sector	
Mining, manufacturing and utilities	15.0
Services	21.4
Individual characteristics	
Less than upper secondary education	7.7
Upper secondary education	18.4
More than upper secondary education	33.7
High-skilled occupations	31.0
Medium-skilled occupations	12.4
Low-skilled occupations	6.3
Total	**17.3**

Source: Bassanini and Brunello (2003).

increase the productivity of the worker only in his/her current job).[60] Examples of the first type are the ability to drive a car or use a computer, whereas examples of the second category are the ability to operate a specific piece of machinery or to use software developed purely for the company's needs. An increase in generic human capital raises the market value of a worker, whereas an increase in firm-specific human capital leaves his/her value unaffected for all firms other than the current employer.

It is easy to 'prove' that in a competitive labour market, where the ongoing wage reflects the average labour productivity, no firm will accept paying for the cost of training for general human capital, since it will be compelled by competitive forces to pay a wage corresponding to the augmented productivity of the worker, without being able to recover the training costs. Should it try to reduce the wage below the labour productivity, the trained worker would be hired by competitors, and the training investment would be lost. Seen from the point of view of competitors, the incentives operate in a complementary way: the best strategy is to wait for a worker to be trained by another firm, and then 'steal' him/her (a common practice, often referred to as *cherry-picking*). The aggregate outcome is that no firm will be available to invest in training for general human capital, and workers will be forced to meet the cost of training themselves. This does not necessarily require a direct monetary payment, since there are alternative ways to charge workers with the cost of their training: for example, think of apprenticeship contracts providing for a reduced wage during the training period. Whenever financial markets are imperfect and workers are liquidity-constrained (or risk-averse), the likely outcome is under-investment in training for general human capital. In contrast, if we consider investment in firm-specific human capital, a worker will be reluctant to pay the cost, since once out of the firm this investment will be wasted. In such a case, this investment will materialise if, and only if, the firm meets the cost.

Despite these strong theoretical predictions, in the real world we observe that firms quite often pay for the general training of their workers. A typical example is given by the training that takes place during working hours. To account for this phenomenon, there are two alternatives: either we introduce imperfect information on workers' ability (and therefore the training acts as a screening device, whereby the expected gain is given by improved information) or we abandon the paradigm of perfect competition in the labour market (if a firm has monopsonistic power, it will set the wage below productivity, thus recovering its training costs).[61]

While useful from a theoretical point of view, the distinction between general and specific human capital is also empirically vague. Take the case of skills that are sector-specific – neither firm-specific nor completely general. In addition, the generality of skills depends on the work organisation within a firm: multi-tasking assignments favour the development of general skills, whereas a rigid organisation tends to transform any task into a firm-specific one. The generality of training also depends on the external vocational system: the provision of official certification (as in the well-known German system) favours the adaptability of skills outside the firm where the training has taken place.[62] If a syndicate of firms offers the training, this reduces the competition between firms and increases the generality of skills; in addition, it also renders more likely the training in small-sized firms, which may be quite unwilling to invest in general human capital.

Table 6.3 shows the cross-country variety of institutional solutions to the training problem. National systems differ in terms of where training takes place (whether within firms or outside them, in external schools), who is financing it (the public authority, firms, workers, or any combination of them) and the potential existence of certification. A crucial factor is also given by the average educational attainment in the population: since training is more likely when educational attainment is higher, an educated labour force constitutes a favourable precondition for the development of general and firm-specific skills.[63] Eventually, the way in which the secondary school system is organised matters: some educational systems are characterised by early tracking (Germany, Italy), while others provide comprehensive education (United Kingdom, United States). If tracking reduces workers' adaptability then some national systems may be more favourable to general human capital formation than others.[64]

6.6 Measuring the return on education

In the previous section we discussed alternative explanations for the positive correlation between acquired education and earnings. If we are interested in measuring the extent of monetary returns (for example, to make comparisons among individuals from different age cohorts, birth regions or countries), we resort to a general principle in financial economics, which states that the internal rate of return of any investment project corresponds to the discount rate that equalises the (discounted) flow of revenues to the (discounted) flow of outlays.[65] In order to explain this general principle, we consider the simplest case of a person living for just two periods and facing the following alternative: either not going to school and working in both periods as an unskilled worker, obtaining a wage W_1 (assumed constant in both periods); or attending school with a direct cost γ in the first period, and working as a skilled worker in the second period for a wage W_2.[66] It is obvious that there exists a monetary incentive to acquire education if, and only if,

Table 6.3 National training systems

Training system	Countries	Essential features
Apprenticeship	Germany, United Kingdom (before 1980), Netherlands	Co-determination (firms, trade unions, local authorities) Cost-sharing Skill certification Good results in schooling activities taken into account when firms hire apprentices
Within-firm training	Japan	Life employment reduces job turnover Firms provide both general and specific training On-the-job training Skills are homogeneous at school exit
Vocational training in state-run schools Training financed by specific taxes on firms	Sweden, Norway, United Kingdom (after 1980) France, Australia	Funding from the central government Training contents are defined at school level The burden is spread across a wide range of taxpayers No guarantee that low-skill workers and/or employees in small-sized firms will be trained
Vocational training in state-run schools and/or on-the-job training	United States, Canada	Greater variety in training possibilities Lack of nationwide certification Most of the training is firm-specific

Source: Adapted from Lynch (1994, table 2).

$W_2 > W_1$. The different wage profiles associated with these two alternatives are reported in figure 6.3 (p. 186), where the dashed line (denoted by the • bullet) corresponds to the unskilled profile, whereas the solid line (denoted by the ○ bullet) describes the skilled profile.

If now we want to find what the internal rate of return associated with the choice of attending school in the first period is, we have to take into account costs and benefits. The former are given by the algebraic sum of direct and indirect costs ($\gamma + W_1$), the latter are given by the skilled–unskilled wage premium $\Delta W = W_2 - W_1$. Since the costs are incurred in the first period, while the benefits accrue in the second period, we discount the benefits with the discount rate $(1 + \beta)$. By equalising costs and benefits we get

$$\gamma + W_1 = \frac{W_2 - W_1}{1 + \beta} \tag{6.26}$$

or, alternatively, we introduce the *net present value* of the investment project associated with attending school, defined as

$$NPV = \underbrace{-(\gamma + W_1)}_{\text{costs}} + \underbrace{\frac{W_2 - W_1}{1 + \beta}}_{\text{benefits}} \tag{6.27}$$

The internal rate of return is given by the value of β that satisfies equality (6.26) (or, equivalently, that sets $NPV = 0$); that is

$$\beta = \frac{W_2 - W_1}{\gamma + W_1} - 1 \tag{6.28}$$

The equation (6.28) shows that the return on education rises with the benefits (the numerator) and declines with the costs (the denominator). The general principle can, obviously, be extended to a multiperiod context. If we consider the case of a given school order lasting m years, a direct cost of school attendance γ_t, wage rates associated with the choice of not attending or attending s years of schooling (respectively, W_t and W_t^s) and a working life lasting n years, the return on education associated with school attendance β satisfies

$$\sum_{t=1}^{s} \left[\frac{\gamma_t + W_t}{(1 + \beta)^{t-1}} \right] = \sum_{t=s+1}^{n} \left[\frac{W_t^s - W_t}{(1 + \beta)^{t-1}} \right] \tag{6.29}$$

Equation (6.29) is the multiperiod equivalent of equation (6.26).[67] Since it includes only the costs and benefits borne by an individual undertaking the choice of school attendance, β represents a *private rate of return* that does not take into account the costs and benefits accruing to the society as a whole.[68] If we now add to the left-hand side of equation (6.29) the cost E_t borne by the public budget for school attendance, and to the right-hand side the potential benefits associated with a better-educated labour force, we obtain a measure of the *social rate of return* β_{soc}:

$$\sum_{t=1}^{s} \left[\frac{\gamma_t + W_t + E_t}{(1 + \beta_{soc})^{t-1}} \right] = \sum_{t=s+1}^{n} \left[\frac{W_t^s - W_t}{(1 + \beta_{soc})^{t-1}} \right] + externality$$

(6.30)

It is evident that $(1 + \beta_{soc}) < (1 + \beta_{priv})$ whenever there exists public subsidisation of education (i.e. $E_t > 0$) and externalities are hard to grasp. However, if, for example, growth externalities are significant (because a better-educated labour force is associated with higher participation rates and lower unemployment rates, and/or allows for the introduction of more productive technologies), the social rate of return may exceed the private one.

The calculations implied by equations (6.29) and (6.30) (often called the *full* or *integral method*) are cumbersome, since they require information about educational expenditures and wages over the entire lifespan of individuals. For this reason, whenever possible economists have resorted to alternative methods to measure the private return on education. The most common strategy is based on estimates of the determinants of individual earnings (typically referred to as the *Mincerian function*, from Jacob Mincer (1974), who originally proposed it). Table 6.4 shows private and social rates of return, computed under alternative methods. It is easy to see that private returns consistently exceed social ones, with a gap that widens with higher school orders. In addition, in accordance with the decreasing marginal productivity assumption, these returns tend to decline with the increase in the level of educational attainment in the population.

In order to show the implicit assumptions underlying the earning function approach, let us go back to equation (6.29) and introduce the following hypotheses:

(i) direct private costs for acquiring education are mainly given by forgone incomes (alternatively, labour incomes obtained during the educational career just match the direct costs of attendance – $\gamma_t = 0, t = 1, \ldots, s$);

(ii) the working life has to be identical for everyone, irrespective of the number of years of school attendance.[69]

Table 6.4 *Returns on education, private and social: regional averages of published estimates*

	Integral method						Earning function	
	Private return on education			Social return on education			Average years of education	Private return
	Primary	Secondary	Tertiary	Primary	Secondary	Tertiary		
Sub-Saharan Africa	41.3	26.6	27.8	24.3	18.2	11.2	5.9	13.4
Asia	39.0	18.9	19.9	19.9	13.3	11.7	8.4	9.6
Europe/Middle East and North Africa	17.4	15.9	21.7	15.5	11.2	10.6	8.5	8.2
Latin America and the Caribbean	26.2	16.8	19.7	17.9	12.8	12.3	7.9	12.4
OECD countries	21.7	12.4	12.3	14.4	10.2	8.7	10.9	6.8
World	29.1	18.1	20.3	18.4	13.1	10.9	8.4	10.1

Source: Psacharopoulos (1994, tables 1 and 4). Figures are percentages.

In such a case, equation (6.29) can be re-expressed as

$$\sum_{t=1}^{s}\left[\frac{W_t}{(1+\beta)^{t-1}}\right]=\sum_{t=s+1}^{n+s}\left[\frac{W_t^s-W_t}{(1+\beta)^{t-1}}\right] \qquad (6.31)$$

or, rearranging terms,

$$\sum_{t=1}^{n}\left[\frac{W_t}{(1+\beta)^{t-1}}\right]=\sum_{t=s+1}^{n+s}\left[\frac{W_t^s}{(1+\beta)^{t-1}}\right] \qquad (6.32)$$

Equation (6.32) compares the earnings profile of an uneducated worker (the left-hand side) with the profile of an educated worker (the right-hand side); it suggests that, in order to observe both choices in a population of otherwise identical individuals, at the margin they must offer the same returns.

Adding the further hypothesis of:
(iii) constant wages across the life cycle,[70]
  equation (6.32) can be rewritten as

$$W=\frac{W^s}{(1+\beta)^s} \qquad (6.33)$$

Taking the logarithms of both sides and rearranging terms, we get

$$\log(W^s)=\log(W)+s\cdot\log(1+\beta)\cong\log(W)+s\cdot\beta \qquad (6.34)$$

Recalling that log differences approximate percentage variations, equation (6.34) indicates that percentage wage differences between two individuals who attended a different number of years of schooling must be proportional to the gap in years of schooling, and the proportionality factor corresponds to the internal rate of return.[71] Equation (6.34) is known in the literature as the base of the *Mincerian equation*, and it allows the direct estimation of the rate of return on education using data from a representative sample of the working population (once work experience is taken into account). If we can identify the factors that systematically affect individual earnings independently from acquired education (for example, age, gender, ethnicity, marital status, local labour market conditions, residential area, and so on), and we generically indicate them with the vector Z_i, equation (6.34) can be replaced by

$$\log\left(W_i^s\right)=\alpha'Z_i+\beta\cdot s_i+\varepsilon_i \qquad (6.35)$$

Equation (6.35) indicates that the labour income of individual i depends on systematic factors Z_i affecting the sample population, on educational attainment s_i and on an idiosyncratic component ε_i, which cannot be predicted by an external observer (such as chance or unobservable ability).[72] Equation (6.35) is consistent with equation (6.34), since two generic and otherwise identical individuals i and j (such that $Z_i = Z_j$) exhibit an earnings gap that is systematically proportional to the difference in their educational attainment:

$$\log(W_i) - \log(W_j) = \beta \cdot s_i - \beta \cdot s_j + \varepsilon_i - \varepsilon_j$$
$$= \beta \cdot (s_i - s_j) + (\varepsilon_i - \varepsilon_j) \qquad (6.36)$$

By taking sample expectations on both sides of equation (6.36) one may retrieve a sample estimate of the return on education $\hat{\beta}$, but this invokes two further assumptions. The first is just a corollary of the previous statement of 'otherwise identical' individuals: if they are identical they face similar work opportunities, they possess identical abilities and therefore they experience the same return on education.[73] When this is not the case (i.e. when $\beta_i \neq \beta_j$), we can obtain only estimates of the returns for population subgroups, which are specifically affected by exogenous variations (see next section). The second assumption derives from extending the bilateral comparison between two generic educational attainments, s_i and s_j, to all potential comparisons, while maintaining the same return rate. This is equivalent to postulating a (semi-log) linear relationship between earnings and years of education, which does not seem contradicted by empirical evidence.[74] In a similar way, one may want to consider the role of work experience and/or job tenure as specific determinants of earnings. In order to take into account the inverted U-shaped wage–life profile, it has become common practice to estimate equation (6.35) in the following form:

$$\log\left(W_i^s\right) = \alpha' Z_i + \beta \cdot s_i + \theta_0 \cdot e_i + \theta_1 \cdot e_i^2 + \varepsilon_i \qquad (6.37)$$

where e_i measures the work experience of individual i. When this piece of information is absent in a data set, economists have resorted to the concept of potential experience (equal to age less schooling plus the starting age of schooling) or directly to age, to avoid potential collinearity with schooling. Independently from the way in which experience is measured, $(\theta_0 + 2\theta_1 \bar{e})$ represents the marginal return on experience

Table 6.5 *The return on education in Europe, mid-1990s (OLS estimates)*

	Men			Women		
	Potential experience	Actual experience	Age	Potential experience	Actual experience	Age
Austria (1995)	0.069	—	0.059	0.067	—	0.058
Denmark (1995)	0.064	0.061	0.056	0.049	0.043	0.044
Finland (1993)	0.086	0.085	0.072	0.088	0.087	0.082
France (1995)	0.075	—	0.057	0.081	—	0.065
Germany (West) (1995)	0.079	0.077	0.067	0.098	0.095	0.087
Greece (1994)	0.063	—	0.040	0.086	—	0.064
Ireland (1994)	0.077	0.068	0.050	0.105	0.100	0.089
Italy (1995)	0.062	0.058	0.047	0.077	0.070	0.061
Netherlands (1996)	0.063	0.057	0.045	0.051	0.042	0.037
Norway	0.046	0.045	0.037	0.050	0.047	0.044
Portugal (1994/95)	0.097	0.100	0.079	0.097	0.104	0.077
Spain (1994)	0.072	0.069	0.055	0.084	0.079	0.063
Sweden (1991)	0.041	0.041	0.033	0.038	0.037	0.033
Switzerland (1995)	0.089	0.088	0.075	0.092	0.086	0.082
United Kingdom (1994–96)	0.094	0.096	0.079	0.115	0.122	0.108
Mean	0.072	0.070	0.057	0.079	0.076	0.066

NB: The year in brackets is the sample year from which the estimates are obtained.
Source: Brunello, Comi and Lucifora (2001, table 4).

(at sample mean $\bar{e}$) and $\frac{\theta_0}{2\theta_1}$ the age at which the average individual achieves his/her maximum earnings during his/her working life. The way in which experience is measured has a direct impact on the measured return on education, as it can be assessed by looking at table 6.5, which reports OLS estimates of the return on education β under alternative definitions of work experience (potential experience, actual experience, when available, and age). In all cases the variable used for experience is considered in levels and squares.

We now move to the econometric problems posed by the attempt to estimate the return on education from equation (6.35) in a representative sample of a working population.

6.7 Estimating the return on education

A direct measure of the private return on education can easily be obtained by an OLS estimator applied to a sample of working individuals:

$$\hat{\beta}_{OLS} = \frac{Cov(\log(W), s)}{Var(s)} \tag{6.38}$$

However, the pioneering paper by Griliches (1977) also warned that OLS estimates could be biased and inconsistent, and therefore unreliable for policy advice. Griliches disputed the – at that time – general opinion of an upward bias in OLS estimates, arguing for the equivalent possibility of a downward bias. More recently, Card (1999) has expressed the opinion that the downward and upward biases could almost offset each other, thus restoring some trust in OLS estimates.

Let us review the sources of potential bias, which we generically indicate as problems of regressor endogeneity.[75] We summarise the problem at hand with the following two equations:

$$s_i = \mu'\mathbf{Z}_i + \eta_i \tag{6.39}$$

$$\log(W_i) = \alpha'\mathbf{Z}_i + \beta \cdot s_i + \varepsilon_i \tag{6.40}$$

where $\mathbf{Z}_i$ is a vector of individual characteristics of individual i, s_i is the amount of education (measured by years of school attendance), W_i is individual earnings and η_i and ε_i are error components. We assume that $E(\mathbf{Z}_i\eta_i) = E(\mathbf{Z}_i\varepsilon_i) = 0$; that is, all individual characteristics but education are orthogonal with the residuals of equations (6.39) and (6.40). The problem of endogeneity in the case of the schooling variable s_i derives from its correlation with the residual η_i – that is, from $Cov(\varepsilon_i, \eta_i) \neq 0$. Whenever $Cov(\varepsilon_i, \eta_i) \neq 0$ applies, the OLS estimate of the return on education β is biased and inconsistent. Endogeneity comes from three potential sources: omitted variables, measurement errors and the heterogeneity of returns in the population (Griliches, 1977; Card, 1999).

The case of omitted variables potentially applies whenever the researcher is unable to control for family background and/or for individual ability, because both groups of variables could raise earnings independently from human capital variables (education, experience) and from other controls in the wage function. A typical example is given by unobservable ability: more talented persons achieve more education because it is easier for them to do so, and at the same time they are more productive when working. If we indicate individual ability with A_i, its omission implies that the error component in equation (6.40) consists of

$$\varepsilon_i = \delta A_i + \sigma_i \tag{6.41}$$

But, if ability also affects educational attainment, we have

$$\eta_i = \lambda A_i + \omega_i \tag{6.42}$$

It is obvious from (6.41) and (6.42) that $Cov(\varepsilon_i, \eta_i) \neq 0$, thus providing biased estimates of the β coefficient; in fact, from (6.38) we see

$$
\begin{aligned}
\hat{\beta}_{OLS} &= \frac{Cov(\log(W), s)}{Var(s)} = \frac{Cov(\alpha'Z + \beta s + \varepsilon, s)}{Var(s)} \\
&= 0 + \beta \frac{Cov(s, s)}{Var(s)} + \frac{Cov(\varepsilon, \mu'Z + \eta)}{Var(s)} \\
&= \beta + \frac{Cov(\delta A + \sigma, \lambda A + \omega)}{Var(s)} = \beta + \delta\lambda \frac{Var(A)}{Var(s)} \neq \beta
\end{aligned}
\tag{6.43}
$$

It is easy to see that the sign of the bias depends on the signs of δ and λ. The first one is expected to be positive (abler individuals are more productive, and therefore better rewarded), while the latter has an uncertain sign. On the one hand, it could be positive, since more intelligent and disciplined persons also perform more ably as students, thus achieving longer schooling. In such a case, the OLS estimate will be upwardly biased. However, we could also have the case of a negative λ coefficient, whenever better-endowed individuals face a higher opportunity cost in attending school, and they may end up leaving school earlier. In such a case, the OLS estimate will be downwardly biased. Similarly, ambiguous conclusions arise when we take into account the fact that educational investment decisions are taken by parents. On the one hand, efficiency considerations suggest that parents want to invest more in more talented children (λ positive); on the other hand, equity considerations could produce the opposite result, whenever parents tend to compensate for the differences in ability endowments among their children with financial resources (λ negative). Overall, in the case of omitted variables related to ability and/or parental investment, a priori we are unable to assess the direction of the bias in the OLS estimate of the return on education.

Measurement error is a second source of endogeneity. It implies that the measure for educational attainment s that we observe is equal to the true measure s^* except for an error component $\chi \sim (0, \sigma_\chi^2)$; that is,

$$s_i = s_i^* + \chi_i \tag{6.44}$$

If we have $\sigma_\chi^2 > 0$, the OLS estimate of β is biased and inconsistent. In fact,

$$
\begin{aligned}
\hat{\beta}_{OLS} &= \frac{Cov(\log(W), s)}{Var(s)} = \frac{Cov(\alpha'\mathbf{Z} + \beta s - \beta\chi + \varepsilon, s)}{Var(s)} \\
&= 0 + \beta\frac{Cov(s, s)}{Var(s)} - \beta\frac{Cov(\chi, s^* + \chi)}{Var(s^* + \chi)} + 0 \\
&= \beta\left(1 - \frac{Var(\chi)}{Var(s^*) + Var(\chi)}\right) < \beta
\end{aligned}
\tag{6.45}
$$

The factor $\frac{Var(s^*)}{Var(s^*) + Var(\chi)}$ is indicated in the literature as the *reliability factor* of observed schooling.[76] In such a case, OLS estimates will be downwardly biased, the extent of the bias depending on the magnitude of the variance of the measurement error.[77]

Finally, the third source of bias derives from the heterogeneity of the coefficient to be estimated in the population. According to Card (1995), there are two potential sources of such heterogeneity. The first derives from the fact that differences in abilities are reflected in differences in productivities, such that abler individuals face a higher return schedule for an identical amount of education (*the ability bias*). The second comes from the fact that, under financial market imperfections, differences in family backgrounds imply different marginal costs in acquiring education, so that children from poorer families face a higher cost for education (*the cost bias*). The consequence of both distortions is that the subset of the population with low educational attainment will be composed of individuals with lower returns (less able) and by individuals facing higher costs (poorer background). Since the underlying model implies that each individual will optimally select the amount of education that will equate his/her expected return to his/her marginal cost, the population estimate of the return on education will depend on sub-group composition. If the group of less able individuals prevails, we observe a positive correlation between education and error component ε in the wage function, and therefore the OLS estimate will be upwardly biased. Otherwise, when the group of individuals from poorer families prevails, the opposite situation will occur, and we will observe a downward bias.

An application of the last case deals with the problem of sample distortion due to participation decision. When we regress labour income onto educational attainment, we are typically including the population sub-sample holding a paid job. But what about when participation in the labour market is affected by sample selection? A typical case is given by the female component in the labour supply. If only abler women enter the labour market, the estimate of the return on education is upwardly biased with respect to an average effect for the entire population. An econometric technique to deal with this distortion has been proposed by Heckman (1979), and is based on the idea of modelling the selection process.[78] The crucial issue following this approach is the possibility of modelling the participation decision in an (at least partially) independent way from the determinants of the return on education. In the absence of this identifying restriction, the decision to participate is indistinguishable from an econometric point of view, the sample selection problem cannot be taken into account properly, and least square estimates of the return on education cannot be used to make inferences for the entire population.

Notes

1. There are several reviews of this literature about the return on education, and particularly on the causal effect of education on earnings: among the most recent ones, see Card (1999, 2001), Bowles, Gintis and Osborne (2001a) and Harmon, Oosterbeek and Walker (2003). Earlier references can be found in Willis (1986).
2. See Ashenfelter and Rouse (1998, 2000) for an analysis of an American sample of twins, and Mulvey, Miller and Martin (1997) for an Australian one. Additional references are to be found in Harmon, Oosterbeek and Walker (2003).

3. Hence the conclusion from the traditional twins model is that the estimated return on schooling for males of 7.1 per cent is comprised of 2.3 per cent due to the 'true' returns on schooling, 4.2 per cent due to the effect of family background and 0.7 per cent due to the influence of genetic factors (Mulvey, Miller and Martin, 1997, p. 130). Similar conclusions are reached by Ashenfelter and Rouse (2000): 'Although part of the correlation between income and schooling may be due to family background characteristics, the intrafamily correlation between income and schooling indicates that most of the relationship between income and schooling is due to something else.' They report an ability bias in the order of one-fourth of the estimated return of 8 per cent per year, which compensates almost exactly for measurement errors in schooling.

4. This is also consistent with the findings by Cameron and Heckman (2001): 'It is the long-run factors that promote scholastic ability that explain most of the measured gap in schooling attainment and not the short-run credit constraints faced by students of college-going age that receive most of the attention in popular policy discussions' (p. 490).

5. Ashenfelter and Rouse (1998) estimate a rate of return between 10 per cent and 12 per cent using individual estimates, and a rate between 7 per cent and 10 per cent using differences between twins. The estimated correlation between family ability and returns (the γ coefficient) is found to be significant, but is sometimes positive and at other times negative. They take the negative occurrence as evidence for the compensatory role of schooling in reducing the impact of natural ability.

6. Mulvey, Miller and Martin (1997) state that the correlation between self-reported education and the sibling's report is about 0.7, suggesting the presence of significant measurement errors, which lower by almost one percentage point the return on education. See section 6.7 below for further discussion.

7. However, the list of individual characteristics X_i must include all the potential variables that may affect both education and earnings (such as cognitive ability, motivation, and so on). If this is not the case the least square estimate will remain biased, as the schooling coefficient β will capture some of the effects that would otherwise be attributed to the omitted variable. See Harmon, Oosterbeek and Walker (2003).

8. More complete surveys can be found in Card (1999) and Harmon, Oosterbeek and Walker (2003).

9. See Card (2001).

10. Trostel, Walker and Wolley (2002) find a similar order of magnitude when comparing IV and OLS estimates for a sample of twenty-eight countries over the period 1985 to 1995, using parental and spouse education as instruments.

11. 'These results suggest that changes in the institutional structure of the educational system can affect the mapping between individual ability and educational outcomes, leading to a violation of assumptions such as independence or homoskedasticity needed for a conventional IV (instrumental variable) estimator to yield a consistent estimate of the average marginal return on education' (Card, 2001, p. 1140). See also the evidence reported in table 6.1 (p. 189).

12. 'When the instrument is formed on the basis of membership of a treatment group the IV estimate of the return to schooling is the difference in expected log earnings between the control group and the treatment group, divided by the difference in expected schooling for the two groups. This implies that if all individuals in the population have the same marginal return the IV estimate is a consistent estimate of the average marginal rate of return. However, if the return to schooling is allowed to vary across individuals the IV estimate is a weighted return, where the weights reflect the extent to which the subgroup is affected by the treatment or instrument. If only one subgroup is affected by the intervention, the IV estimator will yield the marginal rate of return for that subgroup' (Harmon, Hogan and Walker, 2003, p. 143). This is known in the literature as the LATE (local average treatment effect) estimator. It represents a possible explanation as to why the IV estimates exceed those obtained under OLS: see the discussion on this issue in Card (2001). Harmon, Hogan and Walker (2003) explicitly consider the possibility of heterogeneity of returns, using a random coefficient estimator, without finding significant differences between these estimates and standard least square ones.

13. In the same vein of natural experiments, a growing literature on randomised experiments in educational resources shows that earnings are affected by the schooling experiences of agents. For a cursory but enlightening review of this literature, see Krueger (2002).

14. Freeman (1986) presents a nice example of the relevance of this problem with respect to the market for engineers in the United States, applying the cobweb model of delayed delivery to the market: when returns to engineering degrees are high, there is a strong incentive to take that subject, but as long as new graduates enter the market the relative return on this choice declines. The next generation of students abstains from engineering, and the return rises again.

15. Murphy and Welch (1992) combine supply factors (changes in the age and education structure of the population) and demand factors (increases in import competition from countries endowed with low-skill workforces) to account for the relative wage of skilled workers in the United States during the 1970s.

16. 'Put differently, the labour market institutions that push the wages of these workers up make their employers *the residual claimant* of the increase in productivity due to technology adoption, encouraging the adoption of technologies complementary to unskilled workers in Europe' (Acemoglu, 2003, pp. 128f.). The alternative implication is an increase in relative unemployment, also observed for unskilled workers in Europe.

17. One implication of this perspective is the negative correlation of the measured return on education and average educational attainment. Similarly, if workers with various levels of education are perfect substitutes, earnings inequality is also negatively associated with average educational attainment. Empirical evidence partially contradicts these propositions: see Bils and Klenow (2000) and Teulings and vanRens (2002).

18. Recent surveys of this literature are to be found in Krueger and Lindahl (2001) and in Sianesi and Van Reenen (2003).

19. 'An attractive feature of Mincer's model is that time spent in school (as opposed to degrees) is the key determinant of earnings, so data on years of schooling can be used to estimate a comparable return to education in countries with very different educational systems' (Krueger and Lindahl, 2001, p. 1103).

20. If w represents log-income (as in the standard Mincer model) then $\bar{w}$ represents its geometric mean.

21. Both propositions have been tested in the modern theory of growth. Lucas (1988) considers the stock of human capital of the representative agent as an input of the aggregate production function, assumes that human capital grows according to the share of time devoted to education and derives the steady-state conditions under which human capital and output grow at the same rate. Romer (1990a) includes the stock of human capital as a productive input, but technical progress expands the variety of the commodity at a rate that is a positive function of the existing stock of human capital. Thus, the two classes of models originated by these seminal models have different empirical implications: the growth of human capital (i.e. enrolment rates) in the Lucas model should affect output growth, while the stock of human capital should affect growth in the Romer model. See Aghion and Howitt (1998) for details and Gemmell (1996) fur further discussion.

22. Romer (1990b) uses the literacy rate as a proxy for the stock of human capital, finding that its initial level (but not its change) affects subsequent growth. Gemmell (1996) distinguishes between the educated labour force and the educated population, dividing education into three levels; he finds a positive impact from the initial stock of human capital on output growth, and a positive correlation between investment in

fixed capital (relative to output) and school enrolment rates. Primary education seems crucial for the poorest less developed country (LDC), while secondary education affects output growth in intermediate LDCs and tertiary education has an impact only on OECD countries.

23. As in the case of imperfect recall across twins, consider the case of possessing two noisy measures of true schooling S^*, $S_1 = S^* + \varepsilon_1$ and $S_2 = S^* + \varepsilon_2$, where $\varepsilon_i, i = 1, 2$ are measurement errors. If ε_1 and ε_2 are uncorrelated, the fraction of variability in S_1 due to measurement error can be estimated as $R_1 = \frac{Cov(S_1, S_2)}{Var(S_1)}$ (the reliability ratio).

24. 'This is an enormous return to investment in schooling, equal to three or four times the private return to schooling estimated within most countries. The large coefficient on schooling suggests the existence of quite large externalities from educational changes (Lucas 1988) or simultaneous causality in which growth causes greater educational attainment' (Krueger and Lindahl, 2001, p. 1120). However, their final conclusion is much more sceptical: 'The macroeconomic evidence of externalities in terms of technological progress from investments in higher education seems to us more fragile, resulting from imposing constant-coefficient and linearity restrictions that are rejected by the data' (p. 1130).

25. Sianesi and Van Reenen (2003) discuss the issue at length, but they also are rather cautious about the size of the externality effect: 'We join Topel (1999) – "the magnitude of the effect of education on growth is vastly too large to be interpreted as a causal force" – in finding too hard to view such huge effects as uniquely the result of economy-wide externalities generated by the increase in average educational attainment' (p. 188).

26. Altonji and Dunn (1996) analyse school quality, family background and IQ tests as determinants of (possibly heterogeneous) returns on education, using representative samples of Americans. They find that parental background (in particular the mother's education) is by far the most important factor, with IQ remaining significant and school quality measures (the student/teacher ratio, expenditure per student, teacher's salaries) exhibiting inconsistent effects. Murnane, Willet and Levy (1995) divide up the general contribution of education to earnings using information on specific subjects taken during college, finding a substantive increase in the return on mathematics scores. Murnane et al. (2001) include among the determinants of wages academic ability, the speed of problem solving and self-esteem, finding a positive contribution from all three measures. Green and Riddell (2003) propose a model in which earnings depend on cognitive and non-cognitive skills, which in turn are produced by education, experience and family background. By inference from signs and significance in a reduced form estimated on

Canadian data (which use literacy scores as measure for cognitive ability), they conclude that cognitive ability depends on years of education and parental background, but not on work experience.

27. The contribution to explained variance is negligible, the mean value of ΔR^2 being 0.01, its median equal to 0.007 with a range of variation between -0.15 and 0.04.

28. A classical exposition of the concept of 'human capital' is to be found in Becker (1993, chap. 2), where the author discusses the implication of greater human capital on fertility choices.

29. Weiss (1995) stresses the same point with different examples: better-educated people exhibit less absenteeism, are less likely to smoke, drink or make use of drugs, and are generally healthier. A firm minimising its absenteeism cost will be prepared to pay a wage premium in order to attract a better-educated labour force.

30. See the critique reported by Bowles and Gintis (1975).

31. There is a large literature on the adoption of efficiency wages under alternative assumptions: as a solution to the problem of adverse selection in hiring (Weiss, 1990); to reduce hiring costs and/or the turnover among employees (Layard, Nickell and Jackman, 1991, chap. 3). For contingent renewal models, two classical references are Shapiro and Stiglitz (1984) and Bowles (1985); a more recent one is Bowles, Gintis and Osborne (2001b). The obvious implications in terms of the inefficiency of contingent renewal and the effectiveness of the redistribution of property rights are discussed in the introductory chapter by Bowles and Gintis in Bowles, Gintis and Gustafsson (1993).

32. Bowles, Gintis and Osborne (2001a, 2001b) define these traits as *incentive-enhancing preferences*: 'Examples of such profitable individual traits are a low time discount rate, a predisposition to truth telling, identification with the objectives of the firm's owners and managers as opposed to the objectives of co-workers or customers, a high marginal utility of income, and a low disutility of effort' (2001a, p. 1145).

33. In a pioneering piece of research, Edwards (1977) interviewed groups of students and workers, using peer group rating to rank different personality traits. Starting from thirty-two predefined traits, he applied factor analysis, obtaining three factors: *rule* (rule orientation), *depend* (predictability and dependability) and *internalise* (personal identification with enterprise/school goals). Interestingly enough, these three factors exhibit high predictive ability with respect to wages (for workers) and school scores (for students), thus not contradicting the view that schools teach good attitudes that are valuable in the labour market.

34. Analogous models are also reported by Bowles and Gintis (2000) and by Bowles, Gintis and Osborne (2001b).

35. Think, for example, of supervisors monitoring continuously n workers; each worker is inspected a fraction $1/n$ of his/her working time.

36. This corresponds to his/her reaction (best reply) function for any given preannounced wage of the firm and any surveillance structure.

37. A more general formulation replaces u with $\varphi(u)$, $\varphi' > 0$. The second part of expression (6.9), $(W - b) \cdot u \cdot p \cdot (1 - \lambda)$, is indicated by Bowles as the *cost of job loss* that a firm can inflict on a worker by raising the wage rate or the monitoring (or contributing to a higher unemployment rate as a member of the capitalist class).

38. Bowles, Gintis and Osborne (2001b) show that a lower discount rate increases the value of the job rent that is shared between firm and worker when the worker is not shirking.

39. Since the ability to monitor can be job-specific, we have here – potentially – a theory of wage differentials. In addition, the model could also account for wage discrimination, whenever the firm is offering different combinations of 'wage-cum-surveillance' to otherwise identical workers (think of white and blue collars), in order to prevent the formation of a common front of wage claims. See the discussion in Bowles (1985).

40. Similarly: 'We say a parameter b in the employee's utility function is incentive-enhancing if an increase in b shifts the employee's best-response function upward, an increase in incentive-enhancing preferences leading an employee to work harder at every wage rate, holding all else constant' (Bowles, Gintis and Osborne, 2001b, p. 156). In our framework this corresponds to an inner shift of the iso-effort schedule.

41. Even in partial equilibrium analysis we can obtain a positive correlation between wages and education – i.e. a negative derivative of the optimal wage W with respect to α. By computing the first-order derivatives from the λ function in equation (6.12) and plugging them into equations (6.15) and (6.16), we find that $sing\left(\frac{\partial W}{\partial \alpha}\right) = sing(W(2m - 1) - b)$, which is always negative for $m < \frac{1}{2}$, which occurs whenever monitoring becomes extremely expensive.

42. At this point of the discussion it is totally irrelevant whether 'talent' indicates biological abilities or the effects of family background. What is relevant is that agents cannot modify their talent endowments, and that firms cannot freely observe them. In this respect, see the discussion in Goldberger and Manski (1995).

43. See the seminal paper by Spence (1973), in which the equilibrium is defined by self-fulfilling conjectures of the firm: 'Thus, in these terms an equilibrium can be thought of as a set of employer beliefs that generate offered wage schedules, applicant signalling decisions, hiring, and ultimately new market data over time that are consistent with the initial

beliefs' (p. 360). However his claim about the existence of a multiplicity of equilibria, some of which of the 'pooling' type (namely an identical wage paid to all workers), has been criticised as a general equilibrium solution, since it is not robust to deviations by competing firms. Thus, there would be a unique separating equilibrium, as described by Riley (2001, pp. 438–42).

44. This wage offer can be rationalised by the conjecture that talented individuals will obtain more education, and at the same time they are more productive because they are better endowed with talent. See also Weiss (1995) for a discussion of these implications. Belzil and Hansen (2002) find empirical evidence of a convex relationship between education and earnings that they interpret as evidence of 'ability bias'.

45. An implicit assumption of the literature about signalling is the absence of any other obstacles to the acquisition of education. In contrast, if financial markets are imperfect and individuals from poor families are liquidity-constrained then the signal becomes noisy, its informative content vanishes and the recipient is unable to recognise the true message: the absence of education could indicate either low talent endowment or poor family origins. See the discussions of equilibria under these circumstances in Giannini (2001). Bedard (2001) includes the possibility of financially constrained agents, but she assumes that firms can observe those who are prevented from acquiring education.

46. With reference to figure 6.2, this assumption corresponds to the fact that indifference curves for talented individuals are flatter than the corresponding curves for less talented people (often referred to in the literature as the 'single-crossing property').

47. In principle, less talented individuals are indifferent between points **A** and **B**. However, a firm could always leave out less talented individuals by shifting to the right of point **B**, along the $W = \beta_2 S$ line, since the utility reduction for less talented individuals is of first-order magnitude, whereas it is only of second-order magnitude for talented individuals. This also explains why it is possible to get a continuum of separating equilibria (see Riley, 2001, for discussion).

48. While the original model proposed by Spence (1973) allowed for the existence of pooling equilibria, Riley (2001) claims that this result is possible only as a partial equilibrium case, because under firm competition it always pay to deviate in order to attract the best workers, unless firms are already offering a wage associated with a zero-profit condition.

49. Even if formally a simultaneous game, it could be modelled as a sequential game (as in Spence, 1973, fig. 1, p. 359).

50. Stiglitz (1975) advances an interpretation of the entire educational system as a screening mechanism working for the benefit of potential employers. That paper inspires most of the following discussion.

51. However, the private return on screening for talented workers is still positive, because the right-hand side of inequality (6.23) can be rearranged as $\frac{W_2 - W_1}{\gamma} > 1$. By contrast, the social rate of return (which is a weighted average of private rates of return, including firms' profits) is negative.

52. When firms are risk-neutral and there are decreasing returns on ability in production, they have an incentive to pay for screening, since $\overline{W} > n W_2 + (1 - n) W_1$, where $W_i = f(A_i)$, $f' > 0$, $f'' < 0$. However, this depends on the relative cost of screening, which must not exceed the expected gain – i.e. $\gamma < \overline{W} - [n W_2 + (1 - n) W_1]$. Under the linearity assumption made in the text, $W_i = \varphi A_i$, $i = 1, 2$, this obviously never occurs.

53. See, for example, Brown and Sessions (1999), who investigate the employee/self-employment divide using Italian data, finding evidence supportive of the 'weak screening hypothesis': [W]hilst the primary role of schooling is to signal, it may also augment inherent productivity' (p. 397). However, their results do not take into account the fact that data on earnings and worked hours for the self-employed are much less reliable than the corresponding data for dependent employees.

54. Lang and Kropp (1986) find that compulsory attendance laws increase the educational attainment of individuals who are not directly affected by the reforms, using American aggregate census data. In contrast, Chevalier et al. (2003) find no impact from increasing the compulsory leaving age in England and Wales for the lowest educational attainers, thus arguing against the screening hypothesis.

55. The impact of educational attainment on the slope of the age–earnings profile in Europe (using the European Community Household Panel) is analysed by Brunello and Comi (2004).

56. In a pooling equilibrium, a related prediction would be the decline of wages for workers below the average talent endowment. However, this could not be observed in institutionalised contexts, where minimum wage legislation and workers' union pressure may prevent this drop.

57. In the language of the model presented in section 6.3, a rising wage represents a greater cost of job loss, thus becoming a powerful deterrent to shrinking and/or quitting. See also the discussion of the promotion policies in Lazear (1995, chap. 5).

58. The unweighted sample correlations of GDP per capita (measured in PPP terms) with offer and participation are, respectively, 0.55 and 0.48.

59. According to the OECD (2001, table C2.1), the share of secondary enrolment in pre-vocational and vocation-oriented schools is lowest in Ireland (20.6 per cent), Portugal (25.0 per cent), Greece (25.8 per cent) and Spain (31.2 per cent), and is highest in Austria (77.9 per cent), the United Kingdom (66.7 per cent) and the Netherlands (66.1 per cent).

60. See Becker (1993, pp. 36–40). See also the discussion in Acemoglu and Pischke (1999).

61. Suppose, for example, that firms have an informational advantage over the true workers' productivity obtained from training investments. If they do not reveal it (and they have no incentive to do so), they will pay a wage below productivity, and therefore will be willing to afford the cost of training in order to realise this gain: see Acemoglu and Pischke (1999). In the same vein, Bassanini and Brunello (2003) show that compression in wage distribution favours the incidence of workers' training.

62. Soskice (1994) stresses this point. Acemoglu and Pischke (2000) present a model in which certification provided by an external authority is capable of partially solving the asymmetry of information between the training firm and its competitors, which cannot observe the effective outcome of training on workers' productivity. An equilibrium with training is Pareto superior to an equilibrium without training, and in a symmetrical framework the firms, which possess an informational advantage over workers' productivity, pay the cost of training.

63. See Brunello (2003) for an empirical analysis of this link. The idea that an educated labour force is favoured by employers because it is more easily trained was originally proposed by Thurow (1975).

64. See Brunello and Giannini (2004).

65. An alternative way to express the same concept is to identify the discount rate that sets to zero the net present value (NPV) of the investment, where the net present value is defined as the discounted flow of all differences between inflows and outflows.

66. We neglect here the possibility of different employment probabilities associated with different educational attainments, but the wages could easily be reinterpreted as expected wages.

67. However, equation (6.29) implies an additional complication, since it describes a polynomial of $(n-1)$-th degree in $(1+\beta)$, thus admitting $(n-1)$ roots. The problem of root indeterminacy in returns is well known in the financial literature, which has not yet provided a convincing explanation for the common practice of selecting the positive real value that is closest to unity.

68. A further simplifying assumption implicit in equation (6.29) is given by the fact that each individual takes the wage rates W_t and W_t^s as given when considering the choice of school attendance. While this is

reasonable on an individual basis, it does not hold in the aggregate, because, whenever all individuals find it convenient (and select) to attend s years of schooling, the expected gain ($W_t^s - W_t$) declines, with a potential reversal of intended choices.

69. This is equivalent to saying that, if an uneducated worker stops working at the age of n, a worker who has attended s years of school can work up to the age of $(n + s)$. Many pension schemes are consistent with this assumption, under the rationale that individuals who spent part of their lives investing in their education should be given time enough to recover their investment outlays.

70. At the cost of some additional analytical complication, we could consider the case of wages growing at constant rates.

71. For readers who are more familiar with continuous-time analysis, equation (6.32) can be rewritten as

$$\int_0^n W(t) \cdot e^{-\beta t} dt = \int_s^{n+s} W^s(t) \cdot e^{-\beta t} dt$$

When wages are constant over the life cycle, the two integrals can be solved, yielding

$$W\left[-\frac{e^{-\beta n} - 1}{\beta}\right] = W^s\left[-\frac{e^{-\beta(n+s)} - e^{-\beta s}}{\beta}\right] \quad \Leftrightarrow \quad \frac{W^s}{W} = e^{\beta s}$$

which leads to equation (6.34) without approximations.

72. The unsystematic component ε_i must have zero mean $E[\varepsilon] = 0$. If that were not the case, any systematic component should be included in the z_i vector, which already includes a constant.

73. There is an even stronger presumption in the application of condition (6.29), because each individual has to compare two alternative wage profiles, as if he/she had been able to conduct two alternative lives. Since counter-factuals cannot be observed in reality, agents make inferences from observing the life experiences of similar individuals.

74. See, for example, Krueger and Lindahl (2001, fig. 6.1).

75. The current exposition is based on Card (1995).

76. It corresponds to the linear projection of true schooling on observed schooling under the additional assumption of $Cov(s^*, \chi) = 0$. See Krueger and Lindahl (2001) and Card (2001).

77. A direct assessment of the measurement error is obtained from the comparison between self-reported attainment and administrative records. Alternatively, it can be obtained from interviewing relatives – for example, asking each twin about the educational attainment of the other. In such a case the correlation between self-reported and sibling-obtained measure is in the order of 0.70 (see Ashenfelter and Rouse, 1998, and

Mulvey, Miller and Martin, 1997). This is consistent with the following statement: 'Research in the US over the past three decades has concluded that the reliability of self-reported schooling is 85–90 percent (Angrist and Krueger 1999, table 9), implying that the downward bias is in the order of 10–15 percent – enough to offset a modest upward ability bias' (Card, 2001, p. 1134).

78. See Angrist and Krueger (1999) for a review of the applications of the Heckman two-step procedure.

7 | *Intergenerational persistence*

7.1 Introduction

So far we have considered individual choices of educational investment, to some extent neglecting their implications for aggregate equilibrium in the labour market. We have also glossed over the dynamic consequences of current choices. When an individual is educated, not only does he/she improve his/her future prospects in terms of employment probability, expected salary and job quality, he/she also increases the probability that his/her offspring will get educated as well, not to speak of the positive spillover for society as a whole.

With the help of simple models in the present chapter we attempt to disentangle the different channels through which the educational choices of one generation affect those of future generations. We will also provide some cross-country comparative evidence on intergenerational mobility in educational attainments, as well as speculating about potential determinants of observed mobility.[1]

Before moving to formal models, let us review these channels in a cursory way. As we have already seen in previous chapters, educational choices are conditioned by individual unobservable abilities (labelled *talent*), family cultural background, family financial resources, public resources and – more generally – social capital. Most of these factors exhibit intertemporal and intergenerational persistence.

The transmission of unobservable ability can be genetic, such as race, height, eye colour, beauty, and so on. Despite the difficulty of separating traits that are genetic from traits that are culturally induced (a typical example being the propensity to smoke), the empirical evidence obtained from the samples of twins indicates that the relative contribution from genetics to intertemporal persistence is low. Bowles and Gintis (2002) show that measured IQ test scores contribute little to earnings, and use this evidence to conclude that their contribution to intergenerational persistence must be low.[2]

215

A separate channel consists of cultural influences, and works through the educational system. There is vast empirical evidence to the effect that the children of educated parents are more likely to acquire education.[3] This may be partly due to parent imitation (if they see their parent reading a book, they get the idea that reading is a rewarding activity), but in most cases it works through induced educational choices. An educated parent is better aware of the psychological and economic value of education, and therefore puts more pressure on his/her children to achieve more at school. In addition, if the educational system is not homogeneous, an educated parent always has some advantage in collecting information about school quality, and can reorient his/her child's choices towards better opportunities.[4] A strengthening factor derives from marital choices: as long as there is assortative mating (namely, better-educated persons preferring to pair off with other educated persons), the cultural background within a family is made more homogeneous, and the influences received by each parent reinforce one another.[5]

A third channel of intergenerational persistence derives from liquidity constraints. If access to education is limited by family financial resources, and acquired education gains access to higher-paid jobs, this opens the door to a poverty trap: poor families are prevented from investing in the education of their children by a lack of resources and the inability to access financial markets, their children remain uneducated and poor, and thus they are unable to invest in their grandchildren either.[6] From an empirical point of view it is not easy to distinguish between cultural linkages and financial ones, since education and income are correlated within each generation.[7] However, if we measure intergenerational persistence within the richest section of the population (which is not liquidity-constrained), we can get an approximate indication of the extent of intergenerational persistence attributable to cultural background.

A fourth source of intergenerational persistence emerges from territorial segregation, and is related to family wealth. If residential choices are influenced by the evaluation of local school quality, and school quality affects house prices, then richer families will gain access to better schools by locating closer to them. Better school quality combined with a more homogeneous cultural neighbourhood will yield greater social capital, thus providing a clear advantage to children raised in that environment.[8]

Table 7.1 *Population distribution in accordance with educational attainment*

Educational attainment	Italy		Germany		United States	
	Fathers	Sons	Fathers	Sons	Fathers	Sons
Uncompleted compulsory	47.72	10.84	17.54	7.55	42.04	13.98
Compulsory	41.36	39.63	64.17	64.03	18.61	22.55
Beyond compulsory	12.88	41.24	14.36	17.32	23.24	36.16
Tertiary	3.03	8.30	3.92	11.10	16.10	27.29

While it is not always easy to distinguish between alternative explanations of intergenerational persistence in educational choices, their effects are clearly detectable. If we have data on the educational attainment of two contiguous generations from a representative sample of the population, we can measure the intergenerational persistence of educational attainment. Table 7.1 reproduces the marginal distribution for each generation in three countries according to their educational attainment. In order to improve comparability across countries, educational attainment has been classified according to four achievements, which are country- and cohort-specific: uncompleted compulsory education; completed compulsory education; beyond compulsory education without attaining a university degree; university degree.[9,10]

It is easy to observe that educational attainment has significantly increased in the passage from one generation to the following, thanks to the growth of per capita incomes and the consequent mass scholarisation. The divergence between the marginal distributions of educational attainments in two adjacent generations is what is indicated in the literature as *structural mobility*, and can be attributed to the relaxation of liquidity constraints and/or to the increase in public resources invested in education.[11] However, two adjacent generations could exhibit the same marginal distributions and we could still observe differences between countries in terms of how families interchange their relative positions. This second aspect is typically called *exchange mobility* by sociologists, and refers to the positive association between fathers' and sons' educational attainment.[12] Exchange mobility is likely to be affected by the genetic and cultural aspects of intergenerational persistence.

Table 7.2 *Intergenerational mobility in educational attainment*

Italy (1987)

→ Sons' education ↓ Fathers' education	Uncompleted compulsory	Compulsory	Beyond compulsory	Tertiary
Uncompleted compulsory	20.72	56.67	21.16	1.45
Compulsory	4.34	32.93	56.59	6.14
Beyond compulsory	1.44	13.46	60.10	25.00
Tertiary	0.00	2.04	34.69	63.27

Germany (1986)

→ Sons' education ↓ Fathers' education	Uncompleted compulsory	Compulsory	Beyond compulsory	Tertiary
Uncompleted compulsory	14.77	72.57	11.39	1.27
Compulsory	7.50	70.13	14.65	7.73
Beyond compulsory	1.03	39.18	32.47	27.32
Tertiary	0.00	16.98	32.08	50.94

United States (1990)

→ Sons' education ↓ Fathers' education	Uncompleted compulsory	Compulsory	Beyond compulsory	Tertiary
Uncompleted compulsory	25.46	28.44	33.94	12.16
Compulsory	10.88	27.98	35.23	25.91
Beyond compulsory	3.73	17.84	46.06	32.37
Tertiary	2.40	7.78	28.74	61.08

Table 7.2 shows the intergenerational transition matrices in educational attainment, whereby alternative measures can be computed to ascertain the relative ordering of countries in terms of intergenerational mobility. As a consequence, different rankings emerge using different measures, since each indicator can be obtained by a different set of axioms. Suppose, for example, we are interested in the idea of equality of opportunity in accessing education: this would correspond to the (statistical) independence of the marginal distribution of sons from their fathers. Thus, the (Euclidian) distance of the currently observed matrices of table 7.2 and an ideal matrix reporting the long-run

Table 7.3 *Intergenerational mobility in educational attainment and income*

	Italy	Germany	United States
Rank correlation (Spearman) for educational attainments	0.53	0.38	0.43
Rank correlation (Spearman) for occupational incomes	0.37	0.32	0.35
Regression coefficient between fathers' and sons' occupational incomes [a]	0.364 (15.03)	0.447 (13.34)	0.388 (13.25)

[a] OLS regressions including age and age squared; t-statistics in parenthesis.

distribution of the educational attainment of the population could provide the required measure.[13] Conversely, if we are concerned with the degree of relative immobility in a society, we could sum the population falling in the cells along the main diagonal: this corresponds to families in which nothing has changed in the passing from one generation to the next.[14]

In table 7.3 we have reported alternative measures of (relative) mobility, obtained from either education (the first line) or from incomes (the second and third lines). While Germany emerges as the most mobile country by virtue of its having the lowest association between children's and parent's outcomes, any judgement is heavily dependent on the statistical indicator adopted in the analysis (as witnessed by the third line, where the country order is reversed).

It should, therefore, appear evident that we do not possess a unique and everlasting measure for intergenerational mobility,[15] and that cross-national comparisons should state clearly from the onset which properties they subsume in their interpretation of this concept.[16] In the economic literature the most widely used measure of mobility is the regression coefficient of children's income onto parental income (see a review of the results in section 7.6 below). Its adoption is justified in terms of regression to the mean, which has some bearing on the concept of equality of opportunity. Most recent versions take into account the possibility of structural changes by making reference to the correlation index between the incomes of the two generations, to be corrected with the ratio of the standard deviations in incomes for the two generations. In contrast, the traditional approach followed by sociologists measures relative chances offered to individuals from different backgrounds (*odds ratios* – see Erikson and Goldthorpe, 2002). But the differences between the economic and sociological approaches can hardly be reduced to statistical indicators. Sociologists stress the fact that people are embedded in social hierarchical relations, such as different types of labour contracts, which are beyond individual control.[17] Since embeddedness does not derive from intentional choice, intergenerational persistence looks like a mechanical dynamic law, and scholars are left without the ability to test theoretical predictions. According to Grawe and Mulligan (2002), this is the main advantage to the economic analysis of intergenerational mobility. If agents are depicted as maximising their dynastic welfare flow, they will select optimal money transfers and educational investments in their children (based on their expected abilities) aiming at intertemporal consumption smoothing.[18] An additional implication of the potential existence of liquidity constraints is the possibility of non-linearities in the pattern of intergenerational mobility, with stronger persistence in the lower tail of the parents' income distribution. However, the empirical analysis carried out by Grawe (2004) and Couch and Lillard (2004) suggests that income persistence is higher at both extremes of the distribution. A final implication of optimising agent models is the potential crowding out of private educational investment by public expenditure on education, the evidence for which is rather weak.[19]

The impossibility of achieving definitive conclusions about mobility measurement does not imply that the theoretical analysis of mobility is worthless. On the contrary, theoretical models help us to identify different channels of persistence, which can, in principle, be tested separately using structural models. As an example of the complex interplay of factors affecting intergenerational mobility, let us consider figure 7.1. It depicts each individual i belonging to generation t with a triplet (A_{it}, Y_{it}, E_{it}), where A_{it} is ability endowment, Y_{it} is earnings and E_{it} is education. If we neglect on-the-job training, education is predetermined with respect to labour market status, and therefore with respect to earnings. If we consider ability to increase labour productivity, we should observe that

$$Y_{it} = \beta E_{it} + \varepsilon A_{it} + \omega_{1it}, \quad \omega_1 \sim \left(0, \sigma_1^2\right) \tag{7.1}$$

where the relationship between earnings, education and ability is assumed linear for simplicity. ω_1 is an i.i.d. (identically independently distributed) error term, capturing the idea of luck in the labour market.

Parents' generation (*t*–1)   Childrens' generation (*t*)

Figure 7.1 The individual in the intergenerational process

Following the previous informal discussion, we now consider four potential channels through which one generation may influence the following one (figure 7.2).

If ability is genetically (or mechanically) inherited, we indicate this with the α arrow and we write

$$A_{it} = \delta + \alpha A_{it-1} + \omega_{2it}, \quad \omega_2 \sim \left(0, \sigma_2^2\right) \tag{7.2}$$

Cultural influence can be described by the η arrow. However, we have discussed the possibility of liquidity constraints, reducing the optimal investment in education from poor families. We indicate this channel with the γ arrow and we write[20]

$$E_{it} = \eta E_{it-1} + \gamma Y_{it-1} \tag{7.3}$$

Finally, we may consider the possibility that family networking and neighbourhood effects give access to better job opportunities (Montgomery, 1991; Benabou, 1993). We indicate this channel with the μ arrow, and we amend equation (7.1) by adding a further term:

$$Y_{it} = \beta E_{it} + \varepsilon A_{it} + \mu Y_{it-1}\omega_{1it}, \quad \omega_1 \sim \left(0, \sigma_1^2\right) \tag{7.4}$$

Intergenerational persistence in this framework is a dynamical system that maps $\mathfrak{R}^3 \to \mathfrak{R}^3$, the stability and speed of convergence of which are strictly related to the eigenvalues of the associated gradient. However, without entering into the details of the mathematical analysis, by repeated substitution we can dispense with equation (7.2), since the dynamical system is block-recursive, obtaining

$$\begin{cases} E_{it} = (\eta + \gamma\beta)E_{it-1} + \gamma\mu Y_{it-2} + \gamma\varepsilon A_{it-1} + \gamma\omega_{1t-1} \\ Y_{it} = \beta(\eta - \alpha)E_{it-1} + (\gamma\beta + \mu + \alpha)Y_{it-1} - \alpha\mu Y_{it-2} + \varepsilon\delta + \omega_{2t} - \alpha\omega_{1t-1} \end{cases}$$
$$\tag{7.5}$$

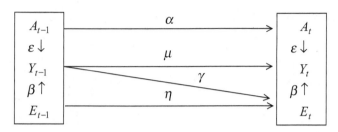

Parents' generation (t–1)   Childrens' generation (t)

Figure 7.2 Intergenerational persistence

By observing the dynamic process described by equation system (7.5), we may infer that income and educational attainment are more persistent the higher the return on education β and the impact of liquidity constraint γ, since the coefficients of E_{it-1} and Y_{it-1} are the eigenvalues of this dynamic process. In addition, income persistence will also depend on genetic inheritability α and on neighbourhood effects μ, whereas schooling persistence is affected by cultural constraints η. Finally, notice that a proper specification of the intergenerational persistence process should take into account grandfathers' earnings Y_{t-2}, which affect educational attainment positively (because parental education is raised) but the earnings dynamics negatively (due to the mean reversion nature of the processes described in equations (7.2) to (7.4)).[21] The utility of such a scheme is to provide interpretative clues when comparing intergenerational mobility estimates across countries (or across years). Other things being constant, this sketch model suggests that intergenerational mobility will be lower whenever returns on education are high or poverty is widespread (and therefore the extent of liquidity constrainedness is high).[22] Similarly, intergenerational mobility in educational attainment should increase as long as schools are able to reduce the impact of family background on educational attainment (the cultural constraint η).[23]

For these reasons, in the following four sections we will review some theoretical models that, in our opinion, shed light on the issue of intergenerational persistence. In the concluding section we will review the existing empirical evidence on intergenerational mobility. Our analysis nonetheless retains a distinctive perspective, since our focus is on persistence in educational attainment, while most of the literature deals with income persistence.

7.2 An initial model of intergenerational persistence

We will begin by presenting a base model, able to account for the alternative channels of persistence mentioned previously.[24] We consider an overlapping generation model, in which each individual lives for two periods. Each individual is born with an ability endowment A_t, obtains an inheritance from his/her parents equal to X_t and (an implicit transfer of) public resources invested in education equal to E_t. Abstracting from the individual choice of time allocation, his/her human capital formation will follow this relationship:[25]

$$H_{t+1} = f(X_t, A_t, E_t) \qquad (7.6)$$
$$\phantom{H_{t+1} = f(} + \quad + \quad +$$

An increase in initial endowments, be it family wealth or public resources, raises human capital formation in the younger generation. Equation (7.6) has to be taken as a mechanical relationship, with no role for individual choice. However, individual heterogeneity in talent endowment leads to the accumulation of different amounts of human capital. Notice also that family human capital has been neglected for simplicity.[26]

In the second period each individual obtains an income Y_{t+1} that is proportional to accumulated human capital:

$$Y_{t+1} = \gamma H_{t+1} + v_{t+1}, \quad v \sim (0, \sigma_v^2) \qquad (7.7)$$

where v_t represents (unpredictable) luck during the working life, and is described by a random error with zero mean. Each individual has a child, allocates his/her income between second-period consumption and inheritance, and then leaves the scene. The budget constraint is given by

$$Y_{t+1} = C_{t+1} + X_{t+1} \qquad (7.8)$$

where C_{t+1} is consumption when old (consumption when young is left out, for simplicity) and X_{t+1} is the inheritance left to the child. Each agent is assumed to be altruistic, and therefore concerned with his/her own consumption and with the future income of his/her child Y_{t+2}.[27] Thus he/she faces a trade-off between his/her own welfare and his/her child's welfare, as described by the following relationship:

$$\max_{X_{t+1}} U_t = U(C_{t+1}, Y_{t+2}) = U[Y_{t+1} - X_{t+1}, \gamma H_{t+2}(X_{t+1}) + v_{t+2}] \quad (7.9)$$

Given the random component v_{t+2} affecting the future income of the child, the optimal choice of the level of inheritance is taken under uncertainty.

Each parent is ignorant of the exact talent endowment of his/her child, but he/she knows that there is some persistence across generations, as described by the following autoregressive process:[28]

$$A_{t+1} = \alpha + \beta A_t + u_{t+1}, \quad u \sim (0, \sigma_u^2) \tag{7.10}$$

It can be proved that the optimal solution (in implicit form) to the problem posed by equation (7.9) is given by

$$X_{t+1}^* = \chi(A_{t+1}, E_{t+1}, r) = \chi(\alpha + \beta A_t + u_t, E_{t+1}, r) \tag{7.11}$$
$$\phantom{X_{t+1}^* = \chi(}{\scriptstyle +} \phantom{A_{t+1},} {\scriptstyle -} \phantom{E_{t+1},} {\scriptstyle -} {\scriptstyle +} {\scriptstyle -}$$

where r is the (average) private return on education.[29] Equation (7.11) indicates that the level of inheritance is positively correlated with the expected ability of the child; thus, more talented children obtain greater resources to be devoted to their education. This may look counterintuitive, since we would have expected an altruistic parent to be willing to compensate for adverse nature depriving the ability endowment of his/her child. However, a more talented child exhibits a greater marginal rate of return, and therefore attracts more resources. For the same reason, public resources invested in education crowd out private resources. The negative sign of the intertemporal discount rate can be explained by the consumption/saving choice of the parent: since investing in the human capital of the child competes with alternative financial assets, when a competing return rises a rational investor will reduce the investment in these assets.

Using recursively equations (7.7), (7.6), (7.11) and (7.10), we obtain the intertemporal link between the income of the parents and the income of the child. We start by endogenising the optimal inheritance choice:

$$\begin{aligned}
Y_{t+2} &= \gamma H_{t+2} + v_{t+2} = \gamma[f(X_{t+1}, A_{t+1}, E_{t+1})] + v_{t+2} \\
&= \gamma[f(\chi(A_{t+1}, E_{t+1}, r), A_{t+1}, E_{t+1})] + v_{t+2} \tag{7.12} \\
&= \varphi(A_{t+1}, E_{t+1}, r) + v_{t+2}
\end{aligned}$$

Then we proceed by linearising the φ function and exploiting equation (7.10):

$$\begin{aligned}
Y_{t+2} &= \varphi_A A_{t+1} + \varphi_E E_{t+1} + \varphi_r r + v_{t+2} \\
&= \varphi_A(\alpha + \beta A_t + u_{t+1}) + \varphi_E E_{t+1} + \varphi_r r + v_{t+2} \tag{7.13}
\end{aligned}$$

By lagging equation (7.13) one period, expressing it in terms of A_t and reintroducing it in the same equation we finally get

$$
\begin{aligned}
Y_{t+2} &= \varphi_A \alpha + \varphi_A \beta \left(\frac{1}{\varphi_A} Y_{t+1} - \frac{\varphi_E}{\varphi_A} E_t - \frac{\varphi_r}{\varphi_A} r - \frac{1}{\varphi_A} v_{t+1} \right) \\
&\quad + \varphi_A u_{t+1} + \varphi_E E_{t+1} + \varphi_r r + v_{t+2} \\
&= \varphi_A \alpha + \beta Y_{t+1} + \varphi_E (E_{t+1} - \beta E_t) + \varphi_r (1 - \beta) r \\
&\quad + v_{t+2} - \beta v_{t+1} + \varphi_A u_{t+1}
\end{aligned}
\tag{7.14}
$$

Looking at equation (7.14), we notice that, under the assumption of perfect financial markets,[30] the autoregression coefficient β describes the intergenerational dynamics of incomes; in addition, the same dynamics is observed in the dynamics of abilities. The higher the β coefficient the more persistent is the (cross-individual) inequality. If we define $\overline{Y}$ as the equilibrium steady state (such that $Y_{t+2} = Y_{t+1} = \overline{Y}$), we can re-express equation (7.14) as

$$
Y_{t+2} - \overline{Y} = \beta (Y_{t+1} - \overline{Y})
\tag{7.15}
$$

Whenever $|\beta| < 1$ individual incomes converge monotonically to their long-run equilibrium value; this convergence is often indicated in the literature as *regression to the mean* (or β convergence). The speed of convergence is higher the lower the β coefficient. Let us suppose a parental income corresponding to double the long-run level; then the child's income will be equal to $(1 + \beta)\overline{Y}$. If β is close to one, we obtain long-lasting persistence: children from rich (above the mean) parents will remain rich for many generations, and, similarly, poor families will remain poor. Conversely, if β is close to zero, the relative position of the parents is almost irrelevant to predicting the future circumstances of the children.

Within the simplicity of the present model, the same persistence can be observed in the level of acquired education. From equation (7.7) we can infer the human capital stock from earned income:

$$
H_{t+1} = \frac{Y_{t+1} - v_{t+1}}{\gamma}
\tag{7.16}
$$

We then use equation (7.16) to re-express equation (7.14) as

$$
H_{t+2} = \frac{\varphi_A \alpha}{\gamma} + \beta H_{t+1} + \frac{\varphi_E (E_{t+1} - \beta E_t) + \varphi_r (1 - \beta) r + \varphi_A u_{t+1}}{\gamma}
\tag{7.17}
$$

where we observe that the same level of intertemporal persistence observed in abilities and incomes can also be traced in educational attainments. By comparing equations (7.10), (7.14) and (7.17) we infer that, under a condition of equality of access opportunities (namely that all individuals face the same financial conditions to invest in their children's education), the observed inequality and persistence in educational attainment is merely the reflection of talent distribution, which can hardly be changed when passing from one generation to the following.

Two assumptions remain crucial for these conclusions:

(i) in order to undertake the optimal investment in their children, parents have to predict the ability of their children, which can be done only when the β parameter is known with certainty;

(ii) there are no other impediments to the accessing of education that are correlated with family incomes.

In the first case, it is obvious that it is impossible to observe the actual intergenerational transmission of ability. However, under the structure of the model, the β coefficient can be estimated by looking at the dynamics of incomes (or even at the dynamics of educational attainment). If we look at the richest portion of the population, it is quite plausible to consider it as financially unconstrained; when current income does not condition educational choices (since borrowing is potentially unlimited, up to the point where the marginal return on human capital investment equates to return on any other financial investment), the only observable intergenerational correlation observed in incomes can be explained by a correlation in abilities.[31] When we consider that the observability of talent transmission is an excessively heroic assumption, we have to take into account the fact that parents' investment is conducted under a veil of ignorance about the true ability of their children. When schools play a screening role with respect to actual student abilities then the incentives to invest in education are modified, since schooling provides information that can be valuable in itself.

As far as the second assumption is concerned, we can easily think of other channels through which family income may limit access to education. The easiest one is residential choices: when school funding is derived from property taxes, we observe a positive correlation between family incomes and resources allocated to education. Unless funding from central government is able to undo the financial segregation of schools, we could observe a positive correlation between family resources and educational investment. In addition, the presence of the private sector in education provision (to which access is typically rationed according to available incomes – see chapters 3 and 5) reinforces this correlation.

Further implications can be derived in similar set-ups, the most important one being intergenerational consumption smoothing (Mulligan, 1997, 1999): this implies that the persistence of consumption across generations must be higher than that in incomes or educational attainments.[32]

7.3 Intergenerational persistence with perfect information on children's talent

The previous discussion suggests that intergenerational persistence in educational attainment is higher than the same persistence in income. Among potential explanations we can list both the intergenerational persistence in talents and the funding of education, partially based on family resources. With respect to the first aspect, the basic model by Becker and Tomes (1986) assumes that parents know their own talent, and that, based on that knowledge, they predict the expected talent of their child; knowing the dynamic evolution described by equation (7.10), the best prediction of the child's talent is $E[A_{t+1}|A_t] = \alpha + \beta A_t$. Despite its wide adoption in the literature, however, this is not always in accordance with the empirical evidence.

In fact, knowledge about the (expected) talent of the child implies that parents take the crucial decision over the educational career of their children once and for all. This may prove appropriate for tracked educational systems (such as the German one), in which, by at the age of thirteen, a child is already destined to become a blue-collar worker, a white-collar worker or a professional, according to his/her school performance up to that point.[33] But it is at odds with comprehensive systems, where educational choices are taken at different stages, with possibilities for revisions and a progressive approximation of the unobservable abilities of a student. Under such circumstances, the more appropriate assumption would probably be the gradual revelation of the hidden talent, thanks to the screening activity of the schools. However, very few papers adopt this perspective,[34] most of them tending towards one or other of the extreme assumptions: *perfect information* (as in the previous case) or an *absence of information* (parents know only the statistical distribution of unobservable talent). Results in terms of persistence depend crucially on which of the two extreme assumptions is adopted. In this section we present two models that retain the basic structure (a two-period overlapping generation model, with educational choices in the first period and work, consumption and inheritance choices in the second period).

The model proposed by Owen and Weil (1998) corresponds to the first approach, since they assume that talent endowment A_t is randomly and independently distributed in each generation, but is perfectly observable before undertaking the educational choice. The educational choice is a discrete one: if the individual is educated, he/she will work in the second period of life as skilled, otherwise he/she will remain unskilled. An important assumption concerns the complementarity/substitutability of skill levels. If we assume that total labour input is obtained from a combination of skilled labour L^s and unskilled labour L^n, considered as imperfect substitutes, we may write total output Y_t as the result of a constant return to scale technology:

$$Y_t = F(L_t, K_t) = \left[L_t^{n\gamma} L_t^{s^{1-\gamma}}\right]^\beta K_t^{1-\beta} \tag{7.18}$$

where K_t is the stock of physical capital. If we assume wage flexibility, we will obtain full employment for both types of workers. Given a marginal rate of return on physical capital R (for example, from foreign financial markets), the wage differential between skilled and unskilled workers (i.e. the incentive to acquire education) is dependent only on the relative supply of skilled workers. To maximise the firm's profit it follows that the wage (per efficiency unit) must equate the marginal productivity of each type of work:[35]

$$W_t^s = \frac{\partial Y_t}{\partial L_t^s} = \beta \left[\frac{K_t}{L^{n\gamma} L^{s^{1-\gamma}}}\right]^{1-\beta} \cdot (1-\gamma) L^{n\gamma} L^{s^{-\gamma}} \tag{7.19}$$

$$W_t^n = \frac{\partial Y_t}{\partial L_t^n} = \beta \left[\frac{K_t}{L^{n\gamma} L^{s^{1-\gamma}}}\right]^{1-\beta} \cdot \gamma L^{s^{1-\gamma}} L^{n\gamma-1} \tag{7.20}$$

Normalising the size of the labour force to unity (such that $L^s + L^n = 1$), we get

$$\frac{W_t^s}{W_t^n} = \frac{1-\gamma}{\gamma} \cdot \frac{L_t^n}{L_t^s} = \frac{1-\gamma}{\gamma} \cdot \frac{(1-L_t^s)}{L_t^s} = f(L_t^s) \tag{7.21}$$

Equation (7.21) indicates that the return on education declines with the increase in the supply of educated people. Each individual accepts as given the existing differential, and ignores the (marginal) impact of his/her choice on the aggregate outcome. If we interpret talent as being equivalent to the number A_{it} of efficiency units obtained as an endowment at birth, each individual compares his/her expected income as a skilled worker ($A_{it} \cdot W_t^s$) with the expected income when unskilled ($A_{it} \cdot W_t^n$).[36] Since acquiring education implies a fixed cost B_t, an individual will acquire such education if

$$A_{it} \cdot W_t^s - B_t \geq A_{it} \cdot W_t^n \tag{7.22}$$

or otherwise if

$$A_{it} \geq \frac{B_t}{W_t^s - W_t^n} \tag{7.23}$$

In order to acquire education one must possess a sufficient level of talent (a sufficient number of efficiency units A_{it}) or face either a sufficiently low cost of acquisition B_t or a sufficiently high wage differential for skilled workers. Under perfect financial markets, the condition (7.23) describes the relevant talent threshold for (economic) convenience in becoming skilled. Under imperfect (or even non-existent) financial markets, educational choices are financed through received inheritances X_t. In such a case, we obtain a double threshold, given by talent and wealth endowments (as represented in figure 7.3).

If we now introduce a standard assumption of homothetic preferences, the inheritance left to a child is proportional to earned income. Since the talent variable A_{it} is assumed to be i.i.d., each individual, irrespective of his/her social origin (whether born of rich and/or educated parents), faces a positive probability of achieving an income that is sufficiently high to leave an inheritance capable of covering the educational cost of his/her child. However, this probability is not independent of the educational attainment of parents, and even grandparents, as can be seen from equation (7.24):

$$A_{it} \geq \frac{B_t}{W_t^s - W_t^n} = \frac{X_t}{W_t^s - W_t^n} = \int_{-\infty}^{B_{t-1}} \left[\frac{\alpha\left(A_{it-1} W_{t-1}^n\right)}{W_t^s - W_t^n} \right] dX_{t-1}$$
$$+ \int_{B_{t-1}}^{+\infty} \left[\frac{\alpha\left(A_{it-1} W_{t-1}^s - X_{t-1}\right)}{W_t^s - W_t^n} \right] dX_{t-1} \tag{7.24}$$

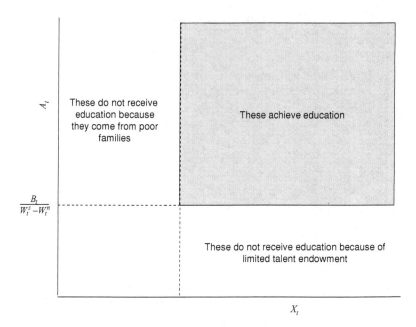

Figure 7.3 Educational choices

where α is the income share devoted to inheritance and where we have adopted the extreme case of non-existent financial markets (up to the point where educational costs can be financed only thorough inheritance). Having a rich grandfather increases the probability of having an educated parent (the second addend on the right-hand side of equation (7.24)), who in turn is more likely to be richer and to leave a higher inheritance. Thus, we observe intergenerational persistence attributable only to liquidity constraints. If these obstacles could be removed, the intergenerational link would cease to exist, because educational attainments and incomes would be based solely on talent, which is randomly distributed in each generation.[37]

As a result, the cost of education is positively correlated with the measure of intergenerational persistence, up to the point of perfect mobility, when parents' achievements are replicated in children's achievements. Owen and Weil (1998) also show that equilibria characterised by low/zero mobility are inefficient,[38] since they prevent talented individuals from fully exploiting their endowment.[39]

In the same model there is also a negative correlation between inequality and mobility. When inequality declines we observe an increase in school attendance, and mobility rises as a consequence. And, conversely, an increase in mobility is accompanied by an increase in the supply of skilled labour, which translates into a decline in wage differentials (see equation (7.21)).[40] Summing up, under the assumptions of perfect observability of talent, the absence of inheritability of talent and imperfect financial markets, the cost of attending education is negatively correlated with intergenerational mobility and positively correlated with income inequality.

7.4 Intergenerational persistence with imperfect information on children's talent

When we remove the assumption of perfect observability of talent, additional factors can be introduced to account for intergenerational mobility. Following Checchi, Ichino and Rustichini (1999), let us suppose that individual talent cannot be freely observed but that it requires schooling experience to achieve a precise knowledge of individual endowment. In such a context, schools operate as a costly screening device. Individuals know only that talent can take two values (A_1 and A_2, with $A_1 > A_2$), and that there is intergenerational persistence in talent transmission. If we indicate with $(1 - \pi)$ the probability of persistence (i.e. the probability for an A_1 parent generating an A_1 child which is identical to the probability of an A_2 parent to generating an A_2 child) and with π the complementary probability of transition, we can represent the dynamic evolution of talent transmission as a first-order Markov process, described by the following matrix:

→ Children's talent ↓ Parents' talent	Low (A_2)	High (A_1)
Low (A_2)	$1 - \pi$	π
High (A_1)	π	$1 - \pi$

When $\pi = 1/2$ we are back to the situation in which talent is randomly distributed in each generation. To retain some persistence in ability transmission, from now on we will maintain that $\pi < 1/2$. In this context, the only way to obtain information about one's talent endowment is to undertake a schooling career, which can be acquired at a fixed cost B.[41] By going to school, an A_1 type expands his/her human capital, his/her income and therefore his/her bequest to his/her child. In contrast, an A_2 type does not acquire any additional human capital and makes losses (equal to the educational cost B). Since, before undertaking the educational choice, an individual is ignorant of his/her own talent endowment, he/she uses expectations based on his/her parents' educational attainment. If his/her parents did not go to school, he/she is forced to search back in his/her memory or in documentation to the point where an ancestor who went to school is found.

To see how this backward induction works, consider initially the case of the child of a parent who went to school. If this parent was successful, he/she was revealed to be of the A_1 type; thus, his/her child has an expected talent equal to $[(1 - \pi)A_1 + \pi A_2]$. Using previous notation, the child will choose to go to school whenever the expected return, net of school tuition, exceeds the certain return of not attending school; that is,

$$(1 - \pi)A_1 W^s + \pi A_2 W^n - B > A_2 W^n \qquad (7.25)$$

which can be rearranged as

$$(1 - \pi) > \frac{B}{A_1 W^s - A_2 W^n} \qquad (7.26)$$

Conversely, the child of a parent who went to school and failed[42] (proving to be of the A_2 type) will face a different arbitrage condition, which is more restrictive than the previous one:[43]

$$\pi > \frac{B}{A_1 W^s - A_2 W^n} \qquad (7.27)$$

In this way we have already introduced intergenerational persistence in educational choices, which depends on the inheritability of talent (even when not directly observed). School failure in one generation lowers the probability of success of all the following generations. The school here plays the role of a screening device, by revealing the talent endowment of any individual undergoing the screening test.

Let us now consider the case of a child of uneducated parents; as a consequence, their talent endowment is unknown. If we indicate with v_t^e the (expected) belief of being of type A_1 that the child attributes to him-/herself, and if it is known that his/her parents held the same belief

v^e_{t-1} of being of type A_1, then coherence in beliefs requires that

$$v^e_t = (1 - \pi) \cdot (\text{probability parents } A_1) + \pi \cdot (\text{probability parents } A_2)$$

$$= (1 - \pi) \cdot v^e_{t-1} + \pi \cdot \left(1 - v^e_{t-1}\right) = \pi + (1 - 2\pi) \cdot v^e_{t-1} \qquad (7.28)$$

When the number of generations about which we do not have information goes up, the repeated application of equation (7.28) yields

$$v^e_t = \pi + (1 - 2\pi)^i \cdot v^e_{t-i} \qquad (7.29)$$

where i is the number of generations for which we do not have information. Since equation (7.29) represents an increasing difference equation of i-th order (since $(1 - 2\pi) > 0$), it converges to 1/2 whatever the level of initial belief regarding ancestors. This implies that, even after a person's school failure (which implies $v^e = 0$), and even if that person's descendants were negatively affected by this failure, the reminiscence of this event will vanish with the passing of time. Sooner or later a new generation will reach a point at which the following condition holds:[44]

$$v^e_t > \frac{B}{W^s - W^n} \qquad (7.30)$$

Even in this context we find that a lower cost of education (or, equivalently, a greater wage differential) raises the fraction of individuals who undergo the screening test of schools, and therefore mobility increases. Thus, the costs of education and social mobility are negatively correlated. Unlike the previous model shown in section 7.3, we cannot argue that there is also an efficiency-enhancing implication. In fact, with high costs of schooling there are individuals of type A_1 who do not dare to go to school for fear of failure, but whenever we lower costs there is an increasing number of type A_2 individuals who go to school and fail, wasting resources.

So far we have abstracted from how individuals obtain funding for their educational choices. If we introduce the further assumption that human capital can be accumulated (and transmitted) across generations, a sequence of successful generations will be characterised by increasing human capital, income and wealth. As a consequence, the implications in terms of inequality are far from straightforward, and depend on the way in which education is financed.

When we consider a *publicly financed schooling system*, all individuals embarking on academic studies will receive the same amount of resources, and they will differ to the extent that parental human capital affects the accumulation of their own human capital. In contrast, when we consider a *private schooling system* (where the amount of resources available for education is strictly dependent on family resources), successful dynasties have a greater incentive to undertake academic studies, since part of their expected gains will spill over to their offspring. In the model by Checchi, Ichino and Rustichini (1999), the relationship between mobility (defined as the population share that attempts to go to school) and inequality holds negative, but varies in accordance with the public/private nature of the schooling system. Everything else being constant, a public schooling system ensures greater equality (thanks to the implicit redistribution operated by tax-financed schooling) at the cost of reduced mobility (since the long-run incentives are lower).[45] The impossibility of transferring financial resources derived from taxation reduces the effort of an individual, thus leading to an under-investment in the accumulation of the dynastic human capital. In contrast, a private schooling system provides the correct incentives, and therefore is characterised by greater mobility, albeit at the cost of greater inequality, since more individuals will put more effort into accumulating human capital, leading to a more uneven distribution of incomes.

7.5 Intergenerational persistence and equilibrium inequality under imperfect information on talent

The relationship between inequality and mobility is discussed in most of the previously reviewed papers, leading to alternative views, often reflecting alternative assumptions. The model presented in section 7.3 suggests a negative relationship between (current) income inequality and intergenerational mobility, since the former strengthen the impact of liquidity constraints. Let us call it the *financing side* of the story. The model presented in section 7.4 adds another aspect, namely that (current) income inequality provides incentive to acquire education and, everything else being constant, implies greater mobility. Let us call this the *incentive side* of the story.[46] But mobility also affects long-run inequality, as clearly stated by Loury (1981, p. 854): '[I]ntergenerational social mobility is a property of the transition probability P, while cross-sectional inequality is (asymptotically) a property of the equilibrium distribution to which P gives rise.'

In order to analyse the relationship between inequality, mobility and growth better, we will introduce some modifications to the model presented in section 7.3.[47] Production technology is still described by a one-commodity economy, in which skilled and unskilled workers are imperfect substitutes[48] (see equation (7.18)). Given competitive labour markets, inequality is measured by the wage differential, which depends on the relative supply of skilled workers (see equation (7.21), here reproduced for ease of reference):

$$\frac{W_t^s}{W_t^n} = \frac{1 - \gamma}{\gamma} \cdot \frac{L_t^n}{L_t^s} = \frac{1 - \gamma}{\gamma} \cdot \frac{(1 - L_t^s)}{L_t^s} = f(\underline{L_t^s}) \qquad (7.21)$$

It is easy to note that inequality disappears and output is maximised when $L^s = 1 - \gamma$; therefore, the economically relevant story occurs in the interval $L^s \in (0, 1 - \gamma)$, since the extreme values are never attained.[49]

Each individual lives for two periods: in the first period he/she receives a bequest that can be consumed and/or used to buy an indivisible unit of education; in the second period he/she works (either as an skilled or unskilled worker) and allocates his/her earnings between consumption and inheritance. Altruism and a preference for consumption smoothing can be represented by the following utility function:

$$U_{it} = U(C_{it}, C_{it+1}, X_{it+1}) = \log C_{it} + \log C_{it+1} + \log X_{it+1} \qquad (7.31)$$

which is maximised under the following budget constraint:

$$\begin{cases} C_{it} + \delta_i \dfrac{B}{A_{it}} = X_{it}, & \delta_i = 0, 1, \quad A \sim (\underline{A}, \overline{A}) \\ C_{it+1} + X_{it+1} = W_{it+1}, & W_{it+1} = W_{t+1}^n \text{ if } \delta_i = 0, \\ W_{it+1} = W_{t+1}^s \text{ if } \delta_i = 1 \end{cases} \qquad (7.32)$$

where C_{it} and C_{it+1} are the consumption levels of individual i when, respectively, young and old, X_{it+1} is the amount of bequest left over, δ_i is the educational choice (whether to go to school or not) and B is the cost of education, which varies inversely with the ability endowment A_{it}, which is randomly selected from a given support in each generation. Financial markets are absent, so only very talented individuals and/or the offspring of very rich families find it convenient to acquire education. Given the homothetic utility function, whatever the earnings obtained in the labour market the optimal choice for the second

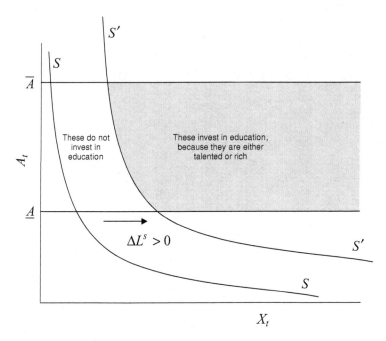

Figure 7.4 Educational choices (under individual specific cost of education)

period will be to allocate half of the income to consumption and the remaining half to the bequest.

By backward induction, the first-period choice (whether to go to school or not) will incorporate the second-period optimal solution. The child will become skilled if, and only if,

$$\log\left(X_{it} - \frac{B}{A_{it}}\right) + \log\left(\frac{W_{t+1}^s}{2}\right) + \log\left(\frac{W_{t+1}^s}{2}\right)$$
$$\geq \log(X_{it}) + \log\left(\frac{W_{t+1}^n}{2}\right) + \log\left(\frac{W_{t+1}^n}{2}\right) \tag{7.33}$$

which simplifies to

$$\frac{B}{X_{it} A_{it}} \leq 1 - \left(\frac{W_{t+1}^n}{W_{t+1}^s}\right)^2 \tag{7.34}$$

The locus described by equation (7.34) can be represented in figure 7.4 as the SS locus, which contrasts with figure 7.3, since now individual talent and family wealth can exactly compensate each other: only the

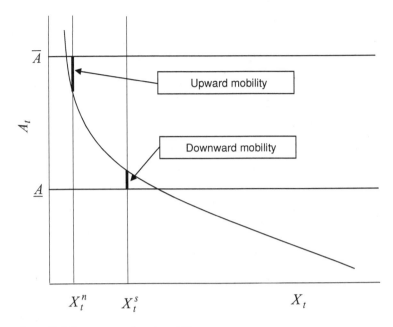

Figure 7.5 Intergenerational mobility

ablest people or children from rich families will become skilled. But the expansion of the supply of skilled workers tends to be self-defeating, since it shifts the locus to the right to $S'S'$, thus reducing the number of people who find it convenient to become skilled.

Given the non-transmittability of talent and the impossibility of money transfer from one period to the next (such that each person is forced to spend all his/her disposable income within each period), in each period we observe only two values for incomes, W_t^s and W_t^n, and as a consequence only two values for inheritance, $X_t^s = \frac{W_t^s}{2}$ and $X_t^n = \frac{W_t^n}{2}$. Among alternative configurations, which are dependent on the initial conditions, we find it worthwhile to discuss the case represented in figure 7.5, which exhibits upward and downward mobility at the same time. Conditional on one of the two levels of inheritance received from the previous generation, X_t^n or X_t^s, some children will obtain from nature an ability endowment high enough to facilitate the acquisition of education, while some others will not. In a steady state the SS locus must remain fixed, and this is possible if, and only if, L^s (the existing supply of skilled workers) remains constant. In turn, this

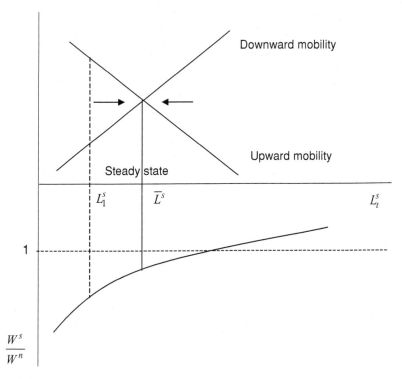

Figure 7.6 Mobility and inequality

requires that the number of upwardly mobile individuals be equal to the number of downwardly mobile ones; under the assumption of the uniform distribution of talent over the $(\underline{A}, \overline{A})$ support, this is equivalent to[50]

$$\overline{A} - \frac{B}{X^n} \cdot \left(\frac{W^{s^2}}{W^{s^2} - W^{n^2}} \right) = \frac{B}{X^s} \cdot \left(\frac{W^{s^2}}{W^{s^2} - W^{n^2}} \right) - \underline{A} \quad (7.35)$$

The working of the model can thus be represented by figure 7.6. When $\overline{L}^s = L_1^s$, the limited supply of skilled workers yields a high wage differential, which has a double impact on mobility: on the financing side it prevents most (unskilled) parents from leaving a bequest high enough to cover educational expenses, but on the incentive side it creates a large reward for becoming skilled. Since the latter effect dominates the former, the supply of L^s increases, progressively reducing the return on education (and therefore earnings inequality) and raising output.[51]

The growth process also reduces the ascriptive component and increases the meritocratic component, since it increases bequests to abler individuals born to uneducated parents and lowers them to less talented individuals born to educated parents. As a consequence, the correlation between ability and education (and income) increases.[52]

7.6 What we know from empirical analysis

When we move from the realm of formal models to the actual world of empirics, we may be surprised by how little has been done so far to test alternative theories. Following Galton's lead, the stage has been dominated by the issue of correctly measuring the extent of mean regression in intergenerational incomes.[53] The article by Becker and Tomes (1979) puts forward an estimate of the intergenerational elasticity of incomes in the order of 0.2, which implies that American society is characterised by a great deal of social mobility. This is in sharp contrast with the analysis of Erikson and Goldthorpe (1992), who maintain the view that class mobility is limited and not very different across countries or years. Part of this divergence was actually due to measurement errors. As has been made clear by Solon (1992) and Zimmerman (1992), whenever the independent variable is measured with errors (and this is certainly the case for parental incomes, because one year's measure does not necessarily represent a good approximation of permanent income, which is the relevant concept from a theoretical point of view) there is an attenuation bias, which is proportional to the variance of the measurement error.[54] An indirect confirmation of this potential bias has come from the study by Atkinson (1981) on UK data (for the city of York), where due to the lack of information on incomes he relied on occupational incomes, finding a higher measure of intergenerational elasticity between 0.39 and 0.46.[55]

A second aspect that has drawn the attention of scholars is the fact that the intergenerational elasticity estimate would not have provided a correct measure of the actual correlation, at least during the transition phases when substantial structural mobility was occurring.[56]

The current consensus is that the intergenerational elasticity is in the order of 0.40, and that the Nordic countries experience more mobility than the Anglo-Saxon countries ones.[57] Beyond the question of correctly measuring the intergenerational elasticity, the real policy issue concerns the ability to decompose this persistence into constituent channels. Only such a decomposition would allow an evaluation of how much of the observed mobility can be altered by appropriate policies. If most of the parental resources are passed from one generation to the next through the educational attainment of children,[58] the understanding of what governs educational choices becomes crucial not only for education economists but also for politicians, since intergenerational mobility shapes long-run inequality. In this respect, some useful results have been obtained.

Solon (1999) reviews several studies on income correlation across siblings (including twins), arguing that this correlation provides information on the relative importance of family and community factors in shaping individual destinies.[59] Even if we may reasonably expect a decline in the direct impact of parental income, the same cannot be said for the overall effect of family background.[60] Ermisch and Francesconi (2001) have drawn attention to the differential role played by mothers and fathers in shaping the educational attainments of their children. Since mothers have fewer outside options (given the existing discrimination in the labour market), they are more likely to take responsibility for supportive activities for their children.[61] The crucial role of mothers in achieving education for their children does not necessarily imply that increasing female participation in the labour market should contribute to a lowering of educational attainment in the children's generation.[62] As Esping-Andersen (2004a, 2004b) has forcefully shown, the impact of family background attenuates in countries characterised by extensive pre-school day care; moreover, additional incomes provided by second wage earners may help boost educational attainment in children.[63] So far, most economic analysis has focused on the impact of family income, testing what has been termed the '*money* → *investment* → *money*' model (Esping-Andersen, 2004a), but the drivers of educational choices are still an area of uncertainty from the point of view of intergenerational persistence analysis. For these reasons, we expect the economics of education to provide fruitful insights into this very issue.

Notes

1. A review of existing approaches to intergenerational mobility from an economist's viewpoint is to be found in Picketty (2000), whereas measurement problems are reassessed in Solon (1999). See also the symposium in the *Journal of Economic Perspective*, volume 16, issue 3, 2002.
2. 'If the heritability of IQ were 0.5 and the degree of assortation, m, were 0.2 (both reasonable, if only ballpark estimates) and the genetic inheritance of IQ were the only mechanism accounting for intergenerational income transmission, then the intergenerational correlation would be 0.01, or roughly 2 per cent of the observed intergenerational correlation' (Bowles and Gintis, 2002, p. 11).
3. Plug (2004) measures the impact of parental education on a sample of adopted children, thus being able to identify a 'pure' family background effect purged of genetic effects.
4. An interesting discussion about the intergenerational persistence of the inequality of opportunities in accessing education is contained in the introduction to Shavit and Blossfeld (1993), which also contains thirteen country studies.
5. See the seminal paper on *marriage markets* by Becker, where he proposes an analysis of assortative mating based on the observable talents in the couple (reproduced as chapter 10 in Becker, 1993). More recent evidence on the relative impact of assortative mating in intergenerational persistence is provided by Ermisch and Francesconi (2002), who use the correlation between parents-in-law's and children's socio-economic status as a measure of this channel. Esping-Andersen (2004c) discusses the contribution of fertility to intergenerational persistence: if richer and better-educated families are more fertile, intergenerational mobility is enhanced. Sweden is taken as an example of the relevance of this claim: 'If my argument holds that universal, high-quality day care reduces the weight of the "cultural" effect, then a society that combines maximum female employment with universal day care should almost by definition produce more mobility and less inherited life chances.' Mulligan (1997) holds an opposite view, since richer families are less altruistic because their cost of child rearing is higher: as a consequence they invest less in their children's education, fostering income convergence across families.
6. The seminal paper by Glenn Loury (1981) was the first to make clear that, in this second-best world, redistributive policies may be efficiency-enhancing: 'If, however, such trades are impossible because the relevant markets have failed, then the distribution of income among parents will affect the efficiency with which the overall training resources are allocated across offspring' (p. 844). Picketty (2000) distinguishes between

poverty traps and *low mobility traps*. In the first case, poor families cannot afford the educational investment because they are liquidity-constrained, and therefore they achieve a lower level of income; a once-and-for-all subsidy can make poverty disappear (as in Galor and Zeira, 1993). By contrast, in the second case mobility is hampered by high interest rates, which are endogenously determined by the supply (from richer families) of and the demand (from poorer families) for funds. In such a situation, the equilibrium is dependent on the initial wealth distribution, and redistribution is less effective (as in Piketty, 1997). Similarly, the wage rate can be made dependent on the initial wealth distribution, obtaining similar results (as in Banerjee and Newman, 1993).

7. Following the suggestion by Becker and Tomes (1986), Mulligan (1997, 1999) identifies liquidity-constrained families as those whose child has not received (and is not expecting to receive) a bequest above $25,000. Ermisch and Francesconi (2001) use the income distribution across parents (and the breaking of marriages between parents as a treatment effect) to distinguish between the 'genetic' transmission of ability and financial bequests: 'Thus if parents do not make gifts or bequests, the correlation between parents and child education is likely to represent primarily a causal effect of parent education. This is because human capital investment is not carried to the point at which the marginal return from education equals its marginal cost' (p. 140).

8. Clearly, the list is not conclusive; see, for example, the following statement by Bowles and Gintis (2002): 'On the basis of this and other empirical regularities, it seems safe to conclude that the intergenerational transmission of economic status is accounted for by a heterogeneous collection of mechanisms, including the genetic and cultural transmission of cognitive skills and noncognitive personality traits in demand by employers, the inheritance of wealth and income-enhancing group membership, such as race, and the superior education and health status enjoyed by the children of high-status families' (p. 4).

9. We make use of the sample analysed in Checchi (1997). The data for Germany (1,351 father–son pairs) are from the public version of the German Socio-Economic Panel Study. These data were provided by the Deutsches Institut für Wirtschaftsforschung. The data for Italy (1,615 father–son pairs) come from the data set developed by A. DeLillo and others, whose results are published – among others – in Cobalti and Schizzerotto (1994). The data for the United States (1,037 father–son pairs) come from the PSID (Panel Study of Income Dynamics) panel developed by the University of Michigan.

10. The educational attainment classification can be derived from the following table (see Checchi, 1997, for details):

	Italy	Germany	United States
Uncompleted compulsory education	No certificate if born before 1952; Licenza Elementare afterwards	No certificate	No certificate
Compulsory education (ISCED 1–2)	Licenza Elementare if born before 1952; Licenza Media afterwards	Mitlere Reife	High School Diploma (grade 12) if born after 1918
Beyond compulsory education (ISCED3–5)	Maturità or Diploma	Abitur or Facharbeiter-brief	Diploma from vocational schools
Tertiary education (ISCED 7)	Laurea or Dottorato di Ricerca	Staats-Diplomprufung or Doktorpru-fungen	Bachelor, Master or Ph.D.

11. See Erikson and Goldthorpe (1992) for a general discussion of the concept of social mobility, which incorporates aspects of both structural and exchange mobility.
12. For an axiomatic treatment of the mobility indices that distinguish between absolute (*structural*) and relative (*exchange*) mobility, see Checchi and Dardanoni (2002).
13. However, given the fact that the long-run distribution is country-specific (as it can be obtained from repeated application of the transition matrices – it corresponds to the eigenvector associated with the second-maximum eigenvalue), this mobility measure is heavily dependent on the choice of the reference point. Using the long-run distribution as a reference point, the Euclidian measures are, respectively, 0.18 for Italy, 0.15 for Germany and 0.12 for the United States.
14. The percentage of families along the main diagonal is, respectively, 33.1 per cent for Italy, 54.2 per cent for Germany and 36.4 per cent for the United States.
15. For an axiomatic approach to the measurement of mobility, see Shorrock (1978), Dardanoni (1993) and Fields (2000).
16. On the recognition of increased mass scholarisation in modern societies, leading to saturation of educational attainment (and therefore to a vanishing influence of social origins), other authors have adopted alternative measures to assess the extent of mobility. For example, the

studies reported by Shavit and Blossfeld (1993) consider age cohort sub-samples to analyse the impact of parental education, lending support to the theory of persistent inequality in access opportunities. Similarly, in the IALS data set Esping-Andersen (2004b) finds a decline in the impact of parental education in the youngest cohorts of Nordic countries (Sweden, Denmark and Norway) but not for Anglo-Saxon ones (the United States, United Kingdom and Germany). Applying an analogous approach to a different data set (TIMSS, 1995), Woessman (2004) compares the extent to which equality of opportunity is offered by different national educational systems; he finds that France exhibits the lowest impact of family background, while the United Kingdom has the highest, and Germany is in between.

17. Erikson and Goldthorpe (1992) give the following definition: 'The aim of the class scheme is to differentiate positions within labour markets and production units or, more specifically, one could say, to differentiate such positions in terms of employment relations that they entail' (p. 37). As an application: '[A] *service* relationship . . . is likely to be found whether it is required of employees that they exercise *delegated authority* or *specialised knowledge and expertise* in the interests of their employing organisation' (p. 42). At the other extreme they envisage standard labour contacts, without any requirement for monitoring (such as piece-rate jobs).

18. Among nine theoretical predictions advanced by Mulligan (1999), two of them have relevance with respect to educational choices: 'vi. human capital investments are less correlated with parental income among unconstrained families. vii. greater public provision of schooling increases intergenerational earnings mobility and decreases intergenerational consumption mobility' (p. S193). His empirical analysis lends little support to most of his theoretical predictions, however, leading him to conclude that, 'because the empirical success of the nine implications is so limited, one can conclude that the observed intergenerational dynamics of measures of economic status are not the result of borrowing constraints' (p. S215).

19. See the discussion of the issue in Grawe and Mulligan (2002).

20. Notice that, for simplicity, we are abstracting from the fact that ability could positively affect educational attainment, since it lowers the marginal cost and raises marginal revenue.

21. Solon (2004) presents a model that has some similarities to the present one. In his model, educational attainment is generated by public and private investment, which are assumed to be perfect substitutes, and ability, which is partially inherited across generations. Altruistic parents allocate part of their income to the education of their children; as a

consequence, the education of the children is positively correlated with the income of their parents. The intergenerational persistence will then be higher the higher the return on education (the β coefficient in our model) and the higher the productivity of the parental investment in education (which in our model is replaced by the size of the impact of liquidity constraints γ). He also takes into account the progressivity of the tax system. A different model is proposed by Bowles and Gintis (2002, appendix), in which genotypes of both parents affect children's genotypes, which in combination with the environment and parental incomes determines children's incomes. A socio-psychological model of intergenerational transmission is presented by Hauser et al. (2000).

22. Both conditions seem to apply in developing countries, where the measured mobility is effectively, low: see Grawe (2004).

23. Once there is agreement on the model structure, and conditional on avoiding causal interpretations, it can be used to decompose observed correlations into constituent components. For example, Bowles and Gintis (2002) propose the following decomposition of an estimated 0.3 correlation between father–son incomes: IQ conditional on schooling (0.04), schooling conditional on IQ (0.07), wealth (0.12), personality traits (0.07).

24. We follow the structure of the model proposed by Becker and Tomes (1979, 1986; also published as chapter 10 in Becker, 1993). The original notation has been modified in accordance with the conventions adopted in the present volume.

25. A crucial assumption for what follows is this: 'Ability, early learning, and other aspects of family's cultural and genetic "infrastructure" [which we denote here as talent A_i] usually raise the marginal effect of family and public expenditure on the production of human capital' (Becker, 1993), p. 262). In symbols, $\frac{\partial^2 H_{t+1}}{\partial A_t \partial j_t} > 0$, $j = X, E$.

26. While it is easy, in principle, to replace equation (7.6) with a more general one that includes parental human capital H_t within its arguments (i.e. $H_{t+1} = f[X_t, A_t E_t, H_t]$), this would introduce a second source of dynamics (in addition to the genetic transmittability of ability described by equation (7.10)), and the long-run dynamics would be more complicated to analyse.

27. In chapter 2 we assumed that altruistic parents were concerned with their own consumption and with the level of inheritance left over. Should the children all be alike, the two approaches would yield the same solution. But in the present context children are different because they are born with different talent endowments. In this case, the inheritance may compensate for the differences in ability.

28. Given the absence of a precise specification of A_t, equation (7.10) may either represent the purely genetic transmission of unobservable ability (clever parents generate clever children) or it may capture the effect of family cultural background (children from correctly speaking parents learn to speak correctly without any effort). Becker and Tomes (1986) make a further crucial assumption, that the parents know their own endowment of ability. In such a case they can compute the expected talent of their child by simply applying the mapping described by equation (7.10). In section 7.4 we will remove this assumption and we will replace it with the more realistic one that talent is revealed by schooling experience (and failure).

29. Under the assumption of a perfect financial market, equation (7.11) can be derived by equating the market interest rate and the return on education for the child. In other words, investing in one's child's education represents an alternative financial asset to achieve (dynastic) intertemporal consumption smoothing; as a consequence, in equilibrium it must ensure the same return as any other asset.

30. The perfect financial market assumption ensures that all individuals obtain the same return on human capital investment. If we abandon this assumption, equation (7.11) has to be replaced by $X^*_{t+1} = \chi(\underset{\pm}{A_{t+1}}, \underset{-}{E_{t+1}}, \underset{-}{r}, \underset{+}{Y_{t+1}})$, because the ability to leave an inheritance is limited by the availability of family incomes. In such a case, the autoregression coefficient β in equation (7.14) rises.

31. This is the route undertaken by Becker and Tomes (1986), who estimate a value of β lower than 0.20 on American data, and argue that the intergenerational transmission of 'genetic' traits is limited. However, Cooper, Durlauf and Johnson (1994) divide the population into three segments, finding different estimates of the β coefficient within each group (respectively, 0.53, 0.13 and 0.43 for the low-, middle- and high-income groups). Similarly, Shea (2000) shows that a two-stage least squares (2SLS) estimate for β (using as instruments the unionisation rate, industry sector dummies and closures of industrial plants – all factors that affect parental incomes independently of parental ability) is not statistically different from zero, whereas the same estimates for a sub-sample of poor families yields an estimate of between 0.32 and 0.79.

32. In its extreme version (the absence of financial market imperfections, the partial revelation of children's talent), consumption should follow a random walk across generations (i.e. the autoregression coefficient must be unitary). But this empirical claim does not find support in the data, forcing the author to introduce an explanation based on different degrees of altruism in line with income distribution (Mulligan, 1997).

33. See the description of the German tracking system by Schnepf (2002).
34. One partial exception is represented by Bertola and Coen Pirani (1998), in which schools screen students in order to reveal their true talent endowment, and the precision of the estimates varies with the amount of resources invested in education.
35. It is possible to recognise that Inada's conditions apply at the boundaries $\lim_{L^i \to \infty} W^i = 0$, $\lim_{L^i \to 0} W^i = \infty$, $i = s, n$. This ensures that, in equilibrium, we do not observe zero values for L^s or L^n.
36. In order to make such a comparison, the number of efficiency units must be perfectly observable, by both the worker and the firm.
37. An alternative possibility, discussed in the original paper (Owen and Weil, 1998), is when the government is able to lower the cost of educational attendance (up to the point where the aggregate output is maximised). Going beyond that level (such as, for example, pushing the educational cost B_t to zero) makes it convenient for everyone to achieve education, thus eliminating the wage differential ($W_t^s - W_t^n$) and creating a situation of overeducation.
38. Intergenerational mobility is measured by the ratio of conditional probabilities (the *odds ratio*). If we define

$$ODDS = \frac{prob(\text{educated child} \mid \text{uneducated parent})}{prob(\text{uneducated child} \mid \text{educated parent})}$$

when ODDS is equal to one we observe perfect mobility, whereas when $ODDS \to \infty$ mobility goes to zero.
39. 'It could achieve the same ratio of educated to uneducated efficiency units by educating some of the wealth-constrained high ability individuals . . . Such a redistribution of education could be achieved at a lower total cost since education costs are allocated per person and not per efficiency unit' (Owen and Weil, 1998, p. 96).
40. A similar result is obtained by Aaberge et al. (2002), for whom the proposed measure of intergenerational mobility is negatively correlated with the inequality measure (provided by the Gini index). The intuition is that greater mobility allows a more intensive reshuffling of income positions, thus lowering inequality when measured on a longer time horizon.
41. In the original model by Checchi, Ichino and Rustichini (1999), this cost is represented by forgone leisure, since the educational production function depends on individual effort. In the present context, we have abstracted from effort supply in order to increase the model's comparability. It is also worth noting that this discussion is, essentially, hypothetical, as schooling is, of course, compulsory in most countries.
42. School failures can take different forms: to be held back (as in the French or Italian systems), to be oriented towards vocational schools (as in

the German system) or simply to drop out from school (as in the US system).

43. Under the condition $\frac{B}{A_1 W^s - A_2 W^n} > \frac{1}{2}$, children from type A_2 parents will never go to school, because it is never convenient to do so. We leave out this uninteresting occurrence by assuming that $\frac{B}{A_1 W^s - A_2 W^n} < \frac{1}{2}$, which implies that the cost of acquiring education never reaches 50 per cent of the potential gain associated with it.

44. Since we have assumed that $\frac{B}{A_1 W^s - A_2 W^n} < \frac{1}{2}$, and it is easy to show that $\lim_{t \to \infty} v_t^e = \frac{1}{2}$, inequality (7.30) will apply with probability one.

45. Iyigun (1999) proposes a model in which school admission is based on academic potential (which is defined as innate ability and parental educational level). This creates ambiguous effects of current (educational) inequality on prospective mobility: 'Thus an increase in the fraction of educated parents in any period has potentially offsetting effects. First, by increasing total output, it expands the supply of educational services. Holding everything else constant, this would make admissions to school less competitive and would increase intergenerational economic mobility. Second, an increase in the fraction of educated parents implies that some members of the young generation have greater academic potential. Everything else constant, this would make admission to school more competitive and would lower intergenerational economic mobility' (p. 698).

46. Hassler, Rodriguez Mora and Zeira (2002) build a model in which inequality and mobility can be either positively or negatively correlated, depending on whether shocks affect the production sector or the education sector. While their model has some similarities with that of Maoz and Moav (1999), they endogenise the cost of acquiring education through the relative wage of skilled workers (on the assumption that teachers are skilled workers).

47. We will present a simplified version of the model proposed by Maoz and Moav (1999).

48. Eeckhout (1999) considers an alternative model, in which two types of workers are not substitutable, but the two types of produced commodities are. Given an increasing return to scale assumption, mobility is a (costly) move from the unskilled sector to the skilled sector. Eeckhout's economy is characterised by multiple equilibria, depending on the initial distribution of worker types.

49. When the supply of skilled workers goes to zero, the wage differential becomes infinite, whereas when it tends to $(1 - \gamma)$ the incentive to acquire costly education vanishes, and no one is willing to buy education. The maximal output can be obtained by setting $dY/dL^s = 0$;

that is,

$$
\frac{dY}{dL^s} = \frac{d\left[\left((1-L^s)^\gamma L^{s1-\gamma}\right)^\beta K^{1-\beta}\right]}{dL^s}
$$

$$
= \left((1-L^s)^\gamma L^{s1-\gamma}\right)^{\beta-1} K^{1-\beta}\left(-\gamma(1-L^s)^\gamma L^{s-\gamma}\right)
$$

$$
\times\left(-\frac{L^s}{1-L^s} + \frac{1-\gamma}{\gamma}\right) = 0
$$

50. It corresponds to the $\overline{L}^s$ such that $\frac{\overline{A}+\underline{A}}{2B} = \frac{W^s(\overline{L}^s)}{W^n(\overline{L}^s)} \cdot \frac{1}{W^n(\overline{L}^s)-W^s(\overline{L}^s)}$, which is highly non-linear in L^s. In the original model, Maoz and Moav (1999) assume that the cost of education B grows with the average wage, thus delaying the convergence to a steady state with mobility. There is a second potential steady state, with zero mobility, which corresponds to the vertical schedules of figure 7.5 crossing the SS locus above $\overline{A}$ or below $\underline{A}$. This represents another example of the poverty traps described by Piketty (2000).

51. 'The growth process, that stems from net upward mobility, decreases the wage earned by educated individuals and increases the wage earned by uneducated individuals. This process has two conflicting effects on future growth: on the one hand, the wage gap – the incentive for investment in education – declines. On the other hand, liquidity constraints on the poor are relaxed, leading to an increase in mobility. Although the cost of education increases with the average wage, liquidity constraints are relaxed since the increase of the wage of the uneducated workers is larger than the increase in the cost of education' (Maoz and Moav, 1999, p. 689). Whether mobility actually increases or decreases depends on the specific definition of mobility that is adopted. If we choose the number of people attaining an educational level different from their parents (the off-diagonal quotas), there is no presumption that mobility declines during the transition from L_1^s to $\overline{L}^s$ it depends crucially on the shape of the upward and downward mobility schedules, which in turn reflect the movements of the vertical schedules in figure 7.5.

52. See proposition 4 in Maoz and Moav (1999).

53. A thorough review of the empirical literature can be found in Solon (1999, 2002).

54. See chapter 6, section 7 of the present volume for a definition of attenuation bias in the context of estimating the return on education.

55. An analogous procedure, also followed by Checchi, Ichino and Rustichini (1999) because of a lack of data, takes the economic approach close to the sociological approach to class mobility, since belonging to

a particular class is typically defined according to occupation. Alternative strategies have been based on multi-year averages when data were available (Solon, 1992) or using instrumental variables (such as parental education or the social prestige associated with particular occupations – Zimmerman, 1992). In all cases, the estimated coefficients under these procedures are higher than single-year estimates. This is confirmed by the estimates provided by Blanden et al. (2004) with reference to the UK case.

56. In a regression such as $y_{t+1} = \alpha + \beta y_t + \omega_t$, the least square estimate of the β coefficient is $\hat{\beta}_{LS} = \frac{\sigma_{t+1}}{\sigma_t} \rho$, where ρ is the true correlation coefficient and σ_t is the (log) standard deviation of parents' incomes. Therefore, if children were experiencing a historical phase of rising inequality, this would be incorrectly perceived as reduced mobility, which is not occurring in the data-generating process. Grawe (2004) calls attention to the variation of income dispersion over the life cycle, showing that the measured mobility varies according to the age distance between parents and children. Following Grawe (2004), Blanden et al. (2004) estimate the underlying intergenerational correlation using the formula $\hat{\rho} = \frac{\sigma_t}{\sigma_{t+1}} \hat{\beta}_{OLS}$, using a correction factor of approximately 1.1.

57. See Solon (2002) and Aaberge et al. (2002). However, the UK ranking is still controversial. Dearden, Machin and Reed (1997), using NCDS data, provide an estimate as high as 0.57 to 0.59 for sons and 0.64 to 0.70 for daughters. Blanden et al. (2004) use NCDS and BCS data (the British Cohort Survey, a longitudinal sample of individuals born in 1970) to show that, if anything, mobility in the United Kingdom has declined between the first and the second cohort. In contrast, Ermisch and Francesconi (2004) make use of BHPS data (the British Household Population Survey, a panel sample of British families) from surveys conducted between 1991 and 1999, producing a much lower estimate using occupational prestige: between 0.15 and 0.30, which more than doubles when potential measurement errors are taken into account.

58. This claim has been challenged recently by Charles and Hurst (2003), who provide estimates of intergenerational elasticity in wealth, and show that asset ownership explains about two-thirds of intergenerational mobility. The different degrees of skewedness of wealth and income distribution suggest a non-linear relationship between intergenerational incomes – an issue explored by, among others, Grawe (2004) (using quantile regressions) and Couch and Lillard (2004) (finding more persistence at the extremes of income distribution). A calibrated model able to replicate these asymmetries has been proposed by De Nardi (2004).

59. 'In that sense, the sibling correlation is an index to the extent to which permanent earnings inequality arises from disparities in families and

community backgrounds' (Solon, 1999, p. 1767). And again: 'The empirical literature on sibling correlations in earnings, mostly focused on brothers in the United States, suggest that somewhere around 40% of the variance in the permanent component of the earnings is generated by variation in the family and community background factors shared by siblings' (p. 1775).

60. With respect to US experience, Mayer and Lopoo (2004) conclude that the decline in the effect of parental income on son's income and wages is steeper when we control parents' education and marital status and son's race, suggesting that some of the correlates of parental income may have become more important to children's economic success at the same time that parental income was becoming less important'. This is in accordance with the findings of Shea (2000), whereas Maurin (2002) still finds strong effects in French data.

61. Ermisch and Francesconi (2001) use UK BHPS data to study the impact of parental education on the educational choices of their children, and use financial transfers as the identifying treatment. 'Thus, if parents do not make gifts or bequests, the correlation between parents' and child's education is likely to represent primarily a causal effect of parent education. This is because human capital investment is not carried to the point at which the marginal return from education equals its marginal cost' (p. 140). They find that the mothers' gradient is higher than the fathers'.

62. Increased female participation in the labour market exerts an ambiguous effect, since on the one hand it reduces the attention paid to children, but at the same time it increases the available income. Ruhm (2004) finds an overall negative impact from working mothers' conditions on the cognitive abilities of children measured at the ages of five and six.

63. Heckman (2000) also expresses similar opinions, stressing the importance of pre-school child care for its complementary role in favouring further educational achievement.

References

Aaberge, R., A. Björklund, M. Jäntti, M. Palme, P. Pedersen, N. Smith and T. Wennemo 2002. Income inequality and income mobility in the Scandinavian countries compared to the United States. *Review of Income and Wealth* 48 (4), 443–70.

Acemoglu, D. 1999. Changes in unemployment and wage inequality: an alternative theory and some evidence. *American Economic Review* 89, 1259–78.

2003. Cross-country inequality trends. *Economic Journal* 113, F121–F149.

Acemoglu, D., and J. Pischke 1999. Beyond Becker: training in imperfect labor markets. *Economic Journal* 109, F112–F142.

2000. Certification of training and training outcomes. *European Economic Review* 44, 917–27.

Aghion, P., and P. Howitt 1998. *Endogenous Growth Theory*. Cambridge, MA: MIT Press.

Alesina, A. 1998. The political economy of macroeconomic stabilization and income inequality: myths and reality. In V. Tanzi and K. Chu (eds.). *Income Distribution and High-Quality Growth*. Cambridge, MA: MIT Press, 299–326.

Alesina, A., and R. Perotti 1996. Income distribution, political instability and growth. *European Economic Review* 40 (6), 1203–28.

Alesina, A., and D. Rodrik, 1994. Redistributive politics and economic growth. *Quarterly Journal of Economics* 109, 465–90.

Altonji, J., and T. Dunn 1996. The effects of family characteristics on the returns to schooling. *Review of Economics and Statistics* 78 (4), 692–704.

Angrist, J., and A. Krueger 1999. Empirical strategies in labor economics. In O. Ashenfelter and D. Card (eds.). *Handbook of Labor Economics* Vol. III. Amsterdam: North-Holland, 1277–1366.

Appleton, S. 2001. User fees, expenditure restructuring, and voucher systems in education. In G. Mwabu, C. Ugaz and G. White (eds.). *Social Provision in Low-Income Countries: New Patterns and Emerging Trends*, WIDER Studies in Development Economics. Oxford and New York: Oxford University Press, 157–85.

Appleton, S., J. Hoddinott and J. Knight 1996. Primary education as an input into post-primary education: a neglected benefit. *Oxford Bulletin of Economics and Statistics* 58 (1), 211–19.

Arnove, R., S. Franz, K. Morse and C. Torres 1997. Education and development. In R. Hillman (ed.). *Understanding Contemporary Latin America*. Boulder, CO: Lynne Rienner Publishers.

Arrow, K. 1962. The economic implications of learning by doing. *Review of Economic Studies* 29, 155–73.

1993. Excellence and equity in higher education. *Education Economics* 1 (1), 5–12.

Arrow, K., S. Bowles and S. Durlauf (eds.) 2000. *Meritocracy and Economic Inequality*. Princeton NJ: Princeton University Press.

Ashenfelter, O., and C. Rouse 1998. Income, schooling and ability: evidence from a new sample of identical twins. *Quarterly Journal of Economics* 113, 253–84

2000. Schooling, intelligence and income in America. In K. Arrow, S. Bowles and S. Durlauf (eds.). *Meritocracy and Economic Inequality*. Princeton NJ: Princeton University Press, 89–117.

Atkinson, A. B. 1981. On intergenerational income mobility in Britain. *Journal of Post–Keynesian Economics* 3, 194–218.

1999. Is Rising Income Inequality Inevitable? A Critique of the Transatlantic Consensus. WIDER Annual Lecture no. 3.

Banerjee, A. 2004. Educational policy and the economics of the family. *Journal of Development Economics* 74 (1), 3–32.

Banerjee, A., and A. Newman 1993. Occupational choice and the process of development. *Journal of Political Economy* 101 (2), 274–98.

Barr, N. 1993. Alternative funding resources for higher education. *Economic Journal* 103, 718–24.

Barro, R. 1997. *Determinants of Economic Growth – A Cross-Empirical Study*, Cambridge, MA: MIT Press.

2000. Inequality and growth in a panel of countries. *Journal of Economic Growth* 5, 5–32.

Barro, R., and J. W. Lee 1993. International comparisons of educational attainment. *Journal of Monetary Economics* 32 (3), 363–94.

1994. *Data Set for a Panel of 138 Countries*. Washington, DC: World Bank.

1996. International measures of schooling years and schooling quality. *American Economic Review*, Papers and Proceedings 86 (2), 218–23.

1997. Schooling Quality in a Cross-Section of Countries. Working Paper no. 6198, National Bureau of Economic Research, Cambridge, MA.

2001. Schooling quality in a cross–section of countries. *Economica* 68, 465–88.

Barro, R., and X. Sala-i-Martin 1992. Convergence. *Journal of Political Economy* 100 (2), 223–51.

Bassanini, A., and G. Brunello 2003. Is Training More Frequent when Wage Compression is Higher? Evidence from the European Community Household Panel. Discussion Paper no. 839, Institute for the Study of Labor (IZA), Bonn.

Bearse, P., G. Glomm and B. Ravikumar 2000. On the political economy of means-tested education vouchers. *European Economic Review* 44, 904–15.

Becker, G. 1993. *Human Capital: A Theoretical and Empirical Analysis, with Special Reference to Education.* Chicago: University of Chicago Press [1st ed., 1964].

Becker, G., and K. Murphy 2000. *Social Economics: Market Behavior in a Social Environment.* Cambridge, MA: Harvard University Press.

Becker, G., and N. Tomes 1979. An eqilibrium theory of the distribution of income and intergenerational mobility. *Journal of Political Economy* 87 (6), 1153–89.

   1986. Human capital and the rise and fall of families, *Journal of Labor Economics* 4, S1–S39.

Becker, S., and A. Ichino 2002. Estimation of average treatment effects based on propensity scores. *Stata Journal* 2 (4), 358–77.

Bedard, K. 2001. Human capital versus signaling models: university access and high school dropouts. *Journal of Political Economy* 109 (4), 749–75.

Belzil, C., and J. Hansen 2002. Unobserved ability and the return to schooling. *Econometrica* 70 (5), 2075–91.

Benabou, R. 1993. Workings of a city: location, education and production. *Quarterly Journal of Economics* 108 (3), 619–52.

   1994. Human capital, inequality and growth: a local perspective. *European Economic Review* 38, 817–26.

   1996a. Equity and efficiency in human capital investment: the local connection. *Review of Economic Studies* 63, 237–64.

   1996b. Heterogeneity, stratification and growth: macroeconomic implications of the community structure and school finance. *American Economic Review* 86 (3), 584–609.

   1996c. Inequality and growth. In B. Bernanke and J. Rotemberg (eds.). *NBER Macroeconomic Annual 1996.* Cambridge, MA: MIT Press, 11–74.

   2000. Meritocracy, redistribution and the size of the pie. In K. Arrow, S. Bowles and S. Durlauf (eds.). *Meritocracy and Economic Inequality.* Princeton NJ: Princeton University Press, 317–40.

Ben-Porath, Y. 1967. The production of human capital and the life-cycle of earnings. *Journal of Political Economy* 75/4 (1), 352–65.

Bertola, G. 1993. Factor shares and savings in endogenous growth. *American Economic Review* 83 (5), 1184–98.

Bertola, G., and D. Checchi 2001. Sorting and private education in Italy. *Lavoro e Relazioni Industriali* 2, 87–124.

Bertola, G., and D. Coen Pirani 1998. Market failures, education and macroeconomics. In G. Barba Navaretti, P. Dasgupta, K.-G. Mäler and D. Siniscalco (eds.). *Creation and Transfer of Knowledge: Institutions and Incentives*. Berlin: Springer-Verlag, 179–207.

Betts, J., and J. Shkolnik 2000. The effects of ability grouping on student achievement and resource allocation in secondary schools. *Economics of Education Review* 19, 1–15.

Bils, M., and P. Klenow 2000. Does schooling cause growth? *American Economic Review* 90 (5), 1160–83.

Birdsall, N., and E. James 1993. Efficiency and equity in social spending: how and why governments misbehave. In M. Lipton and J. Van Der Gaag (eds.). *Including the Poor*. Washington, DC: World Bank.

Blanden, J., A. Goodman, P. Gregg and S. Machin 2004. Changes in intergenerational mobility in Britain. In M. Corak (ed.). *Generational Income Mobility in North America and Europe*. Cambridge: Cambridge University Press, 122–46.

Blau, F. D. 1996. Symposium on primary and secondary education. *Journal of Economic Perspectives* 10 (4), 3–8.

Blöndal, S., S. Field and N. Girouard 2002. Investment in human capital through upper-secondary and tertiary education. *OECD Economic Studies* 34, 41–89.

Bourguignon, F. 1981. Pareto superiority of unegalitarian equilibria in Stiglitz' model of wealth distribution with convex saving functions. *Econometrica*, 49 (6), 1469–75.

    1993. Croissance, distribution et ressources humaines: comparaison internationale et specificités régionales. *Revue d'Economie du Développement* 1(4), 3–35.

Bourguignon, F., and T. Verdier 2000. Oligarchy, democracy, inequality and growth. *Journal of Development Economics* 62 (2), 285–313.

Bowles, S. 1985. The production process in a competitive economy: Walrasian, Neo-Hobbesian, and Marxian models. *American Economic Review* 75 (1), 16–36.

Bowles, S., and H. Gintis 1975. The problem with human capital theory – a Marxian critique. *American Economic Review* 65 (2), 74–82.

    1976. *Schooling in Capitalist America*. London: Routledge and Kegan Paul.

2000. Does schooling raise earnings by making people smarter? In K. Arrow, S. Bowles and S. Durlauf (eds.). *Meritocracy and Economic Inequality*. Princeton, NJ: Princeton University Press, 118–36.

2002. The inheritance of inequality. *Journal of Economic Perspectives* 16 (3), 3–30.

Bowles, S., H. Gintis and B. Gustafsson (eds.) 1993. *Markets and Democracy: Participation, Accountability and Efficiency*. Cambridge: Cambridge University Press.

Bowles, S., H. Gintis and M. Osborne 2001a. The determinants of earnings: a behavioural approach. *Journal of Economic Literature* 39, 1137–76.

2001b. Incentive – enhancing preferences: personality, behavior and earnings. *American Economic Review* 91 (2): 155–8.

Bowles, S., and V. Nelson. 1974. The 'inheritance of IQ' and the intergenerational reproduction of economic inequality, *Review of Economics and Statistics* 56 (1), 39–51.

Brandolini, A., and N. Rossi 1998. Income distribution and growth in industrial countries. In V. Tanzi and K. Chu (eds.). *Income Distribution and High-Quality Growth*. Cambridge, MA: MIT Press, 69–105.

Brown, C. and C. Belfield, 2001. The Relationship between Private Schooling and Earnings: A Review of the Evidence for the US and the UK. Occasional Paper no. 27 National Center for the Study of Privatization in Education, Teachers College, Columbia University, New York (http://www.tc.columbia.edu/ncspe).

Brown, S., and J. Sessions 1999. Education and economic status: a test of the strong screening hypothesis in Italy. *Economics of Education Review* 18, 397–404.

Brunello, G. 2003. On the complementarity between education and training in Europe. In D. Checchi and C. Lucifora (eds.). *Education, Training and Labour Market Outcomes in Europe*. London: Palgrave, 188–210.

Brunello, G., and S. Comi 2004. Education and earnings growth: evidence from 11 European countries. *Economics of Education Review* 23 (1), 75–83.

Brunello, G., S. Comi and C. Lucifora 2001. The returns to education in Italy: a new look at the evidence. In C. Harmon, I. Walker and N. W. Nielsen (eds.). *The Returns to Education in Europe*. Londan Edward Elgar.

Brunello, G., and M. Giannini 2004. Stratified or comprehensive? The economic efficiency of school design. *Scottish Journal of Political Economy* 51 (2), 173–93.

Burtless, G. (ed.) 1996. *Does Money Matter? The Effect of School Resources on Student Achievement and Adult Success*. Washington, DC: Brookings Institution Press.

Cameron, S., and J. Heckman 2001. The dynamics of educational attainment for black, Hispanic, and white males. *Journal of Political Economy* 109 (3), 455–99.

Canton, E., and F. deJong 2002. The Demand for Higher Education in the Netherlands, 1950–1999. Discussion Paper no. 12, Bureau for Economic Policy Analysis (CPB), The Hague.

Card, D. 1995. Earnings, schooling and ability revisited. In S. W. Polachek (ed.). *Research in Labor Economics* Vol. XIV. Greenwich, CT, and London: JAI Press, 23–48.

1999. The causal effect of education on earnings. In O. Ashenfelter and D. Card (eds.). *Handbook of Labor Economics* Vol. III. Amsterdam: North-Holland, 1801–63.

2001. Estimating the return to schooling: progress on some persistent econometric problem. *Econometrica* 69 (5), 1127–60.

Card, D., and A. Krueger 1992. Does school quality matter? Returns to education and the characteristics of public schools in the United States. *Journal of Political Economy* 100 (1), 1–39.

1996a. School resources and student outcomes: an overview of the literature and new evidence from North and South Carolina. *Journal of Economic Perspectives* 10 (4), 31–50.

1996b. Labor market effects of school quality: theory and evidence. In G. Burtless (ed.). *Does Money Matter? The Effect of School Resousces on Student Achievement and Adult Success*. Washington, DC: Brookings Institution Press, 97–140.

Card, D., and A. Payne 2002. School finance reform, the distribution of school spending and the distribution of SAT scores. *Journal of Public Economics* 83 (1), 49–82.

Chapman, B. 1997. Conceptual issues and the Australian experience with income contingent charges for higher education. *Economic Journal* 107, 738–51.

Charles, K., and E. Hurst 2003. The correlation of wealth across generations. *Journal of Political Economy* 111 (6), 1155–82.

Checchi, D. 1997. Education and intergenerational mobility in occupations. *American Journal of Economics and Sociology* 56 (3), 331–52.

2000. University education in Italy. *International Journal of Manpower* 21 (3–4), 160–205.

2003a. The Italian Educational System: Family Background and Social Stratification. Working Paper 2003–01, Deparment of Economics, University of Milan.

2003b. Inequality in incomes and access to education: a cross-country analysis (1960–95). *Labour* 17 (2), 153–201.

2004. Does educational achievement help to explain income inequality? In G. A. Cornia (ed.). *Inequality, Growth and Poverty in an Era of*

Liberalization and Globalization. Oxford: Oxford University Press, chap. 4.

Checchi, D., and V. Dardanoni 2002. Mobility comparisons: does using different measures matter? *Research on Inequality* 9, 113–45.

Checchi, D., A. Ichino and A. Rustichini 1999. More equal but less mobile? Intergenerational mobility and inequality in Italy and in the US. *Journal of Public Economics* 74, 351–93.

Checchi, D. and T. Jappelli 2004. School Choice and Quality. Discussion Paper no. 4748, Centre for Economic Policy Research, London.

Chevalier, A., C. Harmon, I. Walker and Y. Zhu 2003. Does Education Raise Productivity or Just Reflect It? Discussion Paper no. 3993, Centre for Economic Policy Research, London.

Chiu, W. 1998. Income inequality, human capital accumulation and economic performance. *Economic Journal* 108, 44–59.

Christou, C. and M. Haliassos 1994. How do Students Finance Human Capital Accumulation? The Choice between Borrowing and Work, Mimeo, Deparment of Economics, University of Cyprus.

Clapp, J., and S. Ross 2002. Schools and Housing Markets: An Examination of School Segregation and Performance in Connecticut. Working Paper no. 2002–08, Department of Economics, University of Connecticut.

Cobalti, A., and A. Schizzerotto 1994. *La mobilità sociale in Italia.* Bologna: Il. Mulino.

Cooper, S., S. Durlauf and P. Johnson 1994. On the evolution of economic status across generations. *American Statistical Association, Business and Economics Section,* Papers and Proceedings, May, 50–8.

Cornia, G. A. (ed.) 2004. *Inequality, Growth and Poverty in an Era of Liberalization and Globalization.* Oxford: Oxford University Press.

Couch, K., and D. Lillard 2004. Nonlinear patterns of intergenerational mobility in Germany and the United States. In M. Corak (ed.). *Generational Income Mobility in North America and Europe.* Cambridge: Cambridge University Press, 190–206.

Cowell, F. 1995. *Measuring Inequality.* London: Prentice Hall.

Dardanoni, V. 1993. Measuring social mobility. *Journal of Economic Theory* 61, 372–94.

De Fraja, G. 2001. Education policies: equity, efficiency and voting equilibria. *Economic Journal* 111, C104–C119.

    2002. The design of optimal educational policies. *Review of Economic Studies* 69, 437–66.

    2005. Affirmative action and efficiency in education. Forthcoming in *International Economic Review*

De Nardi, C. 2004. Wealth inequalities and intergenerational links. *Review of Economic Studies* 71, 743–68.

Dearden, L., C. Emmerson, C. Frayne and C. Meghir 2003. The Impact of Financial Incentives on Educational Choice. Mimeo, Institute for Fiscal Studies, London.

Dearden, L., J. Ferri and C. Meghir 2002. The effect of school quality on educational attainment and wages. *Review of Economics and Statistics* 84 (1), 1–20.

Dearden, L., S. Machin and H. Reed 1997. Intergenerational mobility in Britain. *Economic Journal* 107, 47–66.

Dee, T. 2003. Are there Civic Returns to Education? Working Paper no. 9588, National Bureau of Economic Research, Cambridge, MA.

Dehejia, R., and R. Gatti 2002. Child Labor: The Role of Income Variability and Access to Credit across Countries. Working Paper no. 9018, National Bureau of Economic Research, Cambridge, MA.

Deininger, K., and L. Squire 1996. A new data set measuring income inequality. *World Bank Economic Review* 10 (3), 565–91.

1998. New ways of looking at old issues: inequality and growth. *Journal of Development Economics* 57, 259–87.

Dustmann, C., N. Rajah and A. van Soest 2003. Class size, education and wages. *Economic Journal* 113, F99–F120.

Eckstein, Z., and I. Zilcha 1994. The effects of compulsory schooling on growth, income distribution and welfare. *Journal of Public Economics* 54, 339–59.

Edwards, R. 1977. Personal traits and 'success' in schooling and work. *Educational and Psychological Measurement* 37, 125–38.

Eeckhout, J. 1999. Educational mobility: the effect on efficiency and distribution. *Economica* 66, 317–33.

Epple, D., and R. Romano 1998. Competition between private and public schools, vouchers, and peer-group effects. *American Economic Review* 88 (1), 33–62.

2002. Educational Vouchers and Cream Skimming. Working Paper no. 9354, National Bureau for Economic Research, Cambridge, MA.

Erikson, R., and J. Goldthorpe 1992. *The Constant Flux*. Oxford: Clarendon Press.

2002. Intergenerational inequality: a sociological perspective. *Journal of Economic Perspectives* 16 (3), 31–44.

Ermisch, J., and M. Francesconi 2001. Family matters: impact of family background on educational attainments. *Economica* 68, 137–56.

2002. Intergenerational Social Mobility and Assortative Mating in Britain. Discussion Paper no. 465, Institute for the Study of Labor (IZA), Bonn.

2004. Intergenerational mobility in Britain: new evidence from the British household panel survey. In M. Corak (ed.). *Generational Income*

Mobility in North America and Europe. Cambridge: Cambridge University Press, 147–89.

Esping-Andersen, G. 2004a. Unequal opportunities and the mechanisms of social inheritance. In M. Corak (ed.). *Generational Income Mobility in North America and Europe.* Cambridge: Cambridge University Press, 289–314.

2004b. Untying the Gordian knot of social inheritance. In A. L. Kalleberg (ed.). *Inequality: Structures, Dynamics and Mechanisms: Essays in Honor of Aage B. Sorensen.* Amsterdam: Elsevier, chap. 7.

2004c. Income Mobility, Human Capital and Fertility. Mimeo, Pompeu Fabra University.

Eurostat 2000. *Continuing Vocational Training Survey* (CVTS 2). *Eurostat,* Brussels.

Feldman, M., S. Otto and F. Christiansen 2000. Genes, culture and inequality. In K. Arrow, S. Bowles and S. Durlauf (eds.). *Meritocracy and Economic Inequality.* Princeton, NJ: Princeton University Press, 61–86.

Fernandez, R. 1998. Education and Borrowing Constraints: Test vs. Prices. Discussion Paper no. 1913, Centre for Economic Policy Research, London.

Fernandez, R., and J. Gali 1999. To each according to . . .? Markets, tournaments and the matching problem with borrowing constraints. *Review of Economic Studies* 66, 799–824.

Fernandez, R., and R. Rogerson 1998. Public education and income distribution: a quantitative evaluation of educational finance. *American Economic Review* 88 (4), 813–33.

1999. Education finance reform and investment in human capital: lessons from California. *Journal of Public Economics* 74 (3), 327–50.

2003. Equity and resources: an analysis of education finance systems. *Journal of Political Economy* 111 (4), 858–97.

Fershtman, C., K. Murphy and Y. Weiss 1996. Social status, education, and growth. *Journal of Political Economy* 104 (1), 108–32.

Fields, G. 2000. Income mobility: concepts and measures. In N. Birdsall and C. Graham (eds.). *New Markets, New Opportunities? Economic and Social Mobility in a Changing World.* Washington, DC: Brookings Institution Press, 101–32.

Figlio, D., and M. Page 2002. School choice and the distributional effects of ability tracking: does separation increase equality? *Journal of Urban Economics* 51 (3), 497–514.

Filmer, D., and L. Pritchett 1999. The effect of household wealth on educational attainment: evidence from 35 countries. *Population and Development Review* 25 (1), 85–120.

Fiske, E., and H. Ladd 2000. *When Schools Compete: A Cautionary Tale.* Washington, DC: Brookings Institution Press.

Flabbi, L., 1999. Effeti redistributivi del finanziamento pubblico dell' istruzione in Italia. In D. Checchi (ed.). *Istruzione e mercato: per una analisi economica della formazione scolastica.* Bologna: Il Mulino, chap. 4.

Flug, K., A. Spilimbergo and E. Wachtenheim 1998. Investment in education: do economic volatility and credit constraints matter? *Journal of Development Economics* 55, 465–81.

Flynn, J. 2000. IQ trends over time: intelligence, race and meritocracy. In K. Arrow, S. Bowles and S. Durlauf. (eds.). *Meritocracy and Economic Inequality.* Princeton, NJ: Princeton University Press, 35–60.

Freeman, R. 1986. Demand for education. In O. Ashenfelter and R. Layard (eds.). *Handbook of Labor Economics* Vol. I. Amsterdam: North-Holland, 357–86.

Friedman, M. (1962). *Capitalism and Freedom.* Chicago: University of Chicago Press.

Galor, O., and J. Zeira 1993. Income distribution and macroeconomics. *Review of Economic Studies* 60, 35–52.

Gambetta, D. 1987. *Were They Pushed or Did They Jump? Individual Decision Mechanisms in Education.* Cambridge: Cambridge University Press.

Ganderton, P. 1992. The effect of subsidies in kind on the choice of a college. *Journal of Public Economics* 48 (3), 269–92.

Gasperoni, G. 1997. *Il rendimento scolastico.* Bologna: Il Mulino.

Gauri, V. and A. Vawda 2003. Vouchers for Basic Education in Developing Countries: A Principal-Agent Perspective. Policy Research Working Paper no. 3005, World Bank, Washington, DC.

Gemmell, N. 1996. Evaluating the impacts of human capital stocks and accumulation on economic growth: some new evidence. *Oxford Bulletin of Economics and Statistics* 58 (1), 9–28.

Giannini, M. 2001. Education and job market signalling: how robust is the nexus? *Economia Politica* 18 (1), 41–54.

Gibbons, S., and S. Machin 2003. Valuing English primary schools. *Journal of Urban Economics* 53 (2), 197–219.

Glomm, G., and B. Ravikumar 1992. Public versus private investment in human capital: endogenous growth and income inequality. *Journal of Political Economy* 100 (4), 818–34.

Glyn, A. 2001. Inequalities of unemployment and wages in OECD countries. *Oxford Bulletin of Economics and Statistics* 62 (special issue), 1–17.

Goldberger, A., and C. Manski 1995. Review article: 'The Bell Curve' by Herrnstein and Murray. *Journal of Economic Literature* 33, 762–76.

Gradstein, M., and M. Justman 1999. The Industrial Revolution, political transition, and the subsequent decline in inequality in 19th-century Britain. *Explorations in Economic History* 36 (2), 109–27.

   2000. Human capital, social capital, and public schooling. *European Economic Review* 44, 879–90.

   2001. Public Education and the Melting Pot. Discussion Paper no. 2924, Centre for Economic Policy Research, London.

   2002. Education, social cohesion and economic growth. *American Economic Review* 92 (4), 1192–204.

Grandmont, J. M. 1978. Intermediate preferences and the majority rule. *Econometrica* 46 (2), 317–30.

Grawe, N. 2004. Intergenerational mobility for whom? The experience of high- and low-earning sons in international perspective. In M. Corak (ed.). *Generational Income Mobility in North America and Europe*. Cambridge: Cambridge University Press, 58–89.

Grawe, N., and C. Mulligan 2002. Economic interpretations of intergenerational correlations. *Journal of Economic Perspectives* 16 (3), 45–58.

Green, D. and W. Riddell 2003. Literacy and earnings: an investigation of the interaction of cognitive and unobserved skills in earnings generation. *Labour Economics* 100 (2), 165–84.

Griliches, Z. 1977. Estimating the returns to schooling: some econometric problems. *Econometrica* 45 (1), 1–22.

Grilli, E. 1994. Long-term economic growth, income distribution and poverty in developing countries: the evidence. In E. Grilli and D. Salvatore (eds.). *Handbook of Economic Development*. Westport, CT: Greenwood Publishing Group, 65–143.

Groot, W., and H. Oosterbeek 1994. Earning effects of different components of schooling; human capital versus screening. *Review of Economics and Statistics* 76 (2), 317–21.

Grossman, H. and M. Kim. 1998. Human Capital and Predation: A Positive Theory of Educational Policy. Working Paper no. 6403, National Bureau of Economic Research, Cambridge, MA.

Gundlach, E., L. Woessman and J. Gmelin 2001. The decline of schooling productivity in OECD countries. *Economic Journal* 111, C135–C147.

Hanushek, E. 1986. The economics of schooling: production and efficiency in public schools. *Journal of Economic Literature* 24, 1141–77.

   1995. Interpreting recent research on schooling in developing countries. *World Bank Research Observer* 10 (2), 227–46.

1996. Measuring investment in education. *Journal of Economic Perspectives* 10 (4), 9–30.

2002. Publicly provided education. In A. Auerbach and M. Feldstein (eds.). *Handbook of Public Economics* Vol. IV. Amsterdam: North-Holland, 2045–141.

Harmon, C., V. Hogan and I. Walker 2003. Dispersion in the economic return to schooling. *Labour Economics* 100 (2), 205–15.

Harmon, C., H. Oosterbeek and I. Walker 2003. The returns to education: microeconomics. *Journal of Economic Surveys* 17 (2), 115–56.

Hassler, J., J. Rodriguez Mora and J. Zeira 2002. Inequality and Mobility. Working Paper no. RWP02–009, John F. Kennedy School of Government, Harvard University, Cambridge, MA.

Hauser, R., J. Warren, M. Hsiung and W. Carter 2000. Occupational status, education and social mobility in meritocracy. In K. Arrow, S. Bowles and S. Durlauf (eds.). *Meritocracy and Economic Inequality*. Princeton, NJ. Princeton University Press, 179–229.

Heckman, J. 1979. Sample specification bias as a specification error. *Econometrica* 47, 153–61.

2000. Policies to foster human capital. *Research in Economics* 54 (1), 3–56.

Heckman, J., A. Layne-Ferrar and P. Todd 1996. Does measured school quality really matter? An examination of the earnings–quality relationship. In G. Burtless (ed.). *Does Money Matter? The Effect of School Resources on Student Achievements and Adult Success*. Washington, DC: Brookings Institution Press, 192–289.

1997. Human capital, pricing equations with an application to estimating the effect of schooling quality on earnings. *Review of Economics and Statistics* 78 (4), 562–609.

Hedges, L. V., and R. Greenwald 1996. Have times changed? The relation between school resources and student performance. In G. Burtless (ed.). *Does Money Matter? The Effect of School Resources on Student Achievement and Adult Success*. Washington, DC: Brookings Institution Press, 74–92.

Helliwell, J., and R. Putnam. 1999. Education and Social Capital. Working Paper no. 7121, National Bureau of Economic Research, Cambridge, MA.

Herrnstein, R., and C. Murray 1994. *The Bell Curve: Intelligence and Class Structure in American Life*. New York: Free Press.

Hoxby, C. 1996a. How teachers' unions affect education production. *Quarterly Journal of Economics* 111 (3), 671–718.

1996b. Are efficiency and equity in school finance substitutes or complements? *Journal of Economic Perspectives* 10 (4), 51–72.

2000a. The effects of class size on student achievement: new evidence from population variation. *Quarterly Journal of Economics* 115 (4), 1239–85.

2000b. *Peer* Effect in the Classroom: Learning from Gender and Race Variation. Working Paper no. 7867, National Bureau of Economic Research, Cambridge, MA.

2000c. Does competition among public schools benefit students and taxpayers? *American Economic Review* 90 (5), 1209–38.

Ichino, A., and R. Winter-Ebmer 1999. Lower and upper bounds of returns to schooling: an exercise in IV estimation with different instruments. *European Economic Review* 43 (4–6), 889–901.

Iyigun, M. 1999. Public education and intergenerational economic mobility. *International Economic Review* 40 (3), 697–710.

Jacobs, B. 2002. An Investigation of Education Finance Reform: Graduate Taxes and Income-Contingent Loans in the Netherlands. Discussion Paper no. 9, Bureau for Economic Policy Analysis (CPB), The Hague.

Johansson, O. 1991. *An Introduction to Modern Welfare Economics.* Cambridge: Cambridge University Press.

Johnson, G. 1985. Subsidies for higher education. *Journal of Labor Economics* 2 (3), 303–18.

Jones, C. 1997. On the evolution of the world income distribution. *Journal of Economic Perspectives* 11 (3), 19–36.

Jones, G. 1993. *The Economics of Education*, London: Macmillan.

Kahn, L. 2000. Wage inequality, collective bargaining and relative employment from 1985 to 1994, evidence from fifteen OECD countries. *The Review of Economics and Statistics* 82 (4), 564–79.

Kamien, M., and N. Schwartz 1981. *Dynamic Optimization: The Calculus of Variations and Optimal Control in Economics and Management.* Amsterdam: North-Holland.

Kane, T. 1995. Rising Public College Tuition and College Entry: How Well Public Subsidies Promote Access to College? Working Paper no. 5164, National Bureau of Economic Research, Cambridge, MA.

Kodde, D., and J. Ritzen 1985. The demand for education under capital market imperfection. *European Economic Review* 28, 347–62.

Krueger, A. 1999. Experimental estimates of education production functions. *Quarterly Journal of Economics* 114 (2), 497–532.

2002. Inequality, too much of a good thing. In J. Heckman and A. Krueger (eds.). *Inequality in America.* Cambridge, MA: MIT Press, 1–76.

Krueger, A., and M. Lindahl 2001. Education for growth: why and for whom? *Journal of Economic Literature* 39, 1101–36.

Krueger, A., and D. Whitmore 2001. The effect of attending a small class in the early grades on college-test taking and middle school test results: evidence from project STAR. *Economic Journal* 111, 1–28.

Krueger, A., and P. Zhou 2002. Another Look at the New York City School Voucher Experiment. Working Paper no. 470 Industrial Relations Section, Princeton University, Princeton, NJ.

Kuznets, S. 1955. Economic growth and income inequality. *American Economic Review* 45 (1), 1–28.

Ladd, M. 2002. School vouchers: a critical view. *Journal of Economic Perspectives* 16 (4), 3–24.

Lang, K., and D. Kropp 1986. Human capital versus sorting: the effects of compulsory attendance laws. *Quarterly Journal of Economics* 101 (3), 609–24.

Layard, R., S. Nickell and R. Jackman 1991. *Unemployment*. Oxford: Oxford University Press.

Layard, R., and G. Psacharopoulos 1974. The screening hypothesis and the returns to education. *Journal of Political Economy* 82(5), 985–98.

Lazear, E. 1977. Education: consumption or production? *Journal of Political Economy* 85 (3), 569–97.

1995. *Personnel Economics*. Cambridge, MA: MIT Press.

1999. Educational Production Function. Working Paper no. 7319, National Bureau of Economic Research, Cambridge, MA.

2001. Educational production. *Quarterly Journal of Economics* 116 (3), 777–803.

Levin, H. 1992. Market approaches to education: vouchers and school choice. *Economics of Education Review* 11 (4), 279–85.

Li, H., L. Squire and H. Zou 1998. Explaining international and intertemporal variations in income inequality. *Economic Journal,* 108 26–43.

Lott, J. 1999. Public schooling, indoctrination and totalitarianism. *Journal of Political Economy* 107 (6), S127–S157.

Loury, G. 1981. Intergenerational transfers and the distribution of earnings. *Econometrica* 49 (4), 843–67.

Lucas, R. 1988. On the mechanics of economic development. *Journal of Monetary Economics* 22, 3–42.

Lynch, L. (ed.) 1994. *Training and the Private Sector: International Comparisons*. Chicago: University of Chicago Press.

Manski, C. 1992. Educational choice (vouchers) and social mobility. *Economics of Education Review* 11 (4), 351–69.

Maoz, Y., and O. Moav 1999. Intergenerational mobility and the process of development. *Economic Journal* 109, 677–97.

Maurin, E. 2002. The impact of parental income on early schooling transitions: a re-examination using data over three generations. *Journal of Public Economics* 85, 301–32.

Mauro, P. 1995. Corruption, country risk and growth. *Quarterly Journal of Economics* 3, 681–712.

Mayer, S., and L. Lopoo 2004. Trends in the intergenerational economic mobility of sons and daughters in the United States. In M. Corak (ed.). *Generational Income Mobility in North America and Europe.* Cambridge: Cambridge University Press, 90–121.

McPherson, M., and M. O. Shapiro 1991, Does student aid affect college enrolment? New evidence on a persistent controversy. *American Economic Review* 81 (1), 309–18.

Mincer, J. 1974. *Schooling, Experience, and Earnings.* New York: Columbia University Press.

Mocan, H. N., B. Scafidi and E. Tekin 2002. Catholic Schools and Bad Behavior. Discussion Paper no. 599, Institute for the Study of Labor (IZA), Bonn.

Montgomery, J. 1991. Social networks and labor market outcomes: towards an economic analysis. *American Economic Review* 81 (5), 1408–18.

Morris, M. 1989. Student aid in Sweden: recent experience and reform. In M. Woodhall (ed.). *Financial Support for Students: Grants, Loans or Graduate Taxes?* London, Kogan Page.

Moulton, B. 1990. An illustration of a pitfall in estimating the effect of aggregate variables on micro units. *Review of Economics and Statistics* 72 (2), 334–8.

Mulligan, C. 1997. *Parental Priorities and Economic Inequality.* Chicago: University of Chicago Press.

1999. Galton versus the human capital approach to inheritance. *Journal of Political Economy* 107 (6), S184–S224.

Mulvey, C., P. Miller and N. Martin 1997. Family characteristics and the returns to schooling: evidence on gender differences from a sample of Australian twins. *Economica* 64, 119–36.

Murnane, R., J. Willett, M. Braatz and Y. Duhaldeborde 2001. Do different dimensions of male high school students' skills predict labor market success a decade later? Evidence from the NLSY. *Economics of Education Review* 20 (4), 311–20.

Murnane, R., J. Willett and F. Levy 1995. The growing importance of cognitive skills in wage determination. *Review of Economics and Statistics* 77 (2), 251–66.

Murphy, K., and F. Welch 1992. The structure of wages. *Quarterly Journal of Economics* 10 (4), 283–96.

Naylor, R., J. Smith and A. McKnight 2002. Why is there a graduate earnings premium for students from independent schools? *Bulletin of Economic Research* 54 (4), 315–40.

Neal, D. 2002. How vouchers could change the market for education. *Journal of Economic Perspectives* 16 (4), 25–44.

Nechyba, T. 1996. Public School Finance in a General Equilibrium Tiebout World: Equalization Programs, Peer Effects and Private School Vouchers. Working Paper no. 5642, National Bureau of Economic Research, Cambridge, MA.

2000. Mobility, targeting and private school vouchers. *American Economic Review* 90 (1), 130–46.

Nehru, V., and A. Dhareshwar 1993. A new database on physical capital stock: sources, methodology and results. *Rivista de Analisis Economico* 8 (1), 37–59.

Nerlove, M. 1975. Some problems in the use of income-contingent loans for the finance of education. *Journal of Political Economy* 83 (1), 157–83.

Okun, A. 1975. *Equality and Efficiency: The Big Trade-Off.* Washington, DC: Brookings Institution Press.

Organisation for Economic Co-operation and Development 1996. *Education at a Glance.* Paris, OECD.

2001. *Education at a Glance.* Paris, OECD.

2003. *Education at a Glance.* Paris, OECD.

Owen, A., and D. Weil 1998. Intergenerational earnings mobility, inequality, and growth. *Journal of Monetary Economics* 41, 71–104.

Perotti, R. 1993. Political equilibrium, income distribution and growth. *Review of Economic Studies* 60, 755–76.

1994. Income distribution and investment. *European Economic Review* 38, 827–35.

1996. Growth, income distribution and democracy: what the data say. *Journal of Economic Growth* 1 (2), 149–87.

Persson, T., and G. Tabellini 1994. Is inequality harmful for growth? *American Economic Review* 84 (3), 600–21.

Piketty, T. 1997. The dynamics of the wealth distribution and the interest rate with credit rationing. *Review of Economic Studies* 64 (2), 173–89.

2000. Theories of persistent inequality and intergenerational mobility. In A. B. Atkinson and F. Bourguignon (eds.). *Handbook of Income Distribution.* Amsterdam: North-Holland, 429–76.

Pistaferri, L. 1999. Informal networks in the Italian labor market. *Giornale degli Economisti e Annali di Economia* 58 (3–4), 355–75.

Plug, E. 2004. Estimating the effect of mothers' schooling on children's schooling using a sample of adoptees. *American Economic Review* 94 (1), 358–68.

Pritchett, L., and D. Filmer 1999. What educational production functions really show: a positive theory of educational spending. *Economics of Education Review* 18, 223–39.

Psacharopoulos, G. 1994. Returns to investment in education: a global update. *World Development* 22 (9), 1325–43.

Ravallion, M., and Q. Wodon 2000. Does child labour displace schooling? Evidence on behavioural responses to an enrolment subsidy. *Economic Journal* 110, C158–C175.

Ridker, R. 1994. *The World Bank's Role in Human Resources Development in Sub-Saharan Africa*. Washington, DC: World Bank.

Riley, J. 1979. Testing the educational screening hypothesis. *Journal of Political Economy* 87 (5), S227–S252.

2001. Silver signals: twenty-five years of screening and signaling. *Journal of Economic Literature* 39, 432–78.

Robertson, D., and J. Symons 1996. Self-Selection in the State School System. Discussion Paper no. 312, Centre for Economic Performance, London School of Economics, London.

Roemer, J. 1986. Equality of resources implies equality of welfare. *Quarterly Journal of Economics* 101 (4), 751–84.

Romer, P. M. 1990a. Endogenous technological change. *Journal of Political Economy* 98, S71–S102.

1990b. Human capital and growth: theory and evidence. *Carnegie-Rochester Conference Series on Public Policy* 32, 251–85.

Rothschild, M., and L. White 1995. The analysis of the pricing of higher education and other services in which the customers are inputs. *Journal of Political Economy* 103 (3), 573–86.

Rouse, C. E. 1998a. Private school vouchers and student achievement: an evaluation of the Milwaukee parental choice program. *Quarterly Journal of Economics* 113 (2), 553–602.

1998b. Schools and student achievement: more evidence from the Milwaukee parental choice program. *Federal Reserve Bank of New York Economic Policy Review* 4 (1), 61–76.

Rubinstein, S., and D. Tsiddon 1998. Copying with Technological Progress: The Role of Ability in Making Inequality so Persistent. Working Paper no. 27-98, Tel Aviv University.

Ruhm, J. 2004. Parental employment and child cognitive development. *Journal of Human Resources* 39 (1), 155–92.

Sander, W. 2001. The Effect of Catholic Schools on Religiosity, Education and Competition. Occasional Paper no. 32, National Center for the Study of Privatization in Education, Teachers College, Columbia University, New York (http://www.tc.columbia.edu/ncspe).

Schnepf, S. V. 2002. A Sorting Hat that Fails? The Transition from Primary to Secondary School in Germany. Working Paper no. 92, UNICEF Innocenti Research Centre, Florence.

Schultz, P. 1988. Education investments and returns. In H. Chenery and T. Srinivasan (eds.). *Handbook of Development Economics* Vol. I. Amsterdam: North-Holland.

Schultz, T. 1963. *The Economic Value of Education*. New York: Columbia University Press.

Sen, A. 1976. Real national income. *Review of Economic Studies* 43, 19–39.

1992. *Inequality Re-examined*. Oxford: Oxford University Press.

Shapiro, C., and J. Stiglitz 1984. Equilibrium unemployment as a worker discipline device. *American Economic Review* 74 (3), 433–44.

Shavit, Y., and H. Blossfeld (eds.) 1993. *Persistent Inequality: Changing Educational Stratification in Thirteen Countries*. Boulder, CO: Westview Press.

Shea, J. 2000. Does parents' money matter? *Journal of Public Economics* 77 (2), 155–84.

Shorrock, A. 1978. The measurement of mobility. *Econometrica* 46 (5), 1013–24.

Sianesi, B., and J. Van Reenen 2003. The returns to education: macroeconomics. *Journal of Economic Surveys* 17 (2), 157–200.

Solon, G. 1992. Intergenerational income mobility in the United States. *American Economic Review* 82, 393–408.

1999. Intergenerational mobility in the labor market. In O. Ashenfelter and D. Card (eds.). *Handbook of Labor Economics* Vol. III. Amsterdam: North-Holland, 1761–1800.

2002. Cross-country differences in intergenerational earnings mobility. *Journal of Economic Perspectives* 16 (3), 59–66.

2004. A model of intergenerational mobility variation over time and place. In M. Corak (ed.). *Generational Income Mobility in North America and Europe*. Cambridge: Cambridge University Press, 38–47.

Soskice, D. 1994. Reconciling markets and institutions: the German apprenticeship system. In L. Lynch (ed.). *Training and the Private Sector: International Comparisons*. Chicago: University of Chicago Press, 25–60.

Spence, M. 1973. Job market signalling. *Quarterly Journal of Economics* 87, 355–79.

Stiglitz, J. 1969. Distribution of income and wealth among individuals. *Econometrica* 37 (3), 382–97.

1974. The demand for education in public and private school system. *Journal of Public Economics* 55 (3), 349–85.

1975. The theory of 'screening', education and the distribution of income. *American Economic Review* 64 (3), 283–300.

Summers, R., and A. Heston 1991. The Penn World Table (Mark 5): an expanded set of international comparisons, 1950–1988. *Quarterly Journal of Economics* 106 (2), 327–68.

Tamura, R. 1991. Income convergence in an endogenous growth model. *Journal of Political Economy* 99 (3), 522–40.

Teulings, C., and T. vanRens 2002. Education, Growth and Income Inequality. Discussion Paper no. 3863, Centre for Economic Policy Research, London.

Thurow, L. 1975. *Generating Inequalities*. New York: Basic Books.

Tibaijuka, A., and A. Cormack 1998. Financing the Social Sectors in Sub-Saharan Africa: A Review of the Literature. Unpublished manuscript, WIDER/United Nations University, Helsinki.

Tiebout, C. 1956. A pure theory of local expenditure. *Journal of Political Economy* 64, 416–24.

Topel, R. 1999. Labour market and economic growth. In O. Ashenfelter and D. Card (eds.). *Handbook of Labor Economics* Vol. III. Amsterdam: North-Holland, 2943–84.

Torvik, R. 1993. Talent, growth and income distribution. *Scandinavian Journal of Economics* 95 (4), 581–96.

Trostel, P., I. Walker and P. Wooley 2002. Estimates of the econometric return to schooling for 28 countries. *Labour Economics* 9 (1), 1–16.

United Nations Development Programme 1997. *Human Development Report 1997*. Oxford: Oxford University Press.

2001. *Human Development Report 2001*. Oxford: Blackwell.

United Nations Educational, Scientific and Cultural Organization 1998. *Statistical Yearbook*. New York: United Nations.

Weiner, M. 1991. *The Child and the State in India*. New Delhi: Oxford University Press.

Weiss, A. 1990. *Efficiency Wages: Models of Unemployment, Layoffs, and Wage Dispersion*. Princeton, NJ: Princeton University Press.

1995. Human capital vs. signalling explanation of wages. *Journal of Economic Perspectives* 9 (4), 133–54.

Willis, R. 1986. Wage determinants: a survey and reinterpretation of the human capital earning functions. In O. Ashenfelter and R. Layard (eds.). *Handbook of Labor Economics* Vol. I. Amsterdam: North-Holland, 525–602.

Woessman, L. 2003. Schooling resources, educational institutions, and student performance: the international evidence. *Oxford Bulletin of Economics and Statistics* 65 (2), 117–70.

2004. How Equal are Educational Opportunities? Family Background and Student Achievement in Europe and in the United States. Working Paper no. 1162, Center for Economic Studies (Cesifo), University of Munich.

Woessman, L., and M. West 2002. Class Size Effects in School Systems around the World: Evidence from Between-Grade Variations in TIMSS. Discussion Paper no. 485, Institute for the Study of Labor (IZA), Bonn.

World Bank 1998. *World Bank Data on CD-ROM*. Washington, DC: World Bank.

Wright, R. 1999. The Rate of Return to Private Schooling. Discussion Paper no. 92, Institute for the Study of Labor (IZA), Bonn.

Zimmerman, D. 1992. Regression towards mediocrity in economic stature. *American Economic Review* 82, 409–29.

Subject index

Author index

Made in the USA
Lexington, KY
06 July 2015